Drawing on America's Past

Drawing on America's Past

Folk Art, Modernism, and the Index of American Design

Virginia Tuttle Clayton / Elizabeth Stillinger / Erika Doss / Deborah Chotner

NATIONAL GALLERY OF ART, WASHINGTON

THE UNIVERSITY OF NORTH CAROLINA PRESS, CHAPEL HILL AND LONDON

The exhibition was organized by the
National Gallery of Art, Washington.

The exhibition and catalogue were made
possible by the Henry Luce Foundation.

Exhibition dates
27 November 2002 – 2 March 2003

This book was produced by the Publishing Office,
National Gallery of Art, Washington
www.nga.gov

Editor in Chief, Judy Metro
Editor, Ulrike Mills
Production Manager, Chris Vogel

Designed by Savitski Design, Ann Arbor, Michigan
Typeset in Centennial and printed on 150 gsm Xantur
by Amilcare Pizzi, S.p.A., Milan, Italy

Front endpaper: Lucille Chabot, *Angel Gabriel Weather
Vane: Demonstration Drawing*, 1939, National Gallery of
Art, Washington, Index of American Design

Back endpaper: Lucille Chabot, *Angel Gabriel Weather
Vane*, 1939, National Gallery of Art, Washington, Index of
American Design

Frontispiece: Charlotte Angus working on rendering of
Appliqué Sampler Quilt Top (cat. 46), 1940, National
Gallery of Art, Washington, Gallery archives

Note to the Reader
NMAH, SI, indicates National Museum of American History,
Smithsonian Institution

*Library of Congress
Cataloging-in-Publication Data*

Clayton, Virginia Tuttle
   Drawing on America's past : folk art, modernism, and the Index of
American Design / Virginia Tuttle Clayton, Elizabeth Stillinger, Erika Doss.
      p. cm.
Catalog of an exhibition organized by the National Gallery of Art,
Washington DC, Dec. 2, 2002–Mar. 2, 2003.
Includes bibliographical references and index.
   1. Index of American Design—Exhibitions. 2. Decorative arts—United
States—Exhibitions. 3. Folk art—United States—Exhibitions. 4.
Decorative arts—Washington, D.C.—Exhibitions. 5. Watercolor
painting—Washington, D.C.—Exhibitions. 6. National Gallery of Art
(U.S.)—Exhibitions. I. Stillinger, Elizabeth. II. Doss, Erika Lee.
III. National Gallery of Art (U.S.) IV. Title.
   NK805 .C58 2002
   745'.0973'074753—DC21
                                        2002013894

ISBN 0-89468-295-4 (alk. paper, softcover)
ISBN 0-8078-2794-0 (alk. paper, hardcover)

Hardcover edition copublished by
The University of North Carolina Press
P.O. Box 2288
Chapel Hill, NC 27515-2288
1-800-848-6224
www.uncpress.unc.edu

Contents

Director's Foreword

Sixty years ago the National Gallery of Art acquired the Index of American Design, an extraordinary collection of more than 18,000 watercolor renderings of American folk, popular, and decorative art. The Index was the product of a government-supported program that operated from 1935 to 1942 as a unit of the WPA's Federal Art Project, offering relief work to some of the many artists unemployed and impoverished during the Great Depression. After the project ended, Federal Art Project director Holger Cahill favored the allocation of the Index of American Design to the National Gallery because he understood that the Gallery would properly care for and exhibit this incomparable survey of Americana. The National Gallery eagerly accepted the offer of this unique compendium of watercolors and over the past six decades has committed its curatorial and conservation resources to maintaining the Index and organizing many exhibitions of its renderings that have traveled throughout the United States. In 2000 the Gallery received a grant from the Save America's Treasures program of the United States Department of the Interior, National Park Service, to perform new conservation on the watercolor plates, and this work has now been successfully completed.

To celebrate the sixtieth anniversary of the Gallery's acquisition of the Index, the National Gallery is presenting *Drawing on America's Past: Folk Art, Modernism, and the Index of American Design*, an exhibition of about eighty outstanding Index renderings that reunites nearly half of them with the actual artifacts they portray—for the first time since the project was in operation. In the essays for the exhibition catalogue, Virginia Clayton, Elizabeth Stillinger, and Erika Doss examine the organization and day-to-day functioning of the Index project, its relationship to American art between the two world wars, and the role it played in forming our present notions of what is American in American art. Deborah Chotner's catalogue entries contribute up-to-date information about the works of folk, popular, and decorative art depicted in the Index.

We are indebted to the Henry Luce Foundation for providing the generous support that allowed us to realize this exhibition and its catalogue. We are also grateful to all the public institutions and private collectors who graciously allowed us to borrow for the exhibition the original artifacts portrayed in the Index of American Design.

Earl A. Powell III
Director, National Gallery of Art

Acknowledgments

Many colleagues at the National Gallery and other institutions have contributed to the preparation of this exhibition. I especially want to thank Elizabeth Stillinger and Erika Doss for their stimulating essays in the catalogue; Deborah Chotner for agreeing to both write catalogue entries on such a broad range of subjects and find information on artists whom posterity has often not treated with generosity; and Louisa Ransom for volunteering to help with numerous organizational tasks and for writing some of the catalogue entries.

Marian Dirda not only performed outstanding conservation work on the renderings but also spent many hours with me scrutinizing the watercolors under a microscope and discussing what we saw, so that I could finally understand each artist's individual technique in creating such astonishing works of art. Ulrike Mills was an excellent and patient editor for the catalogue, and I am greatly indebted to her. Both Francis V. O'Connor and Charles Brock kindly read early drafts of my essay and made some important suggestions. Mark Leithauser has, as always, designed the exhibition with rare artistry and imagination. Rick Block photographed the renderings with great care and skill. Virginia Crockett, a former intern, offered invaluable help during the early stages of planning the show, as did Victoria Foster, formerly with the department of modern prints and drawings, and Jonathan Walz, formerly of the department of exhibitions. Ruth Fine, Carlotta Owens, and Charlie Ritchie in the department of modern prints and drawings were generous with their time and advice as the project advanced. Greg Jecmen, my colleague in the department of old master prints, willingly shouldered the increased burden my work on this exhibition left him to bear.

Others at the Gallery who contributed substantially to the effort include Susan Arensberg, Ira Bartfield, Jeanette Beers, Bill Bowser, Sara Sanders-Buell, Julia Burke, Rio DeNaro, Michelle Fondas, Mari Forsell, Debbie Kirkpatrick, Shan Linde, Missy Muellich, Hugh Phibbs, Michael Pierce, Naomi Remes, Anne Ritchie, Abbie Sprague, Elaine Vamos, and Chris Vogel. National Gallery director, Earl A. Powell III, and deputy director, Alan Shestack, as well as A. W. Mellon senior curator of prints and drawings, Andrew Robison, and curator of old master prints, Peter Parshall, editor in chief, Judy Metro, and chief of exhibitions, D. Dodge Thompson, all offered their support for the show at critical moments.

I had help from many quarters in finding the sometimes elusive original artifacts. Paul D'Ambrosio, Nancy Druckman, Stacy Hollander, Gerry Kornblau, and Ralph Sessions all provided leads that allowed me to locate some of the works included in the exhibition. Nancy and Chuck Purdue at the University of Virginia spent an afternoon with me, discussing my plans for the exhibition and offering valuable insights based on their extensive research on WPA projects in Virginia. Deborah Chotner, Louisa Ransom, and I many times benefited from the expertise of our colleagues in other museums as we wrote our catalogue entries, and we are grateful to them all. My husband, Michael Clayton, endured with grace and good humor the remarkably long process of bringing my initial thoughts about the Index of American Design to fruition in this exhibition and catalogue.

Virginia Tuttle Clayton
Associate Curator of Old Master Prints,
National Gallery of Art

Lenders to the Exhibition

American Folk Art Museum, New York

Brooklyn Museum of Art

Chicago Historical Society

Connecticut Historical Society, Hartford, Connecticut

Allan and Kendra Daniel

Fenimore Art Museum, Cooperstown, New York

Richard Kanter

Mr. and Mrs. Byron H. LeCates

The Mariners' Museum, Newport News, Virginia

The Mattatuck Museum, Waterbury, Connecticut

The Mercer Museum of Bucks County Historical Society, Doylestown, Pennsylvania

The Metropolitan Museum of Art, New York

Museum of Fine Arts, Boston

Nantucket Historical Association

National Gallery of Art, Washington

New Bedford Whaling Museum

The New-York Historical Society

The Newark Museum

Old Sturbridge Village, Sturbridge, Massachusetts

Peabody Essex Museum, Salem, Massachusetts

Philadelphia Museum of Art

Private collections

Shaker Village of Pleasant Hill, Harrodsburg, Kentucky

Shelburne Museum, Shelburne, Vermont

Wadsworth Atheneum Museum of Art, Hartford, Connecticut

Picturing a "Usable Past"

Virginia Tuttle Clayton

*The depression of 1929–? may prove to have been the
best thing that ever happened to American art.*

Suzanne LaFollette
The Nation, 10 October 1936

In his 1918 article, "On Creating a Usable Past,"
literary critic Van Wyck Brooks lamented
what he and many of his colleagues perceived
as the poverty of American culture.[1] He also
identified one of the causes of this deficiency:
the United States did not have a "usable past,"
a cultural memory that could provide American
writers with a comfortable sense of continuity, or
being part of a tradition. Brooks suggested that
since such a cultural memory had no objective
reality but was made up of whichever subjective
characteristics a nation chose to include in it, we
could remedy this apparent failing by simply discovering or inventing a usable past for ourselves.
It was what European nations had done, thus providing their writers with a wellspring of creative
sustenance. Brooks further maintained that our
self-styled cultural history should commemorate
the genuinely American creative impulse he had
encountered among some nearly forgotten, eccentric geniuses who inhabited our past. He argued
that we should discover our aesthetic patrimony
in this "limbo of the non-elect" rather than flaunt
our few acknowledged "masterpieces" in the
European tradition.

Brooks' article became something of an
American cultural resource itself during the two
decades that followed its publication, and his concept of a national art heritage, now enduringly
labeled a "usable past," reappeared often in critical
writings on the visual as well as the literary arts.
The creators of the Index of American Design—
a 1930s government-financed art project that
resulted in an immense pictorial archive of
Americana—repeatedly used Brooks' term in
describing a major purpose of their undertaking:

to provide the background materials needed to
stimulate the development of American culture.

Twenty-four years after his landmark article,
Brooks wrote the preface to a posthumously published book by Constance Rourke, an eminent
cultural historian and folklorist who had been the
editor of the Index of American Design as well as
one of its chief architects.[2] In his preface, Brooks
credited Rourke with the momentous discovery
that Americans did have rich creative resources
in their past—not among the rare masterpieces
of high culture, but in the abundant folk tradition
whose very existence most Americans had hitherto
failed to recognize. It was the goal of the Index
of American Design to acquaint Americans with
this unclaimed cultural legacy and to create what
Michael Kammen has called "an historically based
public culture."[3] To accomplish these ends, artists
employed by the Index produced truly magical
watercolor portraits of the artifacts and implements
that had once served as commonplace companions
to daily life in this country, and they lavished these
portrayals with the most painstaking attention
to form, texture, and detail. They sought uncompromising clarity and objectivity and achieved
astonishing verisimilitude. When we encounter
the mundane objects in these renderings close-up
and seemingly suspended before blank sheets of
paper, as if they had been transported into a time-
less, airless realm, we may at last discover the
startling beauty of the all-too-familiar.

This study of the Index will offer some new
insights into the project and its progenitors. First,
it will demonstrate that the Index was the result
of an ambitious and creative effort to furnish, for
the visual arts, the kind of usable past Brooks had

urged Americans to discover or invent. Additionally, it will show that the founders and administrators of the Index were dedicated modernists, not antiquarians, and that they had a dual agenda. They wanted to assemble visual resources for artists and designers to use in creating a distinctly American modernism in the fine and applied arts, and they wanted to educate Americans about their past material culture, preparing them to recognize American design and to support its future development. The mission of the Index was to amass cumulative, documentary evidence of a uniquely American creative idiom or sense of design, not merely to produce a catalogue of antiques. This, presumably, is why its creators named it the Index of American Design rather than the Index of American Antiques or Folk Art.

For the initiators of the Index project, "design" meant the fundamental character or expressive content of a created object, revealed in its forms and patterns. Design was derived from, and was in turn capable of making visible, the collective spirit of a nation. It was the genius of a people manifest in its works of art, above all its folk art. The perception of folk art as reinforcing ideological definitions of national and ethnic groups was common in the 1930s, although one prescient art historian, Henri Focillon, wisely discouraged such views. In 1931 he cautioned that folk art was more international than national in its essential attributes, that "*national* and *ethnic* frames of reference do not coincide with those of folk art, nor could they possibly do so." Focillon understood that there were "profound accords between peoples, derived from both an extremely ancient community of Man and a natural, general aptitude of Man. Thus our considerations [of folk art] bring us to rise from a provincial plane to a universal."[4] The leaders of the Index of American Design, however, eagerly and perhaps naively, embraced the popular concept of "folk art as evidence of national identity" prevalent in the 1930s—at precisely the moment when European fascism began the process that would eventually betray the consequences of such grouping and stereotyping of humanity, when carried to extremes.

"Folk art" was a term less rigorously examined in the 1930s than it is today. How to define American folk art, how to collect, exhibit, and study it, and even whether folk art can exist in this country without a "folk," are important topics lately of great concern among some art historians, folklorists, and anthropologists in the United States. Such issues, while almost unavoidable in the study of folk art today, did not greatly trouble the Americans who initiated and produced the Index of American Design. In their enthusiasm to popularize American folk art they may at times have been less circumspect in defining and evaluating it than scholars today. Constance Rourke, for example, set wide boundaries for the folk-art domain by claiming that there was a single division in American "arts of design": "[there are] two major classifications, the folk arts, and what… may be called the aristocratic forms. The latter obviously include the work of such distinguished craftsmen as Duncan Phyfe and the fine groups of furniture workers who flourished in…the first half of the nineteenth century. On the other hand, the folk arts run all the way from homespuns and simple furniture and ironwork to the distinctive creative forms of the Pennsylvania German and those of the old Spanish Southwest in painting or sculpture."[5] Holger Cahill, principal administrator for the Index, called folk art "the work of people with little book learning in art techniques, and no academic training," the "honest and straightforward expression of the spirit of a people."[6]

These relatively broad definitions of folk art by the leaders of the Index project, their focus on the aesthetic attributes rather than cultural contexts of objects, and their occasional promotion of it as the simple art of happy craftsmen from an idealized past helped create the tensions that have ignited many recent discussions. Anthropologist John Michael Vlach has despaired that current writings on folk art have often failed to evolve beyond the "joyous manifesto of 1930s discovery" and that some scholars have "continually cited the work of Holger Cahill and seemingly refused to consider the issue in terms of more contemporary studies."[7] Since today's probing questions about American folk art, however, did not penetrate the planning and production of the Index that took place nearly seventy years ago, they are outside the realm of—and cannot be resolved by—this study of the Index.[8]

Not every object included in the Index would fit within even the broadest definition of folk art today. Our contemporary—and often unexamined—notion of what types of artifacts constitute American folk art can ultimately be traced to the selection of objects made by Holger Cahill for folk art exhibitions he organized in the early 1930s, leading up to his work with the Index.[9] Although the Index of American Design includes essentially the same categories of objects as these folk-art shows—among them some works that were mass-produced in factories—Cahill, Rourke, and other Index staff did expand their terminology to describe the content of the Index. Perhaps recognizing the limitations and ambiguities of the term "folk art," they alternately described Index materials as the "humbler arts and crafts," "decorative and utilitarian design," "homely products," "decorative and utilitarian arts," and "decorative, useful and folk arts."[10] In this essay, the most general rubric labels the greatest number of Index objects by referring to them as "folk, popular, and decorative art."

The first part of the essay addresses the history of the Index. It looks closely at the Index's origin and creators, as well as the fundamentals of its structure and day-to-day operation, and culminates with the acquisition of the Index by the National Gallery of Art and a summary of its status since then. The second part considers the purposes of the Index, which I believe represent the ideals of a brief but glorious moment, paradoxically during one of America's bleakest decades. For that moment it seemed possible that folk art, modernism, and industrial design might join to form a new art that was not only recognizably American and modern, but also an integral, gratifying part of everyone's routine life. The third part of this essay weighs the success of the Index in achieving its original goals. Acknowledging that the Index did not, as its founders had hoped, serve as a direct source of inspiration for American artists and designers in the dramatically altered artistic climate after World War II, the third part contends that the value and long-term influence of the Index lie elsewhere. In addition to offering what is still the most comprehensive survey of American folk, popular, and decorative art, the Index is an exceptionally clear and well-documented record of some of the most significant trends and aspirations in American art between the two world wars. Most important, the Index may have contributed substantially to a widely accepted concept of what "American" means in the fine and applied arts.

The question "What is American in American art?" may never be adequately answered because it may not be possible to define any art as purely and exclusively American. The notion is just as elusive as the so-called Englishness of English art.[11]

In the 1930s, however, the Index of American Design popularized a body of artifacts commonly called "folk art" in this country and gave enormous publicity to the idea that these artifacts possessed definitively American qualities, and further, that American folk art was the antecedent to American modernism. The mass circulation of this doctrine by the Index may have helped formulate today's mainstream notion of what looks and feels "American"—in everything from designer sheets and "country" decor to the creative process followed by our most iconoclastic artists. This "Americanness" has evolved as something harder to identify than a national style or common fund of ancestral motifs, especially in the fine arts, and yet as something many believe they are capable of discerning.

Two additional essays in this catalogue examine how the Index fits into the broader picture of twentieth-century American art and culture before World War II. Elizabeth Stillinger places the Index within the little-known history of American folk-art collecting, examining early collections of these artifacts and the reasons for their existence. Erika Doss analyzes the Index as a product of the politically charged connection between national identity and design during the interwar period in the United States. Although cultural nationalism first emerged in Europe during the romantic era, in the 1930s it surged to the foreground of American art, especially in many of the arts programs supported by the Works Progress Administration (WPA). Finally, catalogue entries, primarily written by Deborah Chotner, with contributions by Louisa Ransom and by me, study each rendering included in the exhibition. The aspirations of the Index's founders may have exceeded creating a guide to American antiques, but it is nevertheless an unparalleled fund of knowledge about American folk, popular, and decorative art. The catalogue entries update the information Index researchers gathered in the 1930s about the objects depicted in the renderings and provide further data about their original cultural contexts. Photographs of the actual objects included in the exhibition are reproduced with the catalogue entries. Chotner also researched the biographies of the artists who made these renderings, presenting her findings in an appendix. In many cases, regrettably, public archives and published records have preserved little or no information on the Index artists. In a second appendix I offer a brief description of each state Index project.

History and Operation of the Index of American Design

The enthusiasm and surprise which have greeted exhibitions of Index material throughout the country reveal that our people have a deep affection for these arts of the common man. They seem to recognize that these arts fit very closely into the context of our democratic life.

> Holger Cahill, national director of the
> Federal Art Project, 21 January 1941

The Origin of the Index Project

The Index of American Design's 18,257 watercolor renderings depict in meticulous, breathtaking detail a wide selection of American folk, popular, and decorative art.[12] They portray weather vanes, quilts, toys, tavern signs, figureheads, stoneware, and many other types of artifact made by America's ancestral "common man." Approximately one thousand artists on work relief throughout the United States contributed to this unique compendium of Americana. The project lasted just over six years, from the end of 1935 to the spring of 1942, with no more than four hundred artists— usually fewer—at work at one time. Having proven themselves to be skilled as artists and eligible for relief, they were employed as part of the Index of American Design project, a unit of the Federal Art Project (FAP). The FAP—along with the Federal Music Project, Federal Theater Project, and Federal Writers' Project—was in turn part of Federal Project Number One, sponsored by the WPA.[13] The WPA was established in 1935 to provide work-relief jobs, rather than direct relief, for millions of Americans who were unemployed and destitute during the Great Depression. Federal Project Number One was specifically responsible for serving the desperate needs of the arts community.

Soon after he became president in 1933, Franklin Delano Roosevelt initiated various work-relief programs to help alleviate the dire effects of the depression on American workers.[14] Some of these early "New Deal" programs lasted only a few months, but through eager and creative experimentation, their administrators managed both to codify the theory of federal work relief and to find the means of implementing it. These initial, often short-lived projects substantially influenced the later and more enduring WPA and its Federal Art Project. The early, pioneer programs for the arts bequeathed to their successor, the FAP, the motivating concept of art projects as a form of community service, as well as their system of operating under both federal control and local and state management. Most significantly for this study of the Index of American Design, the first art projects defined one of the patriotic causes that the FAP would continue to serve: to depict the "American Scene" and foster the development of a new and definitively American art.[15]

The official *Index of American Design Manual* enumerated the goals of the project:

1. To record material of historical significance which has not heretofore been studied and which, for one reason or another, stands in danger of being lost.
2. To gather a body of traditional material which may form the basis for an organic development of American design.
3. To make usable source-records of this material accessible to artists, designers, manufacturers, museums, libraries, and art schools.
4. To give employment to painters, graphic artists, photographers, and commercial artists who might otherwise not find employment.[16]

The "Sample Press Release" in the manual further proclaimed that:

> The importance of gathering material of this kind has long been recognized in Europe. European nations have prepared collections of plates in color and have published richly illustrated books on their decorative, applied and folk arts, thus placing the full picture of the native arts of design at the disposal of their scholars, creative workers, and manufacturers. These collections have been considered important not by any means as a basis for imitation but as a wellspring to which all artists and designers may turn for a renewed sense of native tradition. This quality has attracted American manufacturers to the European design market with the consequent neglect of native American talent.[17]

This invidious comparison to Europe—which clearly resonates with that made by Van Wyck Brooks in his 1918 article—apparently struck a chord among Americans. It was paraphrased in countless newspaper and popular magazine articles, transcripts of lectures, and writings for scholarly journals that promoted the Index of American Design during the 1930s. Of all the reasons for supporting the Index, this one proved the most successful at capturing the attention of Americans. The promise and the hope of the Index were, in short, that with its completion, "typical examples of an indigenous American character will be made available for study [and] this material will stimulate the artist, designer, and manufacturer of articles of everyday use to build upon American tradition," rather than copying European tradition.[18]

The original idea for the Index of American Design was formulated by two women in New York City, both directly or indirectly associated with the design profession. Ruth Reeves was an innovative and successful textile designer and a member of the American Union of Decorative Artists and Craftsmen (AUDAC). This group was founded in 1928 with a mission to help bridge the gap between art and industry and to encourage the quality and originality of design in mass-produced goods for American homes.[19] Like her colleagues in the AUDAC, Reeves was determined to escape the European influence that had long dominated American design, and she turned for inspiration to the ancient crafts of South and Central America, as well as to Native American textiles. Early in her career, from around 1918, she had worked as a draftsman for *Women's Wear*, illustrating historic costumes from museum collections to provide fresh inspiration for American textile and fashion designers.[20] From the late 1920s until the mid-1930s, she also made frequent use of the picture files at the New York Public Library, always in search of new ideas, and there she became acquainted with Romana Javitz, head of the library's visual resources.

Romana Javitz, who was also trained as an artist, had begun working at the New York Public Library in 1924.[21] In 1929 she became head of the library's famed Picture Collection, a post she held until her retirement in 1968. Her background in the arts was very helpful in this position since many of her clients were design professionals like Reeves. The Picture Collection, as Reeves later commented, was formed "to feed artists and industrial designers with authoritative pictorial research."[22] The prototype for this compendium was the Picture Collection at the Newark Free Public Library, founded 1904 in Newark, New Jersey, by John Cotton Dana, to further his populist goals by making vast quantities of pictorial information readily available to the general public.[23] These two picture archives ultimately became models for the Index of American

Design, although the Index would consist entirely of images of American folk, popular, and decorative arts.

When Javitz assumed control of the New York Public Library's Picture Collection in 1929, American materials were poorly represented in its files. During the 1930s, demand for images of Americana began to grow, in part because American artists and designers increasingly sought to discover visual resources within their own material culture. Being unable to meet this need sorely frustrated Javitz. She later wrote: "the American designer began to seek his own country, the peoples of his own land and their arts as inspiration for his design. For him pictorial research sources were completely inadequate."[24] She concluded that the United States government should subsidize the publication of a series of volumes illustrating America's folk arts and crafts, like those that had been sponsored by European governments: "I thought of it as an Index…making available, without selective bias, all of the pictorial documentation we could gather and organize that the public may draw on the past to familiarize themselves with our national heritage."[25] It would be a published version of the library's Picture Collection, but specifically focused on American design. The illustrations, she decided, would not need to be great works of art, but they should be accompanied by information about the objects shown. In conformity with Dana's populist ideals, Javitz believed the volumes should be published in large quantities so they might be available in libraries and schools across the country. She repeatedly discussed this idea with Ruth Reeves and other artists and designers who visited the Picture Collection during the early 1930s.

In spring 1935 the inauguration of the Federal Art Project was a prime topic of conversation among the New York art circles to which Ruth Reeves belonged. She quickly recognized that this government work-relief program might offer the perfect opportunity to advance the American picture project she and Javitz had been talking about for years.[26] Reeves and Javitz discussed the idea for obtaining government support through the FAP, and in July 1935 Javitz wrote a formal proposal describing the Index project for New York's Temporary Emergency Relief Administration. Reeves brought the plan to Frances Pollak, head of that project's educational programs, who liked the proposal and acted on it at once. She had been searching for a way to employ commercial

artists in the city who were out of work and on relief. A limited version of what would soon become a national Index of American Design thus began in October 1935 under Pollak's direction as a local, New York City project.

Reeves also traveled to Washington, DC, to meet with Holger Cahill, newly appointed director of the Federal Art Project, to argue that the Index should become a nationwide endeavor as a unit of the FAP.[27] She carried to this meeting two renderings produced by artists in the New York City project, along with a copy of *Weyhe's Ornament*, an encyclopedia of ornamental designs, as a model of what the final outcome of her proposed project might be: a series of portfolios reproducing artists' original watercolor plates.[28] Reeves was more concerned with the aesthetic quality of the renderings than Javitz had been. Years later she recalled recommending at her first meeting with Cahill that the illustrations adhere to the style of "Egyptology-type" renderings, and that they should "all look as if one hand had done them."[29] Less concerned with the historical documentation of the objects, Reeves imagined the results of the project as "tantamount to a *published* Museum of American arts," and definitely an art project rather than "an antiquarian's catch-all."[30]

Although Cahill was immediately intrigued with the idea, he feared that the project was too vast. To contain its scope, he eliminated parts of the original scheme. He decided that architectural ornament and Native American artifacts could be omitted because they were already being recorded by other government projects.[31] He also excluded American folk painting. Reeves greatly regretted the omission of Native American objects, one of her favorite design sources, but with the Index now fixed within more reasonable boundaries, Cahill deemed the project well worth his support, and its national phase began in December 1935. According to Adolph Cook Glassgold, one of the chief Index administrators, operations remained "pretty much uncoordinated experiments" for a few months, but by the spring of 1936 Cahill and his staff began to see the "crystallization of the broad over-all plan of the Index take shape."[32]

Structure and Operation of the Index of American Design

The Federal Art Project, of which the Index made up one unit, was divided into six regions: West Coast, Rocky Mountain States, Midwest, South, New England, and Metropolitan New York, including New Jersey. Each had a regional art director. The regions were subdivided by state, and the states had Index supervisors who reported to state art directors.[33] Each state's FAP administration chose the arts programs in which the state would participate. These included graphic art, easel painting, mural painting, community art centers, teaching projects, and the Index of American Design. Before initiating an art project, the director of the FAP prudently tried to secure local sponsorship through public or quasipublic institutions within the state. These cooperating sponsors provided either a portion of the project's funding or some of its materials.[34]

The national office of the Index of American Design was in Washington, DC, and there, under the direction of Cahill, Index administrative staff outlined the basic content and goals of the project.[35] The first *Index of American Design Manual* defined the main responsibility of this office: "a Central Planning Project in Washington has as its function the co-ordination of the work of the various projects throughout the country. All material collected by the Index of American Design projects in the various states will be edited and correlated by the Central Planning Project."[36] In January 1936, while Romana Javitz remained at her job with the New York Public Library, Ruth Reeves became national supervisor of the Index and was named federal field advisor the following summer. Armed with her advanced technical skills as an artist and with tremendous enthusiasm for the Index, she traveled frequently from Washington to help initiate new state projects, train Index artists, and find local collections of folk and decorative art suitable for rendering.[37] She also presented public lectures, successfully generating interest in and support for the project (fig. 1). She was an omnipresent and tireless contributor who must be counted among the paramount influences on the successful outcome of the Index.

By the summer of 1936, Adolph Cook Glassgold, who had first served as one of the Index editors, became national coordinator of the Index of American Design.[38] He was responsible for developing techniques for rendering, a methodology for research, and a system for accurately cataloguing and filing completed materials.[39] He also made occasional visits to the state projects and met with the artists, both individually and in groups, to discuss their work and to demonstrate methods for making a rendering. Around November 1938 he became the chief arbiter of artistic quality for the project. It was Glassgold who examined and critiqued the thousands of renderings sent to the national office by the state projects, returning those he judged in need of improvement.[40] He also handled the day-to-day administration of the Index from the national office, along with a good portion of the correspondence directed to Holger Cahill. Support staff in the office were three research assistants, a secretary, a clerk-typist, a clerk, and two mat-cutters and framers.[41]

Constance Rourke was first hired in March 1936 as a part-time editorial consultant. Four months later she became a full-time, paid employee of the FAP as editor of the Index of American Design. She helped articulate the objectives and philosophy of the project, made decisions regarding what types of objects should be included, and traveled throughout the United States to initiate and advise state projects.[42] Her prestige as a leading cultural historian added legitimacy to the Index, and her vast knowledge of American folk culture helped the project identify the many regional manifestations of folk art in this country. She also helped advance the program by writing promotional texts as well as a more scholarly article on the Index.[43] The Index depended on Rourke's sound judgment to evaluate collections of Americana, deciding which pieces were the most typically American, of the best quality, and the most historically significant. The original plan of the project was to publish

reproductions of the renderings in a series of portfolios on selected topics.[44] Rourke, more than anyone else associated with the project, tried to keep work organized around the subjects of the portfolios in order not to waste time and effort on renderings that would not ultimately be useful. As she wrote to a colleague: "I have become really passionately anxious to avoid diffusion in the work of the Index. We stand such a good chance of stacking up really notable work in perhaps twenty portfolios...whereas, if we digress too much, we may fall between a good many stools."[45] After devoting a year of full-time work to this effort, she returned to a part-time position for six months, which allowed more time to write her biography of Charles Sheeler and her book on American culture.[46]

Thirty-four states and the District of Columbia eventually chose to take part in the Index of American Design. There were two projects in California (one for the north and one for the south) and two in New York (one for New York City and the other for the rest of the state), a total of thirty-seven projects.[47] From state to state, Index projects varied in size and structure. The largest were those in areas where the highest concentration of business and industry had thrived before the depression, and where, consequently, the greatest number of commercial artists were unemployed and on relief by the mid-1930s. New York City and Pennsylvania employed the largest number of artists and produced the majority of renderings. Cahill and his staff wanted the Index to include every state, but despite their best efforts this was not possible. In some southern and western states, they could not muster a sufficient number of artists from the relief rolls who were trained to perform the meticulous work required by the Index.[48] According to Reeves, there were further problems in the South: "The certification for relief is very severe in South Carolina—and also there are very few persons in these southern states who haven't aunts or second or third cousins who at a pinch could always put one up or share their garden patch. Where we in the North might not even see our first cousins from year's end to year's end, the intricacies of family relationship are very strong in the South. You just don't starve, that's all."[49] Sometimes Cahill also had problems with WPA state administrators who were uncooperative or even hostile toward him and his arts projects.[50]

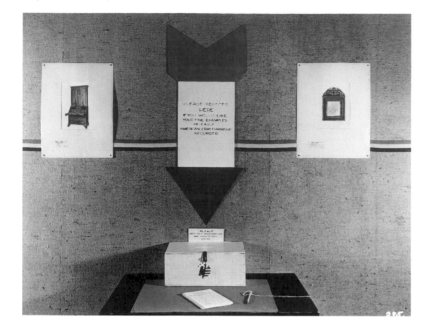

Within some states, Index of American Design projects were concentrated in just a few cities, although artists did venture to more remote locations in pursuit of excellent objects. In only a few projects were many artists simultaneously at work throughout the entire state. The most active centers were in areas that not only offered a sufficient number of highly skilled artists on relief, but also had ample supplies of folk and decorative arts, such as Wilmington, Delaware; San Antonio, Texas; and Chicago.[51] The largest project, in New York City, had an extensive administrative staff with multiple supervisors to oversee the production of renderings of each type of artifact, along with a full staff of research workers.[52] In smaller projects, state supervisors took on broader responsibilities. In Maine, for example, Dorothy Hay Jensen not only was Index supervisor but also was in charge of all WPA art projects. She single-handedly found the objects to render and performed all the research, while hiring and supervising about forty artists. Most of the Maine artists were in the Portland area, but eight or nine were at more distant locations. Jensen tried to visit the artists outside Portland at least once a month, bringing them materials and assignments and monitoring their work.[53]

Establishing Criteria and Locating Objects

One of the first steps recommended in setting up a new state project was to contact local museum directors, chairs of university art departments, women's clubs, state offices of the Daughters of the American Revolution and the Daughters of the Confederacy, antique dealers, and all local art and state historical organizations.[54] Index supervisors solicited their cooperation and specifically requested their help in locating folk-art collections in the area. Supervisors and research workers made surveys of the materials available to the Index in both public and private collections. They sent the results of the surveys to Washington, where Constance Rourke or another member of the staff determined which items the state's artists should render.[55] Centralizing the selection process in the Washington office prevented duplication—images of nearly identical objects being contributed by more than one state—and ensured that the artifacts included in the Index were appropriate to its mission. Since an understanding of the historical and geographical contexts of the objects was considered of great importance, an object of uncertain origin would likely be omitted unless its design was exceptional.[56]

The state Index personnel continually added to their surveys as more collections were discovered. Often they were able to find additional material by passing out questionnaires at local exhibitions of Index renderings (fig. 2), inquiring about privately owned works that Index artists might be permitted to record.[57] Newspaper and magazine articles on the Index also alerted collectors to the project and led to additional offers of works for rendering. Occasionally, private collectors were reluctant to allow artists to make renderings of their antiques, either because of concerns about forgers making copies from the Index plates, or because of suspicions that the federal government was using access to private homes by Index artists as a means to secretly evaluate properties and raise taxes.[58] Index supervisors therefore often targeted public collections as the first sources of material to render. They proved the legitimacy and value of the project by establishing connections with prestigious institutions and by completing some high-quality renderings to demonstrate what the project could accomplish. These tactics, along with the publicity generated by the Index through its many exhibitions and related press coverage, did help stimulate interest among private collectors and prompted them to be more forthcoming with their possessions.

In addition to works from public institutions and large private collections, the Index included numerous works of folk, popular, and decorative art that belonged to Americans of modest means.

Figs. 3, 4
Exhibition *Folk Art
Sculpture and the
Index of American
Design* at the
Downtown Gallery
in New York City,
28 September to
9 October 1937,
photographs by
Von Urban,
National Gallery
of Art, Washington,
Gallery archives

Fig. 5
An Index supervisor
at the shop of Helena
Penrose and J. H.
Edgette in New York
City, April 1939,
National Gallery of
Art, Washington,
Gallery archives

Some were heirlooms that families had passed down for generations. Index artists also recorded the diverse and constantly changing inventory of antique shops, especially that of major dealers in New York City. The American Folk Art Gallery in New York, co-owned by Edith Halpert and Holger Cahill, was a prime source of objects for the Index. Much of the folk art sold at the American Folk Art Gallery had come from the northeastern United States, including objects purchased at auction from such premier private collections as that of Elie and Viola Nadelman. In 1937 Halpert staged an exhibition of forty-seven Index renderings paired with their original objects, all from the American Folk Art Gallery (figs. 3, 4). Another excellent source for the Index was the New York antique shop of Helena Penrose and J. H. Edgette (fig. 5). Many of the renderings of toys and kitchen tools in the Index were copied from the stock of Penrose and Edgette (cats. 20, 25, 29, 59–61).

The Index was a national survey, meant to represent all regional variations of America's folk expression, and the renderings illustrate precisely the types of artifacts in which the nation's cultural diversity could be recognized most readily. As Glassgold explained, "from the potter's wheel, the weaver's loom, the cabinet maker's tool chest and the glass blower's furnace came the concrete embodiments of our diverse early American cultures," and we prize these objects because our "democratic spirit…recognizes and welcomes the contributions of ethnic groups."[59] Although Native American artifacts were not a specific focus for the Index, it did include "Indian" crafts (cats. 24, 51). Index artists also illustrated items made by African Americans (cats. 23, 47), despite the fact that most caches of these objects were in southern states with very limited projects, or none at all.[60] Included were craft works from religious communities that were

little known at the time—the Shakers, the Janson-ists, or the Separatists of Zoar—and these became an important part of the Index portrait of America. The art of the Spanish Southwest was still relatively unknown and underappreciated on the East Coast when the Index of American Design began, but it, too, was systematically recorded (cats. 7, 50).[61] Spanish Southwestern was the most fully repre-sented regional art in the Index of American Design, indicating its priority among Index staff.

Although not every state participated in the project, and despite the fact that only a few ren-derings were produced in some of the states, the goal of broad inclusiveness was fairly well accom-plished. In part this was possible because artists depicted any work of folk art currently located in their state, regardless of its origin, and most collections, public and private, included objects that had been made outside their state's borders. Although the Index gave primary consideration to objects made in the state in which the contributing project was located, a New York rendering might, for example, depict a ceramic work made in South Carolina or Pennsylvania (cats. 23, 22), while a Pennsylvania rendering might show a stove plate found and probably made in Virginia (cat. 16).

Many of the works of art illustrated in Index plates were already on public view in museums and historical societies, but these institutions were in diverse locations throughout the United States; a number of scholarly studies of American deco-rative and folk arts had already been published when the project began, yet some of them were not illustrated. As an Index administrator explained, anyone searching for a panoramic view of American design would not only have to "spend much time tracing articles in scattered periodicals, or con-

sulting unrelated volumes…but these would be found…inadequately illustrated, and vast areas… sparsely treated."[62] By compiling images from col-lections throughout the country, the Index brought all these objects together so that they could be seen as a group and in direct comparison with each other. The renderings presented the objects in a format that also made them more accessible than they had been previously. In the early decades of the twen-tieth century, museums and historical societies often arranged their artifacts in period-room settings or locked them in crowded cabinets, making it difficult for artists and designers to scrutinize those works as individual forms. With every object illustrated as a separate entity, a viewer could more easily contemplate and appreciate its design.

The project's administrators sought to include the finest examples of Americana in the Index, but they also welcomed more humble artifacts if the form of those objects embodied what they deemed the spirit of American design. A weather vane rendered in Concord, Massachusetts, for example, might not be among the grandest of all weather-cocks, but its simple, abstracted shape is striking and seems a perfect manifestation of the quintes-sentially American style that Index administrators wanted to document (cat. 80). A scabbard and saw from Chicago, or a toaster from New York, might not be the kind of artifact most highly valued by some collectors, but they were included because of the simplicity and vigor of their forms (cats. 28, 29).

Index Artists
The employment offered by the Index of American Design, like that of all WPA projects, was meant to be temporary. At certain intervals, which varied in length through the project's duration, artists were

Fig. 8 LEFT
Artists at work
in an Index studio
in New York City,
April 1939,
National Gallery
of Art, Washington,
Gallery archives

Fig. 9 RIGHT
Dorothy Hay
Jensen, Index
supervisor in
Maine, makes a
sketch with color
notes while photog-
rapher Dominic
Avanzato takes a
black-and-white
photograph of a
weather vane,
National Gallery
of Art, Washington,
Gallery archives

required to leave their Index jobs and, through examination by a caseworker, requalify for relief, which meant proving they were still indigent.[63] Once they successfully demonstrated need, they could reapply for their work-relief jobs, but there was often a long wait before the job was again open.[64] Many of the artists were embarrassed to be on government work relief but could find no way to support themselves and their families without it during the Great Depression. Despite these reservations, many took great satisfaction in the work they accomplished for the Index of American Design and in later years expressed gratitude for the opportunity to continue working as artists and to participate in what they considered an important and patriotic project.[65]

Artists applying for work with the Index had to prove their talent, usually through a qualifying test administered by the state art director, or by showing samples of their work.[66] A majority of the artists who ended up working on the Index of American Design had been commercial artists and illustrators and brought a high degree of technical proficiency to the task.[67] They were paid the WPA weekly rate for professional work, which was not generous but sufficient to meet basic needs.[68] The rate differed according to the local cost of living; the top rate, paid in New York City, was $23.50 per week.[69] Artists often worked long hours voluntarily because they enjoyed painting; they were officially expected to work at least fifteen, but no more than forty hours every week. The minimum number of hours required of all types of artists was less than that expected of other WPA workers because, as one of the New Deal art administrators pointed out, "a fiddle player can't play forty hours a week. He would be a menace to everyone near and prob-

ably go crazy himself."[70] On this schedule, Index artists usually needed between two and six weeks to complete a rendering, but very difficult pieces might take eight to ten weeks.[71] Timekeepers sometimes checked to be sure the artists were at their jobs during the appointed hours, and artists were expected to submit weekly time reports.[72]

Index artists usually worked on site, directly before the objects.[73] That might be in a museum or a private collector's home, or in an Index studio if the object's owner had agreed to lend it and have it temporarily installed there (figs. 6–8).[74] Occasionally it was not possible to make a rendering directly from the object. Some owners refused to allow the artists into their homes and would not lend objects to the project's studios. Also, especially in rural states, objects available for rendering might be distributed over a wide geographical area, and the Index did not have funds for transportation and temporary housing to allow the artists to travel to and stay in remote locations. In those cases, artists would work from black-and-white photographs and color notations made either by Index supervisors or by the artists during short visits (figs. 9, 11).[75]

Although the vast majority of Index renderings are watercolor, other media such as crayon, chalk, and color pencil were also used, usually in combination with watercolor. Graphite was often appropriate for metallic objects, and opaque pigments were better suited to some objects than transparent watercolor. Some projects, notably in Maryland and western Pennsylvania, hired photographers to make black-and-white photographs rather than artists to make renderings of objects.[76] Color photographs were not considered a suitable alternative to watercolor plates. The photographic color processes available in the 1930s were not cost-effective, sufficiently permanent, or accurate enough in recording color to meet the Index goals. Index administrators also believed that a camera could not capture the "essential character and quality of objects" as an artist could, and this basic spirit of the work was what they aspired to portray in Index renderings.[77]

The Index provided its artists with all materials, which were generally of very high quality. In each state, the Index supervisor was responsible for ordering materials by requisition through the Treasury procurement offices.[78] The Massachusetts project assigned a group of artists to test materials, and the results were shared with all the state projects.[79] Papers were tested for their ability to resist wear and yellowing, and medium-grain paper was selected as generally the best surface for the fine detail required in an Index rendering.[80] Artists used a number of different papers.[81] Whatman, an excellent English watercolor paper, was common, although the artists working in Philadelphia used Strathmore paper.[82] Occasionally renderings were made on Unbleached Arnold, a very fine English paper, or on Arches Watercolor, a French paper. Often artists used paper that the supplier had already mounted on stiff pulp board.[83] Strathmore Drawing Board was another type of support commonly used by Index artists; dense and smooth, it consists of multiple layers of pure cotton paper pasted together.

The Massachusetts project also tested pigments for their permanence and ability to mix with other pigments.[84] Texture was an important criterion. Grainy pigments were specifically avoided because the larger grains of color did not disperse completely in the water and gave a rough rather than smooth and even finish to the colored surface. The recommended colors were ultramarine, Indian red, cadmium orange, alizarin, cadmium yellow pale, and cadmium red.[85] Windsor and Newton, and Rembrant were the artists' two favorite brands of paint.[86] The Index also supplied artists with the best brushes available, for example, a wide selection of sable or camel-hair brushes that tapered to a fine point, and wide ox-hair brushes for applying flat washes.[87]

The artist's first step in creating a rendering was to make a scale drawing of the object on graph paper. Ordinarily the Index supervisor had to approve this drawing before the artist could commence work on the final color plate. Once finished, the artists' renderings were evaluated by the state supervisors and, if approved, sent to Washington, where national coordinator Adolph C. Glassgold again reviewed them.[88] If he considered a rendering not up to Index standards, he sent it back to the state with recommendations for further work. To show exactly where it needed improvement, he laid a piece of tracing paper over the rendering and wrote his recommended changes on it. Sometimes he returned a drawing two or three times before accepting it. Sometimes artists simply gave up and never finished the plates. The plates that were accepted became the property of the federal government, and the staff of the national office stored them in file cabinets (fig. 10).[89] The best renderings circulated frequently in Index exhibitions.

The Renderings

The task the Index project assigned its artists was to make completely accurate illustrations of folk, popular, and decorative art for other Americans to consult in their search for a national vocabulary of design. Although the artists were compiling pictorial resources from which modern artists and designers might derive inspiration, in producing such a compendium they themselves had to resist engaging in the very kind of creative interpretation or abstraction their work aimed to stimulate in others. The renderings would successfully function

Fig. 10
Renderings are stored in file cabinets, National Gallery of Art, Washington, Gallery archives

in the role for which they were intended—conveying information about the heritage of American design—only if they were undistorted visual records of the objects they represented. Describing a similar situation in the writing of historical biography at this time, Alfred Haworth Jones observed that "if [the 1930s] turned to the past as a guide to the present, then landmarks must be accurate and reliable or the lessons would be misleading. Hence meticulous attention to authenticity became a canon of the decade."[90]

Despite these necessary constraints, many of the watercolor plates are exquisite works of art in their own right, and according to an Index administrator in New York, "the main body of Index artists unquestionably felt they were doing a creative job."[91] Restrictions on artists' work are certainly not unique in the history of art; complete artistic freedom is not always granted to artists, who nevertheless have produced excellent works even while submitting to patrons who insist on absolute compliance with their specific wishes. Exceptional artists have often served as anonymous members of disciplined workshops or have generated magnificent sacred art while meeting the strict formal and iconographic demands of religious communities. They have made ravishing depictions of botanical specimens that also fulfill the exacting requirements of scientific accuracy. Even under severe restrictions artists can, and do, make aesthetic choices that distinguish their work from that of diligent artisans.

An observant eye can detect the often subtle evidence of such choices in the Index of American Design. Elizabeth Moutal, for example, chose to artfully arrange pestles inside their mortars for a satisfying composition (cat. 27), and Rosa Rivero animated her rendering of a Texas corner cupboard by deciding to open the cupboard's door (cat. 38)—a choice not made by other Index artists who depicted similar pieces of furniture. The artists' techniques were sometimes complex and clearly the result of aesthetic deliberation. Artists made careful decisions about how to achieve specific effects because they aspired to express some telling quality of an object. Many made the choice to commit all their considerable skills to accomplishing the purposes of the project. M. Rosenschield-von-Paulin, for example, chose to devote exceptional care to the depiction of a mere candle stand (cat. 33), and Albert Rudin to an old pair of roller skates (cat. 63).

Despite the declared goal of the Index to make all the renderings appear to be the work of a single hand, and despite the overall consistency of appearance that was actually achieved, one artist's work can still be distinguished from that of another. A comparison between three sets of renderings of similar objects made by different artists illustrates the diverse means the artists selected to represent like objects—and their choices created renderings whose style, on close examination, is as individual as handwriting.

Both Charlotte Angus and Mae A. Clarke made outstanding renderings of textiles, but no attentive viewer would ever confuse a rendering by Angus with one by Clarke (cats. 46, 44). Angus preferred a light application of primarily transparent colors. She occasionally allowed them to puddle where she wanted to represent a shadow, but more often she waited until the paper was dry and then added some well-considered brush strokes. Her technique was broadly suggestive in the treatment of detail, and yet it conveys a sense of the fabric's weight and feel. Clarke's colors were less watery, more tightly controlled. She was meticulous in indicating each stitch of thread, and she accomplished this by waiting until the pigments were dry and then gouging deep cuts with a pin or knife point, down to white paper. With her exquisite, three-dimensional treatment of the deep puckering around the stitches, she fully communicated her knowledge of both the fabric's softness and the batting's depth. Using distinct stylistic languages, both Angus and Clarke made wholly convincing illusions of textile.

Edward L. Loper and Elmer G. Anderson each made renderings of iron stove plates (cats. 17, 16). Both interpretations of these ponderous objects are utterly convincing, but they could hardly be more dissimilar. Loper relied exclusively on watercolor over a light graphite drawing. After stroking the colors onto the paper, he manipulated them, blotting and scraping and then applying more color to build up layer upon layer of brown, gray, green, and red. Finally he added white heightening to intensify some areas he had already scraped down to the white paper. To portray a similar object, Anderson first pressed deep lines into the paper with a pointed tool. The displaced paper raised a lip on each side of the furrows. The artist then drew on this prepared surface with black chalk. The chalk did not sink into the submerged lines, which remained white, but caught on their

raised edges, making these some of the blackest areas in the drawing. Here and there he drew hard with his pointed chalk, but in most areas he touched the paper lightly, letting the chalk adhere only to the bumps of the medium-texture, cold-pressed paper. He rubbed the chalk over the surface carefully to leave just the right suggestion of graininess.

To illustrate a sgraffito plate, Albert Levone used thin, flat washes of yellow in conjunction with more opaque green and red (cat. 21). Each letter in the text around the rim consists of multiple brush strokes of gray, brown, and black, one laid down after the other as they dried to show the depth of the letters. On the central part of the plate, he also applied successive layers of his medium, sometimes wet paint on wet paint and sometimes wet on dry. By allowing these layers to puddle and bleed into each other, he compellingly re-created the appearance of slip floated on ceramic. He was a master watercolorist who could let the paint flow freely and spontaneously from his brush, knowing exactly how it would react as it met the paper and previous applications of paint. For a rendering of a very similar plate—probably made by the same nineteenth-century potter—New York artist Giacinto Capelli chose a somewhat thicker yellow pigment (cat. 22). He used careful, controlled brush strokes to depict and model the details precisely; in some areas he blotted the wet paint to

lighten it. This artist also added a profile view of the plate below the main image. Levone's and Capelli's renderings are equally successful but very different, clearly the work of two artists, not one.

Suzanne Chapman, the *Index of American Design Manual,* and More about Technique
The extraordinary quality of Index of American Design renderings can be attributed to a great extent to the inspiration and training provided by Suzanne Chapman of the Museum of Fine Arts, Boston.[92] Chapman was hired by the Index as a special supervisor of textile work in spring 1936 and remained with the project until 1937.[93] She had studied at the School of the Museum of Fine Arts in the 1920s, where she benefited especially from the instruction of Alice Morse. Upon completion of her training, Chapman was employed by the museum to make exact watercolor reproductions of textiles and other decorative arts from the museum's collection. After leaving the Index she joined the museum's Egyptian and classical art departments as illustrator for their publications. Emily Townsend Vermeule of the department of classical art described Chapman's drawings as "not only beautiful but honest. This honesty, total accuracy, is a rare quality and part of the character that makes her drawings so highly prized.... The uncompromising eye is allied to a steely force of character.... To look at a vase or fragment with Miss Chapman is to see a dozen things one would have missed. She sees with her pencil."[94]

In February 1936 Index field representative Nina Collier, along with Gordon Smith, who was soon to become the supervisor of the Massachusetts project, met with Gertrude Townsend, curator of textiles at the Museum of Fine Arts. They arrived at the museum with the request that Townsend allow Index artists to make renderings of that distinguished collection of American textiles.[95] Although Townsend was initially very reluctant to admit the Index artists into her realm, she eventually acquiesced. At a subsequent meeting at the museum, Townsend proposed that Chapman supervise and train artists working on the museum's textiles, and the Index representatives enthusiastically agreed. Chapman's work astonished them. It epitomized and even surpassed their fondest hopes for what Index of American Design renderings might be (cats. 39, 40, 41). The techniques Chapman introduced to the project enabled Index artists to produce renderings that defied viewers' certainty as to whether they were looking at watercolor plates or the real objects. These renderings, at their best, could almost be categorized as trompe l'oeil for their capacity to fool the eye, to make it seem incapable of distinguishing between reality and illusion.

Chapman and some of the artists she had trained helped prepare the first written instructions for Index artists and their supervisors, the focus of the *Index of American Design Manual*.[96] Interviews conducted with the artists during the 1980s indicate that the instruction manual was actually less effective in teaching rendering methods than were the "tricks of the trade" the artists shared with one another.[97] The manual, however, is important today as a written record of some of the techniques employed by Index artists and in providing clues to how they achieved some of their brilliant effects. Its introduction stressed that the manual offered practical suggestions gleaned from other artists' experience, not rules that had be followed: "these outlines on technique are compiled from the notes made by artists on the Index of American Design. They are not intended to be mandatory but simply suggest methods that have been found by practice to give excellent results."[98] The manual was a typical set of instructions for watercolor technique and far from being "an attempt by the federal state to control artists' visions and techniques," as one late twentieth-century study has claimed.[99]

The manual addressed "Media and General Methods" with advice on what paper, brushes, and colors might best be used, as well as how to work, when necessary, from photographs (fig. 11). It offered instructions to artists on how to make a preliminary pencil drawing and suggested that they lay a paper "mask" around the image to keep the paper clean while working (fig. 12). It also explained how to make last-minute repairs of mistakes—as well as when to give up and start over. Most important, it carefully described Chapman's technique for keeping the paper wet during the course of an entire day's work, which enabled the artists to perform their fastidious task more slowly and to achieve a soft effect that was particularly desirable for textiles. Once her pencil drawing was done, Chapman soaked her paper, placed it on a wet blotter, and then put paper and blotter on a drawing board covered with oilcloth.

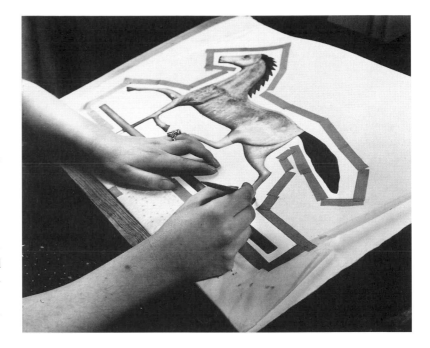

After pushing out the air bubbles with another blotter, she attached the paper to the board with many thumbtacks. At the end of the day she removed the paper from the blotter and allowed it to dry overnight. The next day she would again wet the paper, this time from the reverse side, using a sponge, in order to prevent the previous day's painting from running. She then repeated the process of attaching the wet paper and wet blotter to an oilcloth-covered drawing board and commenced work again.

The Index manual also gave separate consideration to each type of object an Index artist might render. There were detailed suggestions on how to portray ceramics, wood carvings, textiles, and metal objects. It also described how to apply color, "working in" the light areas first and then building up the more intensely colored or darker passages, and how to use transparent washes, applying layer upon layer to achieve the desired effects. The manual provided specific instructions on "stopping out" areas that were to remain uncolored, and on using fixative, erasers, and sandpaper to good effect. Careful examination of a few larger-than-life details further reveals some of the watercolor techniques employed by Index artists.

Enlarged details of Isadore Goldberg's and John Tarantino's *Stoneware Jar* (cat. 20) show the results of the complex work described in the manual, as well as techniques the artists probably brought to the project from their prior experience.

Fig. 12
A mask taped around the figure helps keep the paper clean, National Gallery of Art, Washington, Gallery archives

Goldberg and Tarantino applied multiple layers of wet blue paint that flowed and bled into each other to simulate the uneven resolution of blue slip in the salt-glazing process of stoneware. In the gray areas they seem to have manipulated the still-wet surface with a small, blunt tool—perhaps a pencil eraser—that pushed spots of pigment aside to leave pale, shallow indentations with dark puddles of gray on one side. To heighten this mottled effect they added a few short brush strokes of wash. In some areas they seem to have rubbed off the paint and added new patches of wash. The paper is roughened in these areas and the lifted fibers catch and reflect light, re-creating the effect of illumination on the surface of the actual jar. When the watercolor was dry, and sometimes when it was still wet, the artists scratched white hatching lines through the blue paint with a finely pointed tool, then pricked out tiny points and dug away some big chunks, variably exposing the paper below. These lines, dots, and gouges are sometimes not even visible to the naked eye, and yet they have a tremendous impact on our perception of the rendering, very effectively simulating the irregular, crazed finish of the glaze and the way that light reflects inconsistently off its surface.

Equally instructive are large details of two renderings of wooden objects, John Matulis' *Circus Wagon Figure* (cat. 73) and Marian Page's *Rooster* (cat. 2, page 60). The Index manual advised artists to "model each tiny groove and indentation as carefully as the larger masses. Do not be satisfied with a dark stroke of color as representing a depression."[100] The cracks in the dried-out surface of the circus wagon figure seem real enough for us to touch as they open and close, precisely following the grain of the wood. Matulis has painstakingly modeled each one with flecks of light reflected consistently from the side facing the perceived light source. Page gave equal care to rendering the rough surface of the toy rooster, describing the cracks and lifted chips of paint with an exacting focus worthy of monumental sculpture.

Enlargements of two textile watercolors, Flora G. Guerra's *Money Bag* (cat. 50) and Esther Molina's *Crazy Quilt* (cat. 48), may further increase our sense of wonder at the artists' accomplishments. Guerra and Molina were able to depict each thread as a separate entity, shading and highlighting it to give it form and create the illusion that one thread lies atop the other. The texture of Molina's velvet

seems even more tangible viewed close-up. We can see each irregularity of the quilt's surface and in the threadbare portions actually observe an underlying layer of fabric. The magnified detail shows the fuzzy edge of the piping along the side; this may not be visible to normal eyesight without magnification, but we can feel its presence almost subliminally, slyly convincing us that this is not a watercolor at all but real fabric. In an enlarged view of the top fringe on Guerra's bag, the strands tangle over and around each other, apparently moving above and below the picture surface, and the chords of the blue ornament seem to reach out in every direction.

It was this intense concern with three-dimensional detail that the manual encouraged in Index artists. A passage on rendering embroidery, for example, says: "Each thread is a cylinder...it is important to notice the holes caused by the needle and the puckering of the background where the embroidery draws it, as well as irregularities in contour caused by the necessity of drawing each embroidery thread *between* threads of the ground."[101]

The magic of the Index renderings seems to lie in their uncanny power to make us feel that we are seeing the portrayed object with preternaturally acute vision. Taking as an example Chapman's *Valance* (cat. 39), it seems as if her artistic gift allows us to experience this embroidered textile in all its infinite detail, to gain profound knowledge of its materiality almost at a glance. To understand how the artist achieved this, it is important to remember her training at the Boston Museum School and her career recording artifacts for the museum. Like medical, botanical, or ornithological illustration, the kind of rendering that Chapman executed of the museum's holdings can be more valuable than photography to those whose accurate analysis of a subject depends on an absolutely clear, unambiguous image. The camera, like the untrained eye, detects merely optical information; it records facts uniformly. It may miss important details if they are obscured by shadow or within complex patterns. The artist, on the other hand, can sort and evaluate features, then emphasize those that reveal the most important attributes of an object. The work of such ingenious illustrators—for science, for archaeology, or for the Index of American Design—may reach an almost unnatural perfection because the artists endow these images with factual, intimate knowledge of the subject beyond what is easily seen or quickly learned. The best Index artists would minutely observe and contemplate the tactile qualities of the surface, its luminosity, and its most subtle gradations of color, texture, and form, with a care and affection rational humans rarely commit to inanimate objects. These artists also needed uncommon manual skills and technical expertise to combine and translate all this optically, intellectually, and sensuously acquired data into perfect two-dimensional facsimiles. Studying these renderings under magnification may reveal some of their secrets, but it dispels none of their sorcery.

Early in 1937 an exchange of ideas and renderings began among the state projects, aimed at improving artists' techniques. Step-by-step process plates, such as Chapman's *Valance: Demonstration Drawing* (cat. 40), Lucille Chabot's *Angel Gabriel Weather Vane: Demonstration Drawing* (cat. 79), and possibly Molina's *Crazy Quilt* (cat. 48), were sent to Index supervisors as aids in instructing artists on rendering techniques. There were at least six sets of process plates, and as better ones became available, the older were replaced. Glassgold observed in 1947: "I believe these demonstration portfolios probably played the most effective role in producing generally the almost uniformly high quality of workmanship, and uniformity of method."[102] Starting in 1938, especially gifted artists from Boston and New York City, and occasionally from other states, traveled to provide on-site instruction to their colleagues in other Index projects.[103]

Data Sheets, Portfolios, and the End of the Project
An official "Data Report Sheet" (WPA Form 30A) accompanied each rendering. Compiled by Index staff, these data sheets presented pertinent facts about the original object, sometimes derived from the object's owner and often supplemented with additional research (fig. 13).[104] With the help of librarian Phyllis Crawford Scott, Index administrators organized a team of research workers, but occasionally Index supervisors, or even artists, were responsible for compiling the information on the data sheets.[105] These sheets recorded the name, period or date, maker, and original owner of the object and stated how each of these facts had been verified. They also documented the object's materials, colors, condition, and measurements, as well as the current owner and location. The name of the

artist who made the rendering appeared at the bottom of the data sheet. The Index supervisor dated, signed, and gave a classification number to each form.[106] This classification number identified the state, the category of object, and the number of the object in the state's sequence of that category. For example, a carved figure of a carousel goat rendered by an Index artist in Rhode Island was classified "RI, ca, 67," for Rhode Island, carving, the sixty-seventh (carving) rendered in that state (cat. 8). One copy of the data sheet was attached to the back of the rendering, a duplicate was filed at the national office, and the state art director retained a third copy.

The planners of the Index of American Design project expected it to culminate in the publication of a series of portfolios reproducing a selection of renderings, organized by type of object.[107] There were to be portfolios on furniture, metalwork, Shaker artifacts, stoneware, and other categories of objects, including one on early manufactured and patented goods. By means of these portfolios, which would be distributed in libraries, schools, and private homes throughout the United States, the Index would acquaint a broad cross section of Americans, including artists and designers, with the folk art and crafts of their national past, an aspect of this country's cultural heritage that was relatively little known at the time. As the project progressed, however, the publication of the portfolios was repeatedly delayed. Project administrators were unable to find a satisfactory medium for the reproductions, and they wanted to accumulate a large quantity of

Fig. 13
A research worker completes a data sheet, National Gallery of Art, Washington, Gallery archives

excellent renderings, accompanied by accurate and complete research, prior to making a selection for the portfolios. Before these ideals could be realized and the portfolios produced, the project ended.[108]

Three experimental portfolios were published, but none was a great success in fulfilling the hopes the project leaders had for these volumes. In 1938 the New Mexico project reproduced renderings in hand-colored block prints for the *Portfolio of Spanish Colonial Design in New Mexico*. The preliminary work for this publication was performed by an earlier, local arts project in Santa Fe that had independently set out to reproduce images of saints.[109] When the Index finally was established in New Mexico, the work of this earlier project was used for the experimental portfolio. In 1940 the Pennsylvania project published *Folk Art of Rural Pennsylvania* with silk-screened prints of renderings, and in 1941 the Southern California project produced *Mission Motifs*, also using silk-screened illustrations.

Although the plan to publish the portfolios and to widely disseminate them across the country was not achieved, the goal of familiarizing Americans with these images of their cultural heritage was partially accomplished in another way. During the years in which the Index operated there was an almost feverish effort by Index staff to bring exhibitions of the original watercolor renderings before the American public, in part to help generate goodwill for the project (fig. 14).[110] These exhibitions often appeared in venues that were easily accessible to most Americans—not only in museums and

libraries, but also in department stores, book shops, hotels, banks, and antique stores—and consequently attendance was enormous.[111] In an undated essay from the 1930s, Glassgold wrote:

> About twenty exhibitions have been held in large department stores, including Marshall Field of Chicago, R. H. Macy of New York, Stix Baer & Fuller of St. Louis, Hutzler Bros. of Baltimore, Bullocks of Los Angeles, and Rike Kumler of Dayton. Outstanding museums that have displayed the Index are the Cleveland Museum, the Art Institute of Chicago, the Detroit Art Institute, the Museum of Modern Art, the California Palace of the Legion of Honor, the Dallas Museum, the Milwaukee Art Institute, the San Diego Fine Arts Museum, the Cincinnati Museum, and the Worcester Museum. The material has been shown in about thirty Federal Art Centers and by a large number of cultural organizations, such as the University of Pittsburgh, the University of California, and Yale University.[112]

Through these exhibitions many Americans came to know and cherish the Index of American Design, as well as the folk art that it illustrated.

It was not long after the Index of American Design project began that the federal government started to decrease incrementally its funding to arts programs. In the early days of the Federal Art Project, administrators were permitted to hire a sizable number of nonrelief workers to help with the projects, and most—such as Suzanne Chapman and Constance Rourke—were supervisors and administrators. In fall 1936 the permissible number of nonrelief workers decreased to equal no more than ten percent of the relief workers, and in 1937 it was cut again to five percent. The Appropriations Act of 1937 reduced the whole FAP budget by twenty-five percent. The number of workers employed on all four arts projects went from 39,000 in April 1936 to 28,000 in July 1937.[113] The most drastic reduction occurred in 1939, however, when the project was effectively turned over to the states and the Works Progress Administration was renamed the Work Projects Administration.[114] By April 1942 national unemployment was no longer a serious problem as the United States entered World War II, and Congress shut down the Index project before its staff considered the work complete.

For a short time after the project's termination, the Metropolitan Museum of Art in New York housed and cared for the Index renderings, and Benjamin Knotts, who had succeeded Glassgold as national coordinator of the Index in 1940, acted as its curator.[115] Because the renderings were officially the property of the United States government, a federal institution had to be selected as their final destination. Archibald MacLeish, poet, librarian of Congress, and ardent promoter of Americana, hoped to acquire the Index for the Library of Congress. Cahill, however, considered the newly founded National Gallery of Art a more suitable repository for these works. He convinced Harry Hopkins, former head of the WPA who served as a special assistant to President Roosevelt during World War II, to support him in his effort. Cahill later recalled that Hopkins was fairly preoccupied by events surrounding the Nazi defeat at Stalingrad, "but the Index of American Design was important enough for him to listen to me…. I wanted it to go to the National Gallery, and I got Harry's support, so that no matter what MacLeish did, he was always blocked. Harry was like that. He liked what we had done, and he gave his loyalty to it."[116] Cahill easily convinced David Finley, then director of the National Gallery, to accept the Index as part of its collection.[117]

In 1943 a formal agreement was reached to send the Index of American Design to the National Gallery, and in 1944 it was shipped from New York to its new, permanent home in Washington. Each year since it arrived in Washington, hundreds of Americans have consulted the Index—which is now part of the department of modern prints and drawings at the Gallery—through visits, letters, or telephone calls. During the 1980s Laurie Weitzenkorn, assistant curator in charge of the Index, began to organize existing archival materials on the Index, to locate and conduct interviews with surviving Index artists—an invaluable source of information—and, with Charles Ritchie, assistant curator of modern prints and drawings, to implement a new system of storing the renderings using archival materials. Ritchie, Jane O'Meara, and Victoria Foster all contributed to the cataloguing of the Index. Anne Ritchie, senior archivist and oral historian for the Gallery archives at the National Gallery, directed the massive project of organizing the substantial quantity of documents related to the Index of American Design and the preparation of a finder's guide to this material. Samuel Larcombe, a great advocate of and expert

on the Index, assisted her in this effort. The National Gallery has presented many exhibitions of the Index and, through the Gallery's National Lending Service, has circulated shows throughout the United States. The most comprehensive exhibition of the Index was mounted at the Gallery in 1984–1985, organized by Lina Steel and Nancy Allyn and accompanied by Allyn's excellent brochure.[118] The present exhibition is the first major show on the Index since 1985.

Two authors have published notable surveys of American folk and decorative art using Index renderings as illustrations. Neither author had been associated with the Index during its years of operation and both seem to have been more concerned with the works represented in the renderings than with the project itself. The first was Erwin O. Christensen, who became curator of the Index in 1945. His book is titled *The Index of American Design*, but only the introduction, written by Cahill, concerns the Index project. Clarence P. Hornung reused Cahill's introduction for his 1972 book, *A Treasury of American Design*.[119] A set of microfiche reproducing thousands of Index renderings was compiled in 1980. It was accompanied by *The Consolidated Catalog to the Index of American Design*, edited by Sandra Shaffer Tinkham. Lina Steele and Lisa Fukui contributed to this effort. A selection of renderings is now posted on the National Gallery's Web site.[120]

The Goals of the Index of American Design

Whatever it may mean to the cultural future of America one cannot at this time prophesy, but that its meaning is more than mere antiquarianism is self-evident.

　　Adolph C. Glassgold, "Recording American Design"

An American Modern Art
The primary purpose of Roosevelt's New Deal art projects was to provide work relief for artists. The federal government's massive support for these projects also offered the American arts community unprecedented opportunities to accomplish additional goals. Foremost among these was the chance to respond systematically and constructively to discouraging assessments of American culture that had been promulgated during the preceding decades. The negative self-image so many had

come to accept was one of provincial boorishness. Van Wyck Brooks, along with other critics, despaired that there was no truly American art or even a tradition of art in this country. Critics complained that art was not part of ordinary, daily life—as it presumably was in Europe—and that without such cultural resources to elevate their minds and spirits Americans were doomed to persist in their present, uncouth state.

Pioneers and Puritans were meted an ample portion of blame for these conditions, suggesting that our problems might come from the very roots of our nationhood. Critics claimed that the pioneers' extreme cultivation of industry and thrift as the virtues of survival had resulted in a level of materialism that deadened all finer sensibilities, while the Puritans' repression of earthly joys had extinguished the heart and soul of artistic expression.[121] Despite the dismal state of American culture as they perceived it, many of these critics voiced hope that a dedicated search through our history might reveal previously overlooked materials of value— what Brooks had labeled a "usable past."

Rising to the challenge, American artists, writers, and cultural historians set forth on a patriotic quest for evidence of such a native cultural tradition. In this search for an inspirational American past, they were in fact following the established path of European artists who had taken from folk and other primitive art—not necessarily that of their own countries—direction in developing modern forms of abstraction.[122] Two scholarly investigators intent on uncovering an American cultural patrimony were Constance Rourke and Holger Cahill, who later became, respectively, the editor of the Index of American Design and national director of the Federal Art Project. A third was Edith Halpert who, in a business partnership with Cahill, promoted and sold American folk art as the progenitor of American modernism. Rourke, Cahill, and Halpert contributed to the development of a new concept of American art and presented the Index of American Design as necessary groundwork for the future of our national arts.[123]

Constance Rourke, one of the most devoted advocates of the movement toward cultural self-recognition in America during the 1920s and 1930s, was an earnest believer in the mission of the Index of American Design; she once confided to Cahill her heartfelt conviction that the Index was "basic for the future development of the arts in this country,

and for a full understanding of our cultural and social history."[124] Using the word "design" for the typical artistic expression of a nation, Rourke wrote that if the Index of American Design could be successfully carried to completion, "the questions 'What is American design?' or 'Have we an American design?' may answer themselves"—we might have an answer, in other words, to that nettlesome question: what is American in American art?[125]

Long before she became involved with the Index, Rourke had delved enthusiastically into American popular and practical arts to prove that these unexplored regions of our culture showed recurrent patterns of creative expression and that they amounted to an artistic heritage both creditable and highly "usable." She did this most famously in her 1931 study of American humor, in which she "traced a mythic imagination in American folk tales and literature alike."[126] In her celebration of popular art as evidence of a vibrant, if unrecognized, epicenter of American culture, Rourke was at odds with some of her contemporaries who shared the rhetoric of her search for "genuine Americanness," but who disdained the popular arena and found very little in the American past they wished to own. She also differed from the regionalist painters of the 1930s, whose ideas regarding popular culture and modernity—although not their aesthetics— in some ways resembled her own; she dismissed Grant Wood as having "many times used superficial and transient elements of the American subject without touching its core."[127]

In July 1935—at precisely the moment when Romana Javitz and Ruth Reeves were preparing to launch their proposal for a grand picture index of Americana—Rourke's "American Art: A Possible Future" appeared in the *American Magazine of Art*.[128] In this article she sought to clarify our "full native inheritance" in the arts, to demonstrate, using concepts and terms appropriated from contemporary anthropology, that it was an organic development from the "peculiar and irreducible social forces" of our *total* culture.[129] She asserted that the puritans and pioneers had played a beneficial role in our culture. Puritan New England, she maintained, had taken sensuous delight in the abstraction of simple form and had left this aesthetic pleasure as its legacy to American art.[130] Furthermore, according to Rourke, our national creative genius was most evident in exactly those tools and useful artifacts that the pioneers had perfected through their intense focus on the practical arts.[131] Yet, as Brooks admonished: "her interest was never antiquarian."[132] Although she researched America's folk past, Rourke's true concern was for the present and future of American culture. In 1938, shortly after leaving the staff of the Index of American Design, she published a biography of artist Charles Sheeler, whose work she considered the epitome of modernism, grown wholly from the American tradition.[133]

When Rourke, in her 1935 article on the future of American art, proposed that "the American painter might gain assurance in a contemporary mode if he knew by heart the spare abstract as this appears in many phases of our folk expression," she was describing rapprochements that had already been made between folk and modern art, beginning at an art colony in Ogunquit, Maine.[134] The colony's founder had frugally decorated its cottages with American folk art, a type of American "antique" that was not so highly esteemed or voraciously collected by wealthy colonial revivalists of this time. The painters and sculptors who stayed in these Ogunquit cottages—including Charles Sheeler, Robert Laurent, and Yasuo Kuniyoshi—were astonished to discover that this unfamiliar art embodied aesthetic principles that they had previously understood as purely modern. It was simple yet strongly expressive in form; folk artists had naively achieved the same qualities of abstraction to which modern artists aspired in their work. These modern artists were so smitten by what they saw in Ogunquit that they began to collect folk art themselves, and the first exhibition of this relatively unknown material, at the Whitney Studio Club in 1924, consisted entirely of the works they had amassed.[135] It was the purpose of this groundbreaking show in New York City to proudly display the aesthetic affinities between American folk art and American modernism. A perceptive newspaper reviewer announced that the exhibition amounted to nothing less than "the discovery of our artistic past."[136]

The Ogunquit modernists whose folk-art collections made up the Whitney Studio Club show were all friends and acquaintances of Holger Cahill, who would soon be recognized as a leading authority on both American modernism and folk art.[137] In the late 1910s and early 1920s, Cahill had lived in New York City and worked as a freelance journalist while taking classes at Columbia University and the New School for Social Research from

John Dewey and Thorstein Veblen. During these years, Cahill associated with and wrote about members of the early twentieth-century group of American painters known as the Eight, or the Ash Can School, and founded a dadaist group he called the Inje-Inje. He also was hired to manage publicity for the Society of Independent Artists, a job previously held by the owner of the Ogunquit art colony. Publicity, it soon became evident, was a task at which Cahill excelled.[138] John Cotton Dana, director of the Newark Museum, was impressed by Cahill's success in public relations and hired him in 1921 to help publicize the second Deutsche Werkbund exhibition Dana would bring to the Newark Museum.[139] The next year Cahill became a regular employee of the Newark Museum, writing educational and publicity texts for exhibitions and organizing a series of shows on modern American art. Acknowledging Cahill's expertise in modern art, one of the tasks Dana gave him was to help select for purchase a collection of contemporary American paintings—art that few other museum directors at that time were interested in acquiring.[140]

Cahill left his job at the Newark Museum when Dana died in 1929 but was "lured back" by Dana's successor to organize several exhibitions, including a modern American watercolor show in 1929 and the first two museum shows ever devoted to American folk art, *American Primitives: An Exhibit of the Paintings of Nineteenth Century Folk Artists*, in 1930, followed a year later by *American Folk Sculpture: The Work of Eighteenth and Nineteenth Century Craftsmen*. In 1932 Cahill became acting director in charge of exhibitions at the Museum of Modern Art in New York, where he organized yet another folk-art show, *American Folk Art: The Art of the Common Man in America, 1750–1900*, this one consisting nearly entirely of Abby Aldrich Rockefeller's collection, which he had helped assemble. Held in the first American museum dedicated to the representation of modern art, which had opened just three years earlier, this exhibition emphasized the aesthetic connection that Cahill drew between folk art and modernism. The label the exhibition gave to folk art, the "art of the common man," further linked it to the populist spirit that was so important to Cahill and to this decade of Americans. The show was immensely successful, traveling to six other cities in the United States after closing in New York.

In his catalogue for the show, Cahill referred

to folk art as "the unconventional side of the American tradition...the work of craftsmen and amateurs of the eighteenth and nineteenth centuries who supplied a popular demand for art."[141] After discussing the various categories of folk art in the exhibition, he concluded his introductory essay by observing that the "pioneers" of modern art, rebelling against the "naturalistic and impressionistic tendencies of the nineteenth century," had discovered folk art and recognized its aesthetic relationship to their own art.[142] Also in 1932 Cahill published an article in an American art journal further analyzing the "kinship" modern artists found between their work and folk art. Folk art and modern art, Cahill held, both showed "indifference to surface realism," as well as "honesty...and...a great deal of vigor and imaginative force." Although folk painting and sculpture had their own intrinsic appeal, he maintained they were most valuable for their "definite relation to certain vital elements in contemporary American art."[143]

As Diane Tepfer, biographer of Edith Halpert, has observed, the content of these three initial museum exhibitions of American folk art was

mainly limited "by accident of geography" to the objects Cahill and Halpert could gather conveniently on automobile trips through New England and Pennsylvania.[144] It was not until 1935, when Mrs. Rockefeller paid Cahill's expenses to travel through the South in search of folk art to purchase on her behalf, and not until the federal government funded the Index of American Design, that Cahill could add Southern and Spanish colonial artifacts to his range of expertise in American folk art.

Cahill acknowledged the omission of Spanish colonial art in his catalogue for the *Art of the Common Man*—probably mindful that such modernists as Georgia O'Keeffe, drawn to the Southwest by the majesty of its desert landscapes, had expressed great admiration for the region's indigenous artifacts. Southwestern art was not in the show because it was not represented in Mrs. Rockefeller's collection of folk art, which made up all but one piece in the exhibition. Cahill wrote that although New England and Pennsylvania were the most productive centers for folk art, and although most of the works in the show were from those locations, along with a "fair number" from New York, New Jersey, and the South and Midwest, "there is another type of American folk art, found in the Southwest states, particularly in New Mexico, which is not included in this exhibition. This art has a marked Spanish influence, is largely religious in character, and is related to Mexican colonial art."[145] With the Index project, he was at last able to close the gap, to give America's Southern and Southwestern folk art a more thorough representation. This was particularly true of Southwestern art. The Index holds more than 950 renderings of Spanish colonial artifacts, as compared to about 350 Shaker and about 600 Pennsylvanian German renderings.

Cahill expected Shaker, Pennsylvania German, and Spanish colonial art to have a beneficial influence on contemporary American art and design. In his introduction to Christensen's book with Index reproductions, he wrote that the art of the Shakers was a "forerunner" of modern design in its "severe integrity in handling materials, its discarding of ornament in favor of unadorned surface and its sense of fitness and function." He also hoped Pennsylvania German and Spanish colonial art would make an important contribution: "Pennsylvania German and Spanish Colonial which are related to peasant art seem further away from us. Yet, in their

Fig. 15
William Michael Harnett, *The Old Violin*, 1886, oil on canvas, National Gallery of Art, Washington, Gift of Mr. and Mrs. Richard Mellon Scaife in honor of Paul Mellon

feeling for surface and their stimulating influence on our all but lost sense of vivid and clear color in articles of everyday use they have much of value for the contemporary designer and craftsman." The Index staff was eager to gather a sufficient quantity of Spanish colonial material for a portfolio—a successor to their earlier effort with the New Mexico project—and apparently encouraged Index supervisors in the Southwest to attend to this matter as expeditiously as possible.[146] The Index supervisor in Texas, Thomas M. Stell Jr., wrote to Cahill and Glassgold in June 1939 that he shared their desire to illustrate such artifacts, but that his artists were still learning the Index skills: "the workers need more time to perfect their techniques before starting on the Spanish-Colonial objects, which are so rare that it is desirable that the rendering of each object be done with the greatest perfection."[147]

In 1931, the year in which Cahill organized his exhibition of folk sculpture at the Newark Museum, he went into business selling folk art with Edith Halpert.[148] They opened the American Folk Art Gallery in New York City, upstairs from Halpert's Downtown Gallery on West Thirteenth Street—one of the first galleries to promote and sell modern American art. In the summer of 1927, Cahill had visited Edith Halpert and her husband Samuel, a painter, while they were staying at the art colony in Ogunquit, Maine. Halpert and Cahill, like the artists associated with this colony, were thrilled by the formal similarities between the American modernism and folk art they found there. Although each would have been acquainted with these similarities from the 1924 Whitney Studio Club show and probably elsewhere, it seems to have been their shared encounter with folk and modernism juxtaposed in Ogunquit studios that led to their partnership in the American Folk Art Gallery.

Their business relationship lasted until 1941, although in 1931 Cahill had already begun to question Halpert's method of sharing profits.[149] Cahill did benefit, however meagerly, from the sale of folk art while he promoted it by means of the Index of American Design. The inventory of the American Folk Art Gallery was rendered for the Index—a cooperative venture that was at least as advantageous to the Index as it was to the American Folk Art Gallery. It was certainly no secret that Cahill was a partner in the American Folk Art Gallery—in fact it was probably part of the experience that qualified him for his federal job—and apparently in the 1930s this type of business connection was not considered to be of questionable propriety, as it doubtless would be today.

Halpert and Cahill sold folk art not for its antiquarian interest, one of the primary motivations for many antique collectors of the day, but because it seemed to provide an ancestry for American modernism.[150] They organized three folk art shows titled *Ancestors of American Art*—in 1931, 1933, and 1938—and installed them in Halpert's modernist Downtown Gallery rather than in the American Folk Art Gallery. Their carefully worded press releases emphasized that they were presenting folk art in these exhibitions to demonstrate that modernism was the recognizable and predictable outcome of a continuous American tradition.[151] Folk art was a "usable past," a validation after the fact, for the American modernism that had already begun to evolve without initial recognition of its own rich patrimony. The theoretical genealogy Cahill and Halpert advanced for American modern art originated in American folk art. It moved next to the work of such American trompe l'oeil painters as William Harnett (fig. 15), who had been rediscovered by Edith Halpert in the mid-1930s. She had held the first retrospective of his work in the Downtown Gallery in 1939.[152]

Art historian Wanda M. Corn, while contemplating the "complexities of this modernist gaze into the past," recognized that Cahill, Halpert, and Rourke had constructed a "new paradigm" in the history of American art.[153] This paradigm—which, as Corn notes, persisted until recently in American studies—specified an exclusively American tradition in art that began in the vernacular art of the nineteenth century and was not connected to developments in Europe. As Corn has demonstrated, Cahill, Halpert, and Rourke all cited the work of Charles Sheeler as the evidence that made their paradigm seem most plausible (figs. 16, 17).[154] Sheeler not only collected folk art but frequently portrayed works from his collection in his paintings, drawings, and photographs.[155] He allowed his Shaker furniture to be recorded in renderings for the Index of American Design, perhaps encouraged to do so by Rourke, who was his close friend as well as his biographer. Sheeler's thoroughly modern precisionist paintings, drawings, and photographs—which were as likely to show factories as folk art—not only depicted early American artifacts,

but also seemed to share with these artifacts a purity of form, a reduction to abstract essentials, and simplicity and restraint.

Corn's analysis of the new paradigm invented by Cahill, Rourke, and Halpert focuses on some of the finest works of American art created between the two world wars, and Index renderings are not part of her analysis. Nevertheless, examining parallels between Index plates and these great monuments of American art does help clarify the place of the Index within the context of 1930s art. Like much of Sheeler's work, for example, Index renderings simultaneously recorded the evidence of an American tradition and, through their style, participated in that tradition. For the Index plates, it was the meticulous, trompe l'oeil presentation of their subjects that drew them into alignment with the new paradigm, a point Cahill emphasized when he wrote that "to find their peers in American art we must go back to the still-life of William Harnett and the trompe l'oeil painters of the nineteenth century."[156]

Americans who saw Index exhibitions during the 1930s reacted to the renderings in the same way nineteenth-century audiences had to Harnett's paintings: with astonishment at watercolors that seemed indistinguishable from the actual objects. Lincoln Rothschild, an Index administrator in New York, recollected that "Index artists became so skilled in representation of textiles and embroidery that people seeing plates of such material in exhibitions frequently asked, 'Is that a piece of cloth or a painting?', even expressing tentative indignation 'if a beautiful antique was cut up like that!'"[157] In 1937 Constance Rourke further described viewers' reactions to the Index: "it is no exaggeration to say that the observers have been able to satisfy themselves that the mounted plates were watercolor on paper rather than the actual textile only by the sense of touch."[158] Index artists attested that they tried to make not a picture of an object but the object itself. New York City artist Leo Drozdoff said: "it is meaningless to state that the Index artist 'copies' an object. He does more. Actually he 'recreates' the object."[159]

Yet it was not the goal of Index artists, as it might be of trompe l'oeil artists, to deceive, to trick their viewers into trying to pick up the objects and thus to amuse them with the recognition that reality can be difficult to distinguish from artifice—or to impress their audience with supreme virtuosity.

Index artists had a more sympathetic, less sensational cause: to create such a perfect illusion of the object that the viewer could feel its presence and sense its material qualities with complete conviction. Isolating the images on blank sheets of paper would most often contradict any attempt to convince the hapless viewer that this was the real object, not a watercolor. It is probably because textiles were often mounted for display on white backgrounds that renderings of textiles were most frequently mistaken for the actual pieces.

The compositional format of Index renderings in some ways heightened their trompe l'oeil effect and thus strengthened their link to the paradigmatic American art tradition. By suspending their subjects—the same ordinary objects favored by Harnett and Sheeler—in front of a flat, white background, the artists offered no suggestion of setting or spatial context. This seemed to force the volumetric objects forward, in front of the picture plane, to appear more insistently as part of the real world. Harnett sometimes used a similar technique, setting a still life in front of the flat surface of a door that appeared to be on the same plane as the picture surface, or barely recessed behind it. This blocked any illusion of depth that might accommodate the three-dimensional objects and seemed to project them out of pictorial space into real space. Furthermore, just as each subject of an Index rendering was iconic and self-contained—suspended in the vacuum of its blank, white paper—the objects in Harnett's and Sheeler's pictures often seem strangely, hermetically isolated from one another, even while coexisting in what Corn described as "formal group portraits" (figs. 15–17).[160]

In late August 1935, when Cahill was first weighing Reeves' and Javitz' idea for an Index of American Design project, he apparently considered using black-and-white photographs rather than watercolor renderings for the proposed pictorial archive. He and Reeves seem to have agreed that Sheeler's, Walker Evans', and Edward Steichen's photographs, which pictured a hard-edged, concentrated reality, would be ideal for the Index (figs. 18, 19).[161] They were exemplars of the documentary style that was such an important part of the WPA's writing, music, photography, and art projects, and that Cahill believed was a prominent feature of the American aesthetic.[162] In 1938 Lincoln Kirstein wrote of Walker Evans' photographs: "The sculpture of the New Bedford ship-builders,

Fig. 20
Walker Evans,
*Fireplace, Burrough's
Bedroom, Hale
County, Alabama*,
1936, gelatin silver
print, National
Gallery of Art,
Washington, John
Wilmerding Fund

the face-maps of itinerant portraitists…continue in his camera. We recognize in his photographs a way of seeing which has appeared persistently throughout the American past."[163]

Cahill boasted that Index renderings were among the masterpieces of this genre: "fully one-half of the plates will meet the highest contemporary standards for documentary art, and most of these will set new standards in the field."[164] Documentary art rejected—or pretended to reject—all suggestion of aesthetic subjectivity, handing the viewer just the plain facts devoid of interpretation filtered through individual temperament. Frequently, 1930s pictorial documents pictured what was common or humble—exhausted tenant farmers, dilapidated rural structures, the tired implements of daily life on the margins— and seemed to uncover what was essential in them (fig. 20). The intended reaction was emotional, an overwhelming sense of personal involvement with the matter so starkly at hand. William Stott called this the "direct documentary method," quoting Roy Stryker, head of the Farm Security Administration's photography team, that to be successful a documentary photograph "should tell not only what a place or thing or a person *looks* like…it must also tell the audience what it would *feel* like to be an actual witness to the scene."[165]

Good documentary art, like trompe l'oeil art, had to be so real that it seemed to replace reality, and to achieve that, the artist who performed the magic had to be completely hidden. In Sheeler's work, like Harnett's, the mediating presence of the artist was noticeably absent; there was "no showmanship. Just honest craft."[166] Artist Marsden Hartley said of Harnett: "In the strict sense he was without a personal life—he interpreted nothing… he was only interested in getting down a group of the commonest objects…and expressing every single aspect about them, not merely their shapes in the camera sense, but also their individual textures…there is the myopic persistence to render every single thing, singly."[167] Rourke, in her biography of Sheeler, testified that "the artist remains in shadow, only partially portrayed, and…the cord is there to pull down the shade at any time…. His self-effacement is practically complete."[168] Similarly, according to Reeves, all the renderings produced by the Index of American Design would ideally appear, at least superficially, to have been made by just one hand, not individual artistic personalities.[169]

Drozdoff reiterated these aesthetic goals: "Index plates done in different regions seem to have been done either by one artist or in one technique. This undoubtedly establishes the fact that art employed for documentary purposes can be brought to such a degree of standardization...that, regardless of execution, the finished product is a document."[170] Reviews in the national media during the 1930s applauded the renderings for their lack of "artiness, for their impersonality...and...objective beauty."[171]

This demand for strict objectivity does not betray a nefarious attempt by the FAP to dehumanize the Index artists, however, any more than Harnett and Sheeler were personally diminished by their seeming nonpresence in their works of art. As discussed earlier, the individual styles of different artists are evident to the careful observer. Drozdoff stressed that even within the rigid limits of documentary art, the Index artist "exploits his creative faculty.... Although factual and precise, [the rendering] is created through an understanding and skill that are grounded in the fine arts."[172] Documentary art of the 1930s asserted its modernity by decisively rejecting any communication of the artist's personal emotions or visual "impressions." Artists of the preceding period had aspired to depict these subjective qualities, and 1930s modernists reviled their work for its sentimentality.

The search for a cultural legacy from which a modern American art could evolve was not a new cause when the New Deal art projects began; it was well under way during the late 1920s and early 1930s. What was new, and what did change the entire landscape of this campaign, was the massive financial support and the administrative structure that was committed to this effort through the government art projects. Now a vast army of artists, musicians, and writers could be mobilized to lay the foundations of the definitively American modernism to which so many had committed themselves. Suzanne LaFollette, reviewing *New Horizons in American Art*—a 1936 exhibition at the Museum of Modern Art of works produced by the FAP— wrote that the depression "may prove to have been the best thing that ever happened to American art" because of the New Deal art programs.[173] Similarly, Constance Rourke described the Index as "fortunate," because "except for the depression probably no enterprise of so wide a scope could have been initiated, and scope is essential if basic values in American design are to be revealed."[174]

The Index and American Industrial Design

The creators and administrators of the Index of American Design hoped it would play an important role in the development of an American modernism. The 1930s concept of modernism, however, was not limited to the fine arts. The applied and practical arts, including industrial design, were equally part of the modern ideal. To many Americans and Europeans, the 1930s—with the "machine age" finally at full throttle—seemed like the threshold to a new world that would witness the final collapse of an old hierarchy that had consistently ranked the fine arts as superior to the applied, the handcrafted above the machine-made. Index leaders hoped their project would help accelerate the evolution of American design, enabling industry and its artists to create a new kind of modern art for everyday life. This art would be mass-produced and affordable to everyone, it would defy the existing segregation of the arts, and it would express itself in the nation's own, distinctive cultural language.

One of the goals Holger Cahill set for the FAP was to realize this egalitarian vision of well-designed, mass-produced, utilitarian goods that would serve as modern art for the lives and homes of all people—"from the shaping of a teacup to the building of a city."[175] His populist goals had evolved from the progressive ideals of the previous generation, although they involved much greater governmental support through the New Deal than most progressives would have found acceptable.[176] John Dewey, Thorstein Veblen, and John Cotton Dana—all compelling spokesmen for progressive principles—had served as mentors to Cahill while he formulated ideas about art and its responsibilities to society that would later materialize in his plans for the FAP. From Dewey, Cahill had learned that American democracy should enable a "free and enriching communion" between people and art in all spheres of human endeavor.[177] From Veblen, he had gained appreciation for modern industry as the most effective, democratic means to produce useful goods that would benefit all members of society.[178] From Dana, who shared his admiration for Veblen, he acquired a marked distaste for the notion of art as a luxury product for the elite.[179] The way in which Cahill defined his utopian goals for the FAP sometimes recalls the rhetoric employed by left-wing political activists of the 1930s; it was a tone and vocabulary typical of many writings from this time of acute economic and social crisis, although Cahill was not directly involved with the radical political movements of the day.[180]

Cahill's FAP was going to lay the groundwork for a renaissance of American culture by bringing art back to the people, closing the gap that had separated the artists of this country from their public, and the fine from the practical arts, for the past century.[181] In addition to opening hundreds of community art centers in primarily rural areas and adorning thousands of public buildings throughout the country with murals, the FAP would bring art to Americans through the Index and the influence it would have on the development of American industrial design. After feasting their eyes on the bountiful offerings in the Index of American Design, modern designers and manufacturers would produce items that were handsome, inexpensive, and useful, as well as modern and imbued with an authentically American form. Modern industry would create mass-produced goods that were "the only art that many individuals know."[182] Artists would no longer need to rely on "the whimsical support of museums and private collectors, artists would again have true patrons [among the people] as they had in medieval Europe."[183]

According to Cahill's interpretation of the history of American art, until the mid-nineteenth century art had been part of the everyday life of all people because it had been integrated with crafts. Sign painters, cabinetmakers, shipwrights, woodcarvers, and blacksmiths had supplied the popular demand for art, and their work was "an honest and straightforward expression of the spirit of a people."[184] These years marked a great period of folk and popular art, when "the interests of the common man began definitely to shape American art."[185] After the Civil War, however, everything changed, Cahill explained. The newly rich of the industrial age became the dominant class, and they flaunted overly ornate goods as objects "of conspicuous display." This conspicuous display and waste, which Thorstein Veblen's book *The Theory of the Leisure Class* had brought to the forefront of American consciousness, was a recurrent theme in 1930s writings that heralded the wonders of modern design.[186] Lewis Mumford, for example, complained that "modern industrial design is based on the principle of conspicuous economy [but] the bourgeois culture which dominates the Western World is founded…on the principle of

conspicuous waste." Modern industry, Mumford added, offered the common man hope for the future by producing objects that were inexpensive, plentiful, and functional, and by promising that with machines, "every member of society [would have] an equal share in the essentials of life."[187] The beleaguered middle class, far from losing confidence in American industry during the depression, believed that modern technology could repair the economic devastation of their dark day.[188]

Since the mid-nineteenth century, organizations devoted to the reform of art and society had preached the gospel of a modern art that drew no distinctions between the crafts and so-called higher arts, of a modern art that would infuse the lives of all people with grace and beauty. This utopian scheme—forging connections between art and life—had been one of the motivating ideals of the arts and crafts movement, and it became the legacy of this movement to the various modern design groups that succeeded it.[189] These later groups did change the formula for societal redemption through art in one important respect: they discarded the European arts and crafts movement's romantic, impractical abhorrence of machine-made objects. The modern design movements were determined to reform art and society through the application of the newest and best tools available to them: industry and technology.

One of the earliest of the new design confraternities was the Deutsche Werkbund, founded in Munich in 1907 with the intention of bringing together art and industry, fostering a partnership between fine and commercial art, and promoting the development of a German national design.[190] Walter Gropius, one of the leaders of the Werkbund, later became director of Germany's Bauhaus, the government-supported school devoted to uniting art and industry that became an international symbol of modernity by the mid-1930s.[191] Bauhaus students followed an interdisciplinary program, taking instruction in the fine arts as well as learning about modern industry and its techniques for mass-producing aesthetically pleasing, useful objects. The faculty of the Bauhaus included some of the most outstanding artists of the time, along with craftsmen and designers who had practical experience in manufacturing.

By the early 1930s the concept of a modern art that embraced not just painting, sculpture, and graphic art, but products made by machines, had already captured the imagination of many American modernists.[192] The earliest manifestations of this aesthetic date to World War I and its aftermath. French dada artists Marcel Duchamp and Francis Picabia, for example, who had arrived in the United States at this time, used their provocative wit to convince American artists that they should value the modernity of their popular machine culture as the true pinnacle of American creativity. In 1934 the Museum of Modern Art (MoMA) presented its *Machine Art* exhibition, displaying as works of art such machine-made objects as propeller blades, furnaces, and kitchenware, although in this show the impious humor of the dadaists had given way to a profoundly serious attitude toward industrial art.[193] Also in 1934, Edith Halpert organized a show at the Downtown Gallery in which artists whose work she sold, including Charles Sheeler and Stuart Davis, exhibited objects they had designed for mass production, alongside one of their paintings or sculptures.[194] Sheeler, who had worked in commercial as well as fine art and whose oeuvre included stunning images of modern industry, had designed such utilitarian objects as salt and pepper shakers, eating utensils, and textiles that seem inspired by the Shaker works he collected and portrayed in his paintings, drawings, and photographs.[195]

The widespread and almost messianic campaign during the 1930s to reform industrial design, to facilitate the creation of the mass-produced, affordable goods that many considered the quintessence of modernism and their best hope for the future, coexisted with rampant fear of the machine and its power to enslave and dehumanize.[196] As Marshall Berman has observed, this conflict was, and is, one of the defining features of the modern world: "the basic fact of modern life... is that this life is radically contradictory at its base." The monstrous engines we dwell among are geared as well for destruction as construction, and "to be modern is to find ourselves in an environment that promises us adventure, power, joy, growth, transformation of ourselves and the world—and at the same time, that threatens to destroy everything we have, everything we know, everything we are."[197] In the catalogue for the *Machine Art* exhibition, MoMA's director Alfred H. Barr Jr. examined these competing views of technology and offered a suggestion for how this dilemma might be resolved. He wrote that humanity was "lost in the... treacherous wilderness of industrial and commercial civilization.

On every hand machines literally multiply our difficulties and point our doom." He added that we could force these mechanisms to gently serve rather than menace us if we would just "assimilate the machine aesthetically as well as economically. Not only must we bind Frankenstein—but we must make him beautiful."[198]

When the National Socialists closed the Bauhaus in 1933, the idea of opening a school in the United States that would resume its educational mission had immediate appeal.[199] Once again, the FAP offered the American arts community the opportunity to achieve a significant goal it had conceived but not yet found the means to accomplish. In 1935 the regrettably short-lived Design Laboratory school opened in New York City as a unit of the FAP, its function linked to that of the Index of American Design.[200] The Design Laboratory offered a free education in design to adults who could not otherwise afford it, with a curriculum based on that of the Bauhaus. Like the Bauhaus, the school was government-sponsored and emphasized coordination in the study of aesthetics, industrial products, machine fabrication, and merchandising. Ruth Reeves, one of the designers who helped organize and administer the Index, also served on the staff of the Design Laboratory.[201] In a memorandum Cahill wrote in 1936 to Captain Henry I. Brock, art critic for the *New York Times*, he stated that the Design Laboratory and the Index of American Design were two of the most compelling programs within the FAP and that the Index was "a continuation of the work that was done in the Design Laboratory."[202] The Index of American Design would continue the work of the Design Laboratory by compiling a pictorial archive of folk and popular art for designers to consult in their quest for an ideal prototype of American design.

Holger Cahill, Ruth Reeves, and Adolph C. Glassgold, three of the chief administrators of the Index of American Design, all came to the project with a clear understanding of modern industrial design as the new art of the American people. Reeves and Glassgold, along with Gilbert Rohde, director of the Design Laboratory, had been members of the American Union of Decorative Artists and Craftsmen (AUDAC), the closest organization in the United States to such European design groups as the Deutsche Werkbund.[203] Founded in New York in 1928, the AUDAC was a consortium of artist-designers determined to modernize American

Fig. 21
Holger Cahill on
the cover of *Time:
The Weekly
Newsmagazine,*
5 September 1938,
photograph TimePix

design. AUDAC members, like their counterparts in Europe, represented all fields of design, and some were masters of several. Glassgold correctly observed that "practically every important American designer is an AUDAC member."[204] In 1930 the AUDAC published, as a kind of manifesto, *Modern American Design*, a book of essays in which members expressed their utopian hopes for modern industrial design and in which their works were illustrated. One wrote, for example, that the modern movement must "through the agency of the machine...make available for the masses what is now the luxury of the few."[205] Another insisted that industrial design was necessary, not for "the development of great art, but rather [for] the fostering of quality in ordinary art, of the kind or kinds that daily serve the 'cross-section of the people,' contributing to its comfort, convenience, or pleasure."[206]

Reeves had become a member of the AUDAC after she returned to the United States in 1927 following seven years in Paris, studying under Fernand Léger at the Académie Moderne.[207] She exhibited her textile designs in AUDAC exhibitions starting in 1928, and her work appeared among the illustrations in the AUDAC's *Modern American Design.* Reeves also had important one-woman shows of her work in New York, and she was hired by Donald Deskey to design modern textiles for the opening of Radio City Music Hall, a popular shrine to modernism in the 1930s.

Glassgold, national coordinator of the Index, was also an active participant in the modern design movement in New York during the 1920s and early 1930s. He had been an art instructor at the City College of New York in the early 1920s and later joined the AUDAC. After the AUDAC disbanded in 1931, he became associate editor of *Creative Arts: A Magazine of Fine and Applied Art,* and then curator of museum extension at the Whitney Museum from 1932 to 1934, where he organized a symposium on abstract art in 1933.[208] He wrote a series of articles in the late 1920s and early 1930s proselytizing on behalf of modern design in America while noting that although the modern style emerging in the decorative arts was international, it was still both possible and desirable to work toward creating a distinctly American expression within the outlines of this style.[209] Glassgold was one of the editors of *Modern American Design.* He contributed an essay in which he declared that it was high time for American designers to emancipate themselves from European patterns, that American industry should produce forms suitable for contemporary life, and that the machine must be "a means to the full cultural development of man."[210]

Reeves and Glassgold were both contemptuous of the period-style reproductions so popular in their day. Reeves' own working method, which she hoped would be the approach other artists would take to the Index, was to extract a design concept from a work of a different period or culture and to use it as a "liberating springboard" for her own, original design.[211] Glassgold also maintained that the Index was gathering material to serve as inspiration for design that was appropriate for modern times, not as a picture index of antiques for designers and manufacturers to copy.[212] Reeves, Glassgold, and Cahill were all resolute modernists, determined that the Index would be a resource for the creation of modern, mass-produced goods, not antique reproductions. An article Cahill coauthored for *House and Garden* as publicity for the Index, "American Design: From the Heritage of Our Styles Designers Are Drawing Inspiration to Mould National Taste," began with a firm declaration that antiquarianism was not the motivation of the project: "Antiquarianism would have us set back the clocks, get rid of our machines and gadgets, and build a Chinese Wall against the present. The modern industrial designer and craftsman, and all those who believe in the creative spirit of American decorative art, hold that the past should not mean an atmosphere of quaintness and nostalgia, but a source of vitality and renewal for our own day."[213]

Cahill, like Reeves and Glassgold, had close connections with the contemporary industrial design movement. In October 1927 Cahill, Halpert, and Bee Goldsmith had organized a show integrating modern American painting and sculpture with applied arts at the Venturus Gallery in Wanamaker's Department Store, to coordinate with an adjoining exhibition of modern French design.[214] Glassgold gratefully acknowledged this demonstration of support for modern American applied arts in a review he wrote for *The Arts*.[215] Cahill had worked for eight years at the Newark Museum, where John Cotton Dana had been the first American museum director to promote modern industrial design as a new and thoroughly American art. Throughout his career Dana conducted a tireless crusade to elevate

the applied and industrial arts to the status of fine arts, once claiming, with typical flourish, that "if beauty be the most perfect adaptation of means to ends, then industry is as full of art and beauty as the Milky Way is full of stars."[216] He organized several nontraditional exhibitions in Newark. One, in 1915, included a roomful of bathtubs, and another consisted of handsome household goods that were mass-produced and cost no more than ten cents each.[217] By means of these unorthodox shows he endeavored to prove the two central tenets of his ideology: that art and industry could go hand in hand, and that "beauty has no relation to price, rarity, or age."[218] In 1936, seven years after Dana's death, Cahill acknowledged his profound debt to his mentor in a lecture he presented at the Newark Museum for the opening of an exhibition of art produced by the FAP, saying that the show might have been titled, "Homage to John Cotton Dana."[219]

It was probably the connection to industrial design that engendered enthusiasm about the Index among such a broad spectrum of Americans, from conservative businessmen and -women to liberal idealists. It seemed to conjure for them all the inspiring dream of a future when all Americans would partake in their national cultural heritage and when enlightened, democratic industry would provide useful, artistically designed products for American homes.[220] Reeves recollected, years later, that the promise of the Index to "inspire fresh and more distinguished designs in America's design-for-living industries...was, right from the start... one of our strongest selling points in our effort to win public and congressional approval for the Index project."[221]

Cahill, a former journalist and publicist, knew how to enlist the popular media for his cause, to convey his message about the FAP and "art for the people" to millions of Americans. *Time* magazine, with a circulation of approximately 800,000 in the late 1930s, reported in its 5 September 1938 cover story that the FAP was "getting people all over the U.S. interested in art as an everyday part of living and working" (fig. 21).[222] This article also noted that Cahill was fond of saying, "you don't often find mountains where there is no plateau," meaning that a nation had to have a widespread, popular art movement before great masters would emerge.[223] Lewis Mumford, who had once joined the critical chorus deploring the starved and stunted development of America's arts, proclaimed in the *New Republic* that through the good offices of the FAP, the American artist "at last…has been brought into working relations with his fellow citizens."[224] Similarly, E. M. Benson—the associate editor of the *American Magazine of Art* who had led the crusade for opening an American school to continue the mission of the Bauhaus—claimed that the FAP "has helped to heal the breach between the artist and the man in the street. It has helped to convert art from a luxury and a confection into a useful and necessary element of our daily life."[225]

Fortune, a magazine whose readership included the captains of American industry, actively promoted modern industrial design during the 1930s, even commissioning Sheeler to paint a series of images of industry for its covers.[226] In May 1937 *Fortune* published a glowing evaluation of the New Deal art projects. The article—unsigned, but authored by Archibald MacLeish—praised the art projects for having substantially enriched American life, reaching many people who had never had the opportunity to experience art and thereby preparing the soil for the flowering of a "genuine art movement" in the United States.[227] The art projects, the article claimed, were also performing a remarkable service in documenting American life, "piling up the kind of raw cultural material…which is so necessary to artists and particularly to artists in a new country."[228]

The following month MacLeish singled out the Index for special consideration in a sequel to his article on the FAP. He began by citing familiar complaints about the lack of an American tradition in the arts: "[American art] has no roots in the depths of the American soil. It has no relation to the life of the American people. It rests on no peasant handicrafts, no popular taste, no anonymous workmanship."[229] Anyone who believed these criticisms, MacLeish contended, would find the Index of American Design "something of a shock" because in the popular and practical arts it portrayed—"the so-called lower levels of anonymous and useful workmanship"—the spirit of American art has survived. The article concluded with the prediction, "if the publication of the plates of the *Index of American Design* does not profoundly influence the work of modern designers of articles of use, the loss will be ours—and the designers.'"[230]

The Accomplishments of the Index of American Design

The Index taught the nation that…what had been considered curios for the delectation of collectors or the exploitation of dealers were in reality the material deposit of the artistic genius of the common man.

> William F. McDonald, *Federal Relief Administration and the Arts*, 1969

As author Joan Didion pondered her recurrent visual memory of Boulder Dam—a 1930s symbol of the coming utopia promised by American technology—she thought about the great bronze sculptures that adorn the site, lifting sheaves of wheat toward the heavens and defying its thunderbolts. She called them "muscular citizens of a tomorrow that never came."[231] The anticipation of a glorious future in which all people might equally thrive, a golden age in which those heroic bronze figures might comfortably dwell, was endemic to the 1930s and its WPA art projects, despite—or perhaps because of—the prevailing economic misery. The Index of American Design was the creation of true believers with a noble cause. It was going to influence the course of American art and design to the great and lasting benefit of the American "common man." This, too, may seem a tomorrow that never came.

As art historian Wendy Kaplan has observed, not only the most liberal segments of society embraced the idea of folk design forms as epitomizing a national identity, but the most conservative as well: "Romantic nationalism was both progressive and conservative, modern and anti-modern."[232] While Cahill and his colleagues were conducting their quest for a national art grown from the American folk tradition, hoping to further the cause of modernity and the cultural enfranchisement of the common man, fascists in Europe were cultivating national cultural forms as part of their program for the annihilation of alien groups, individual freedom, and modern art. Following the prolonged agony of World War II, nationalism and the conceptual linking of folk art to the expression of a national persona became suspect in America through association with fascism.[233] In 1949 H. W. Janson exclaimed, "The whole question of 'American style' smacks strongly of cultural nationalism and is in danger of involving extra-artistic criteria."[234] Even Holger Cahill demurred at this time, "I don't think it is particularly important to ask whether or not a work is American."[235]

Representational art seemed to reverberate with memories of the brutal realism of fascist art—and, after the war, with the social realism adopted by the totalitarian communist state. Janson, apparently disgusted by American popular taste, referred to the "artistic doctrines of Hitler" and wrote that "leafing through the illustrations of 'healthy' and 'degenerate' art...it is difficult to suppress the feeling that a vast majority of the American public, given the choice in the matter, would agree with the policies of the *Reichskulturkammer*."[236] He also deplored the alliance certain artists had made with industry, reminding his readers that industry, "unlike the genuine art patron," only appreciates art as a means to make money, not for its own sake.[237] Alfred H. Barr Jr. worried even more about communism: "the more conservative and popular styles which the ignorant suppose...are peculiarly American have their counterparts...above all in the U.S.S.R. where 'modern art' was strangled twenty years ago."[238] "Mass Culture" became a pejorative term and critics, including Clement Greenberg, Dwight Macdonald, and Gilbert Seldes, defined it as "kitsch," a debased continuation of folk art into the twentieth century.[239] Harold Rosenberg concluded that "mass culture threatens not merely to cretinize our taste, but to brutalize our senses while paving the way to totalitarianism."[240]

The art that found approval by some leading 1950s art critics was the art that aspired to be all that fascist and communist totalitarian art were not. It had to be universalist rather than nationalist; it had to be nonrepresentational and abstract, like the "degenerate" art that Nazis and communists repressed; it could not convey political messages; and most of all, it could not address or cater to the masses.

With its dreams of a national aesthetic idiom that would synthesize the fine and applied arts for the enrichment of Everyman now fallen into disrepute, the Index of American Design was evidently not going to lead the way into the promised land of an American modernism. Instead, it settled into a quiet but useful life after the war as an antiquarian's catalogue of Americana, its old ideals rarely mentioned or even remembered. The trompe l'oeil, documentary style that the Index artists had perfected was no longer in demand in the marketplace of American art; in some quarters it was even con-

demned as a threat to democracy. The concept of modernism that had, in the 1920s and 1930s, motivated such artists as Charles Sheeler to design household items for mass production, lost momentum in the aftermath of World War II; in the 1950s, the Museum of Modern Art discontinued its landmark series of design exhibitions.[241]

Whatever else it may or may not have accomplished, the Index of American Design spared many American artists extreme hardship during the depression. Furthermore, nearly seventy years later it is still the most extensive and inclusive pictorial representation of American folk, popular, and decorative arts. As its administrators predicted, many of the original objects captured by the Index have been either lost or badly damaged since they were rendered and would be unknown today. It seems nothing short of miraculous that the Index of American Design managed to produce such an extraordinary body of material, regardless of whether it achieved its goal of having a lasting impact on American art.[242]

Looking beyond the immediately obvious, what else can be said for the Index? In fact, a great deal. We can acknowledge that it participated in, and perhaps even dominated, the prewar effort to enshrine folk art as the true visual record of the American spirit. It also conveyed this idea far outside the limited group of American modernists and their patrons who might otherwise have been the only ones to learn about it, and instilled in a wide cross section of Americans the notion that folk art mirrored the soul of American design.

It is impossible to specifically identify and separately quantify the impact of the Index of American Design among all the cultural forces that joined in the search for a "usable past" for the sake of a modern future in the United States. The Index was neither the first nor the only proponent of this quest. During the years of the project's operation, however, Americans did recognize the Index as contributing significant momentum to this cause. As the leading historian of the WPA art projects concluded in 1969: "The Index of American Design did more than record the 'usable past'; it popularized, as museums and art associations had never done, American folk art.... The Index taught the nation that...what had been considered curios for the delectation of collectors or the exploitation of dealers were in reality the material deposit of the artistic genius of the common man."[243] The Index had spent its considerable energies and influence promoting among the citizens of this country the notion of Americana as the epitome of "American-ness." Once this idea became a mainstream concept, it was not forgotten, even though the Index itself was scarcely remembered as one of its principal messengers.

Although the Index of American Design does not appear to have played a meaningful role in the development of the major art trends that evolved in America during the second half of the twentieth century, it does seem to have had a significant impact on how we perceive the art of this period— on the way we have defined our art of the late twentieth century as American, as an extension of ourselves and our national history and environment.

Harold Rosenberg, one of the leading art exegetes of the 1950s, had a theory about what made abstract expressionism so distinctly American. He called this indigenous quality "coonskinism" and even cited Constance Rourke as the source of his folksy label.[244] Coonskinism, he wrote, was the uniquely American way of creating art without reference to any preexisting tradition or preconceived method. In explicating this theory he allowed folk art to slip back into the modernist discourse in its respectable prewar guise of the true Americana. Rosenberg cited American folk art as an example of what he meant by coonskinism: "As made-up art, folk painting in America is the mass-product of Coonskinism…. Folk art has no development; its successes are a sum of individual pot shots; in sum, it lacks history."[245] Folk art and abstract expressionism, according to this theory, were both the products of an archetypal American creative process. Folk art did not bequeath anything to abstract expressionism, which, as a proper coonskin art, did not rely on or draw from anything outside itself. Folk art did provide an earlier, unconnected example of the same independent creative impulse, a precedent that set abstract expressionism in a context and perhaps even gave it a kind of tradition.

In the late 1960s Jonathan Holstein and Gail van der Hoof began collecting American quilts, admiring their intrinsic aesthetic qualities as outstanding, if primitive, examples of American abstract art. Their friend, abstract expressionist painter Barnett Newman, eagerly agreed with this assessment of the quilts. He asked if he could show them to a German critic who was interviewing him;

he wanted the quilts to illustrate his definition of American creativity.[246] He did not perceive them as sources for art like his own, but as documentation of American qualities that his art, without inspiration from the past, also spontaneously expressed.[247] In 1971 the Whitney Museum exhibited Holstein's and Van der Hoof's collection as *Abstract Design in American Quilts*. Hilton Kramer, art critic for the *New York Times*, shared the enthusiasm of Holstein, Van der Hoof, and Newman for the quilts, and wrote: "The question remains whether or not the native genius for visual expression found its most powerful expression [in nineteenth-century 'high art']…. In many quarters the suspicion persists that the most authentic visual articulation of the American imagination in the last century is to be found in the so-called 'minor' arts—especially in the visual crafts that had their origins in the workaday function of regional life."[248]

Holstein and Van der Hoof were not the only Americans with a bright new interest in folk art at this time. Lynda Roscoe Hartigan, writing about the collection of Herbert Waide Hemphill Jr., has noted that a second wave of folk-art collecting had begun to build momentum in the 1960s, and that artists were again, as they had been in the early twentieth century, among the first to amass new collections of folk art: "in both phases, folk art was a beacon for artists committed to change."[249] Andy Warhol began rummaging through Second Avenue antique shops for folk-art bargains as early as the 1950s, reportedly believing that these works "confirmed his own artistic sensibility."[250]

Some American art critics marked the transition from modernism to postmodernism with the advent of pop art. Using the same strategy employed by earlier colleagues who had explicated and promoted modernism between the two World Wars and abstract expressionism in the 1950s, some pop art advocates presented it to the public as an art in the true American spirit by citing American folk art and the paintings of William Harnett as early parallels. In 1962 critic Dorothy Gees Seckler wrote that pop artists were "again dealing with that same concrete and hard-edged object and invoking that same sense of locale that has been a hallmark of native expression. Is it possible that the cycle of styles has moved in a wide enough circle to permit the crossing of the cultural orbits of a Harnett and Jasper Johns?"[251] Like folk art, pop situated itself squarely and without apology within popular culture.

It completely eschewed the expression of personal emotions and interpretations and betrayed "a certain native humor."[252] In these attributes, and in its iconic presentation of the most ordinary objects of daily life, some pop art actually resembles the renderings of the Index of American Design. Despite these similarities, however, pop art did not find its inspiration in American folk art or, certainly, the Index of American Design. As art historian Lucy Lippard remarked, "the flag gates, nineteenth-century trade signs, whimsies, and weather vanes of folk art provide amusing counterparts to Pop Art but are unimportant sources."[253]

In the second half of the twentieth century, American artists and their commentators did not regard folk artifacts as a source for their new art. Artists inserted motifs from earlier works into their paintings as if they were pictorial quotations, but they did not draw inspiration from earlier art. Only occasionally would designers cite such Americana as Shaker crafts as precedents for their modern work; period reproductions were still common in American homes. The Index does not seem to have served as its creators had hoped it might, as an abundant "wellspring" of creative inspiration "to which all artists and designers may turn for a renewed sense of native tradition."[254] Yet the folk art the Index did so much to popularize did offer artists and those who interpreted their work a valuable precedent or parallel. Folk art helped confirm—after the fact—that the "coonskin" approach the later artists had taken to making art was typically American, granting convincing visual evidence that even if these artists had not contemplated folk art during their aesthetic process, they were apt to arrive at a similar artistic destination because they were American.

According to the prescription of Van Wyck Brooks, the past did not have to supply exemplars for direct inspiration to be usable. It only had to provide artists with a sense of cultural identity, of being part of a larger purpose. The Index accomplished that by helping to make commonplace and indelible in American culture the idea that folk art was the quintessential expression of a purely American brand of creativity. Holger Cahill called folk art "the unconventional side of the American tradition in the fine arts," and, in large measure through the efforts of the Index of American Design, folk art became our abiding proof that what was unconventional was American.

Notes

1 Brooks 1918, 337–341.

2 Rourke 1942; the essays in this book are fragments of a work in progress, a comprehensive study of American culture that Rourke left incomplete when she died prematurely as the indirect result of a fall. See Rubin 1980, 40.

3 Kammen 1991, 299. Kammen's book is a massive "history of patriotism" in the United States from 1870 to 1990. Unfortunately, he misunderstood the Index, which he described as "published in book format and...expanded steadily ever since," 476.

4 Henri Focillon, "Introduction" to *Art Populaire* (Paris, 1931), a published collection of the papers presented at the First International Congress of Folk Art in Prague, 1928, trans. Robert F. Trent, in Trent, *Hearts and Crowns: Folk Chairs of the Connecticut Coast, 1720–1840, As Viewed in the Light of Henri Focillon's Introduction to Art Populaire* (New Haven, 1977), 17, 20.

5 Rourke in O'Connor 1975, 166.

6 Exh. cat. New York 1932, 3, 6.

7 Vlach 1980, 345. In "The Index of American Design: From Reference Tool to Shoppers' Guide," in *Wood and Wood Carvings from the Index of American Design* [exh. brochure, Guild Hall Museum] (East Hampton, N.Y., 1988), 7–13, Vlach reveals his sore disappointment that the Index was not what he believes it ought to have been: primarily a written reference guide for the study of folk art. He regrets that it was instead an art project and fails to recognize what the Index founders really intended to achieve—a foundation for a new American modernism. He suspects the project's administrators of having had "ulterior motives...not openly articulated," that diverted the Index from its loftier, less art-focused aims midway through the project.

8 As a starting point in reviewing the controversial issues related to folk art today, see exh. cat. Winterthur 1977, Quimby and Swank 1980, and Vlach and Bronner 1992.

9 On Cahill's exhibitions, see below, 21. See also Rumford in Quimby and Swank 1980, 23, 36. Curiously, Vlach states that "works of folk art and folk craftsmanship constituted the primary content of the Index" ("Index of American Design: From Reference Tool to Shoppers' Guide," 12), a judgment with which few careful observers would agree.

10 Glassgold in O'Connor 1975, 167; Rourke in O'Connor 1975, 166; NGA/GA, Index Manual 1938, 1. In 1950 *Antiques* magazine acknowledged the problems attendant on the words "folk art:" "This is a name that is easy to use but hard to define, and we use it in a fairly broad sense," and published symposium proceedings on "What Is American Folk Art?" illustrated with renderings from the Index of American Design. One contributor, Frank O. Spinney, wrote:

> The gushing proprietress of the antique shop cooed that it was "quaint" when she sold it to the dealer searching for "American primitives." Observing it in the dealer's gallery a critic described it as a piece of "pioneer art" to his friend, a collector of "provincial painting." The collector gave it to a museum where the curator put it on exhibit along with other examples of "American folk art." There it was admired by visitors including some who spoke knowingly of "untutored art" by an "anonymous" "self taught" artist. Finally it was seen by a suburban matron doing the museums on her day in town. "Isn't it quaint?" she remarked.... Pity the poor writer in a plight like this! What is the proper word or phrase to adopt in referring to the work of our early non-academic American artists?

Antiques 57 (May 1950), 354, 362.

11 Sir Nikolas Pevsner, *The Englishness of English Art* (New York, 1956).

12 Although nearly all are watercolor, some of the drawings are graphite, some are gouache, and some combine other media with watercolor. There are also black-and-white photographs, such as a series made at Hancock Shaker Village in Pittsfield, Massachusetts, and a group of fire marks produced by the Pennsylvania project (see Appendix II). The exact number of renderings was not determined until the 1990s, when the National Gallery initiated a new, comprehensive system of accession numbers for all works of art in its collection. As part of this endeavor a new accession number was assigned to each Index rendering. The previous numbering system for Index renderings had been instituted during the operation of the project in the 1930s, when a state Index supervisor allotted a number to each rendering at the time the work was assigned to an artist (see below, 17). Each state employed its own sequence of numbers, and within each state there was a separate sequence for each type of object. Since the renderings were numbered before they were complete, and since many were never finished and added to the Index—in fact, some were never even begun—these series of numbers had many gaps. The numbering system made it difficult to be sure of the total number of renderings, but the Gallery's new system required each to be numbered as part of one sequence.

13 For the most complete coverage of the New Deal art projects see McDonald 1969. Other histories of the New Deal art projects include O'Connor 1972, McKinzie 1973, O'Connor 1975, Park and Markowitz 1977, Mangione 1983, Harris 1995, and Bustard 1997.

14 Roosevelt inaugurated the Federal Emergency Relief Administration (FERA) shortly after he assumed office. Within a year he also instituted the federally operated, but state- and locality-sponsored Civil Works Administration (CWA) and, shortly thereafter, the Civil Works Service (CWS). The CWS, unlike the FERA, principally provided employment for white-collar workers. It also promoted cultural projects as a form of community service. In December 1933 the CWA, through a grant to the Department of the Treasury, initiated the first program that was intended to employ artists, the Public Works of Art Project or PWAP. The PWAP, CWA, and CWS operated only for a few months.

15 McDonald 1969, 341–376, outlines the beginning of federal support for the arts in a chapter that begins: "The Federal Art Project was the dramatic expression of two tendencies in American artistic thought: a greater awareness of art on the part of the American people, and a greater awareness of America on the part of the American artist. These two developments complemented each other and promised, if fostered, to create artistic maturity in the United States."

16 "Purposes of the Project," in NGA/GA, Index Manual 1938, 1.

17 NGA/GA, Index Manual 1938, "Appendix," n.p.

18 NGA/GA, Index Manual 1938, 2.

19 On Reeves and Javitz, as well as other women who served in developing the Index, see Claire Richter Sherman, "The Tradition Continues (1930–1979)," in *Women as Interpreters of the Visual Arts, 1820–1979*, ed. Claire Richter Sherman with Adele M. Holcomb (Westport, Conn., 1981), 82. On Reeves, see Carlano and Shilliam 1993, 31–34, and Allyn 1982, 17–19. For Reeves' account of the start of the Index idea, see AAA, Reeves to Cahill 1949; on the AUDAC, see below, 29–30.

20 AAA, Reeves to Collier 1950, 3.

21 On Javitz, see exh. cat. New York 1998, 2; and Troncale 1995, 115–138. For Javitz' version of the origination of the Index, see AAA, Javitz to Cahill 1949.

22 AAA, Reeves to Collier 1950, 3.

23 He had started the nation's first picture collection in 1889 in the Denver Public Library. On Dana see Peniston 1999 and, in the

October 1929 issue of the Newark Museum's journal, *The Museum,* a collection of letters and obituaries celebrating Dana at the time of his death.

24   From AAA, Javitz to Cahill 1949, 2.

25   AAA, Javitz to Cahill 1949, 2. Javitz had traveled to Europe in 1925 and 1926 to study government-supported picture files and had found many, along with publicly funded museums and books, devoted to acquainting citizens with their indigenous costumes and folk culture.

26   AAA, Reeves to Cahill 1949, 3.

27   There were subsequent meetings on 6–8 December 1935 at which the Index was discussed with administrators of other units of Federal Project Number One. Brief reports of these meetings are preserved as "Index Reports" (National Archives, WPA, Record Group 69, Box 14).

28   It is significant that Reeves considered *Weyhe's* a prototype because—like the Index—such books usually were produced to reform contemporary patterns of design. See, for example, the introduction to *Weyhe's*: "The times in which we live are felt to be a turning point. The break with all traditions is realized more and more emphatically and distinctly. But, as yet, there has been no innovation." Helmuth Theodor Bossert, *Ornament in Applied Art [Weyhe's Ornament]* (New York, 1928), vII; and the preface to Owen Jones, *The Grammar of Ornament* (London, 1856), 1: "I have ventured to hope that…I might aid in arresting that unfortunate tendency of our time to be content with copying, whilst the fashion lasts, the forms peculiar to any bygone age." On ornament and reform, see Ernst H. Gombrich, *The Sense of Order: A Study in the Psychology of Decorative Art* (Ithaca, N.Y., 1984), 33–62.

29   AAA, Reeves to Cahill 1949, 2.

30   AAA, Reeves to Cahill 1949, 2.

31   Architecture was recorded by the Historical American Building Survey; in 1935 the Office of Indian Affairs at the Department of the Interior initiated the Indian Arts and Crafts Board under the direction of René d'Harnancourt (McDonald 1969, 414; Bustard 1997, 30); according to Cahill, a record of American Indian design was begun by Frederick Douglas in 1932, employing artists from government art projects from 1933 to 1938 (Cahill in Christensen 1950, xi).

32   NGA/GA, Glassgold to Christensen 1947, 1.

33   The state art directors, according to Glassgold, were not always artists. They included "museum people, some art gallery dealers, some writers, etc."; all the Index supervisors were artists with professional experience, and they were responsible for training the artists in their projects (NGA/GA, Glassgold to Christensen 1947, 3).

34   "It is desirable that some public or quasi-public institution indicate local interest in each project and co-operate with the Works Progress Administration in sponsoring the project…. The District Supervisor of Projects and Planning and the Art Directors and Supervisors…should circulate to all public and quasi-public agencies which might be interested in becoming Co-Operating Sponsors the Form 320…. On this form the prospective sponsor may indicate that it is willing to aid, financially or otherwise, in setting up a project…. It is expected that art projects will have Co-operating Sponsors. However, since the Federal Art Project has been sponsored by the Works Progress Administration, art projects may be set up even when no local public agency is the Co-operating Sponsor," AAA, Cahill FAP/WPA, 7–8.

35   The address of the national office was 1734 New York Avenue, NW. On the staff of this office, see Allyn 1982, 34–35.

36   NGA/GA, Index Manual 1936, 3.

37   Reeves' job as federal field advisor is described in AAA, Cahill FAP/WPA, 1–2.

38   Glassgold's friends and colleagues called him "Cook" or "Cooky," and that is probably why his name often appears incorrectly as C. Adolph Glassgold or C. A. Glassgold—even in his own publications. Glassgold's obituary, with some biographical information, appeared in the *New York Times*, 15 February 1985, 24(A). He remained in the position of national coordinator of the Index until 1940, when he was succeeded by Benjamin Knotts.

39   Glassgold described his job in NGA/GA, Glassgold to Christensen 1946, 1.

40   NGA/GA, Glassgold to Christensen 1947, 3–4.

41   For a diagram of the administrative structure of the FAP and Index, see AAA, Cahill Papers, reel 1105, frame 1091; for a list of personnel in the national office and their salaries, see "Personnel of the Index of American Design" (National Archives, WPA, Record Group 69, Box 10, folder 5).

42   See Rubin's biography of Rourke, which regrettably includes very little information about her work with the Index. For her "Employment Record" Rourke described her two successive positions with the Index: "As Editorial Consultant on the Index of American Design, under salary from the American Council on Education, I made surveys of collections of Index material, and consulted with supervisors or directors of the Index, as well as with the National Director of the Federal Art Project as to objectives and plans for Index work"; "Editor, Index of American Design. This position, involving consultation, supervision, assistance in selection of material, travel to various units of the Index, organization of work, and writing" (National Archives, WPA, Record Group 69, Box 14, Folder 5).

43   Rourke 1937, 207–211, 260.

44   See below, 17–18.

45   Constance Rourke letter to Hildegarde Crosby, 5 May 1937 (National Archives, WPA, Record Group 69, Box, 4), 2. William Warren, state director of the Index for Connecticut, expressed his appreciation for Rourke's organizational skills in a letter of 17 May 1937: "Our short talk proved to me that you are attempting to guide the Index activities in a definite direction" (National Archives, WPA, Record Group 69, Box 4), 1

46   Rourke 1938; Rourke 1942 (see above, note 2).

47   An alphabetical list of the states, noting the FAP programs in which they elected to participate, is filed among Cahill's papers (AAA, Cahill Papers, reel 1105, frames 1009–1010). Glassgold evaluated the success of each state project in NGA/GA, Glassgold to Christensen 1946, 6–8. See Appendix II for a description of the state projects.

48   Cahill later reported: "After we had allocated the Index of American Design to the National Gallery of Art, David Finley, who was then the Director, said to me, 'The thing that disappoints me about this Index of American Design is that I don't see anything from my native state of South Carolina, and there are lots of things down there.' 'Well,' I said, 'nobody could be more conscious of that than I am. I would certainly like to record a great many things in South Carolina, but there weren't any artists in South Carolina who had the training that we required for that kind of work. We could have given some work to people in that field in South Carolina, if we could have sent four or five supervisors. I tried, but we had to do two things. We had to get the consent of the administrator (like Somervell, in New York) to pay these people, and then we had to get the consent of South Carolina, or any such state, to accept them. But even if we found them and paid them and sent them to South Carolina, as Somervell agreed to do, the South Carolina administrators refused.' It was only partly because of local patriotism…. There was another element in it: the people from the outside would be paid higher rates than those in South Carolina, because the wage scale was fitted to what somebody had worked out in relation to the cost of living…. That irked the administrators down there…. It's a very invidious thing…. That sort of thing went on all the time" (Cahill 1957, 519–520).

49   Memorandum from Ruth Reeves to Holger Cahill, Thomas Parker, and Cook Glassgold, 22 August 1936 (National Archives, WPA, Record Group 69, Box 4, Ruth Reeves folder).

50   For example, "Mary Curran was appointed Director of the Pennsylvania project. But in the meantime, Mary Curran was in the doghouse with the State Administrator. At that time, the way the Federal Project was set up, no funds could be released for art in his

state unless I OK'd it with the Treasury Department, and no funds could be spent there unless he made them available, so there we were in an impasse, you see. It went on a good deal that way" (Cahill 1957, 346–347). Cahill claimed his problem getting projects started in Texas had resulted from interference by the vice president of the United States: "the Vice President at that time was 'Cactus' Jack Garner—Roosevelt's first Vice President.... He had told the [WPA] administrator down there in Texas..:'You be careful of those art projects.' And it was just impossible to get a project started there until we got a man by the name of Thomas Stell who started an Index of American Design project, and they did some very nice work" (Cahill 1957, 349–350). Cahill gave yet another example: "the Missouri project was a sad project, until I went out there one time. I went to St. Louis to give a talk in a department store which was holding a big exhibition of the Index.... I went out there to set up an Index...project... and I inadvertently said something about the fact that I had come out there to set this up, and this administrator heard about it. He just blazed. He said, 'You! *You're* going to set up an Index of American Design project!' I said to him, 'have you never been misquoted by a newspaper? I don't think I said it just that way.' There was always that sort of stuff, that pulling and hauling" (Cahill 1957, 348–349). Assuming that he was likely to encounter problems in the South, Cahill sought the help of Thomas C. Parker, a Virginian, and made him assistant director of the FAP. He later described hiring Parker: "I said, 'You know, it has been my idea to hire you for this reason: because you're a Southerner, and you will be recognized by people in the South as not just a damned Yankee'" (Cahill 1957, 343).

51 In 1939 an Index project opened in San Antonio (it was the only unit of the Federal Art Project in Texas), and it produced renderings of remarkable quality. In a letter to Cahill dated 15 June 1939, Thomas M. Stell Jr., supervisor of this Index project, described the wealth of folk material found in that region of Texas (National Archives, WPA, Record Group 69, Box 2642, file 651.3155).

52 Cornelius in O'Connor 1975, 170–172.

53 On Jensen, see Appendix I; see also NGA/GA, Jensen Talk 1985, and NGA/GA, Jensen Interview 1986. See also Jensen 1987, 78–81, 103.

54 NGA/GA, Index Manual 1938, 5; "Federal Art Project, Works Progress Administration, Index of American Design: Suggested Procedure for Setting Up Index Projects" (National Archives, WPA, Record Group 69, Box 5, Folder 7), 1–3.

55 NGA/GA, Index Manual 1938, 6.

56 NGA/GA, Index Manual 1938, 6.

57 NGA/GA, Index Manual 1938, 5. A sample questionnaire is included in the manual's appendix, n.p.

58 NGA/GA, Warren Interview 1965, 7. Also, Nina Collier reported: "One of the chief difficulties now being encountered is that of persuading collectors and owners of Americana to have anything to do with a WPA project. Many of these owners are particularly opposed to the New Deal policies and refuse to attach their names to any enterprise of this administration," Memorandum from Nina Collier to Cahill, 12 February 1936 (National Archives, WPA, Record Group 69, Box 8), 2. On an especially difficult relationship with Edward and Faith Andrews, collectors of Shaker furniture, see Allyn 1982, 55–62. Jonathan Harris mistakenly believed that the Andrews were a company and that they wanted to donate their collection of Shaker artifacts to the Index ("the Andrews Company collection of Shaker materials, which the company wished to donate to the Index," Harris 1995, 100).

59 AAA Glassgold 1939, 1 and 3. A revised version of this text was published as Glassgold in O'Connor 1975, 167–169.

60 Glassgold, in a lecture on the Index, spoke of the goal of inclusiveness and described "a canvas bedspread embroidered in cotton by Indians for the wife of a Texas rancher in which a distinctly floral New England design is interlarded with Indian religious motifs and primitively organized" (AAA, Cahill Papers, reel 1107, frame 1308). A 1937 report on the progress of the FAP states that "in North Carolina the chosen subject is the state's red-glazed slave pottery" (AAA, Cahill Papers, reel 1105, frame 1281). When he specified the ways in which he would supplement the Index if the project were to start again, Glassgold mentioned that "Indiana with its Shaker and 'river steamboat' material and Georgia with its 'slave made' products would be significant additions to the Index," and that Illinois' "material from religious communities [were] not fully exploited," nor were "cowboy materials" in Arizona and Texas, and "early settler material" in Kansas (NGA/GA, Glassgold to Christensen 1946, 5–7).

61 As Glassgold explained, "were it not for the Index of American Design the superb costumes, saddle trappings, furniture and 'santos' from the old Spanish Southwest might not be recorded. As it is, New Mexico, Colorado, and Southern California projects are making plates which when published, will come as a pleasant surprise to many" (Glassgold in O'Connor 1975, 169).

62 Glassgold in O'Connor 1975, 167.

63 In 1939 the length of time an artist could remain on an FAP job was set at eighteen months.

64 Jacob Kainen recounted the demoralizing process of being periodically fired and rehired (Kainen in O'Connor 1972, 163–164). Kainen was in the graphic arts division, but the same rules applied to Index artists.

65 NGA/GA, Chabot Interview 1986, 13; NGA/GA, Davison to Steele 1983, 2.

66 "The first step in setting up a project is the determination of the talents or skills of personnel on relief. In order to determine this, District art supervisors shall request local offices which have been designated by the United States Employment Services to refer all relief personnel registered as artists, art teachers or craftsmen in the arts to the person or committee authorized to pass on the qualifications of artists.... Persons eligible to participate in art projects will be certified as stated above to the State and District Art Supervisors," AAA, Cahill FAP/WPA, 3. On evaluating artists' skill, see also NGA/GA Jensen Interview 1986, 3; NGA/GA, Kottcamp Interview 1985, 2; NGA/GA Davison to Ritchie 1985, 4–5.

67 "Among the most highly skilled artists, from the viewpoint of the Index, were those whose training had consisted in the development of a coordination between eye and hand capable of producing visual reproductions, such as architectural renderings or illustrations for catalogues. Such orientation toward the object, and experience in producing an accurate image, were exactly the requirements of the Index program." Rothschild in O'Connor 1972, 178.

68 There was a "skill classification" for the FAP: those rated professional and technical artists were "experienced in their skill and... capable of producing creative work of a high standard of excellence"; below the rank of professional and technical, artists were evaluated as skilled, intermediate, and unskilled (AAA, Cahill FAP/WPA, 5–6).

69 Rothschild in O'Connor 1972, 184. In 1985 New Hampshire artist Lucille Lacoursiere Gauthier recalled that she had been paid $20 each week (NGA/GA, Gauthier Interview 1985, 1). Cahill reported that artists in South Carolina were paid about $75 per month (Cahill 1957, 520).

70 Arthur Goldschmidt, acting director of professional projects, quoted in McDonald 1969, 182.

71 NGA/GA, Jensen Interview 1986, 16; NGA/GA, Kottcamp Interview 1985, 7.

72 Rothschild in O'Connor 1972, 184; Kainen in O'Connor 1972, 163; AAA, Cahill FAP/WPA, 10.

73 A series of memos to Cahill from Charles O. Cornelius, Index supervisor of the New York City Project, reports where Index artists were working each week. Among the locations named for the week ending 26 February 1937: Metropolitan Museum (twenty-three artists), Brooklyn Museum (thirteen artists), Museum of the City of New York (eleven artists), Federal Building (thirty-three artists), Mrs. Kuttner, private collection (one artist), M. Davenport, private collection (four artists), McKearin's Antiques (three artists) (National Archives, WPA, Record Group 69, Box 14, folder 1).

74 William L. Warren, Index supervisor in Connecticut, later recounted, "the Wadsworth Atheneum gave us a room where artists could go and work...and [for] private homes, instead of artists going there, why we'd borrow it and bring it to the Atheneum...and they'd record it there." NGA/GA, Warren Interview 1965, 4.

75 It was permissible to work from a photograph if the object was inaccessible to the artist, *"but it is most essential that a color sketch be made directly from the object* [with] absolutely true color" and in as great detail as possible. "Working from Photographs," NGA/GA, Index Manual 1938, 26. See also NGA/GA, Jensen Interview 1986, 7, 12–13.

76 See Appendix II.

77 Cahill in Christensen 1950, xxv.

78 See the January 1937 letters from Hildegarde Crosby, Index supervisor of the Illinois project, to Cahill; to Thomas Parker, assistant director of the FAP; and to Audrey MacMahon, assistant to the director of the FAP, describing her difficulties in securing the best watercolors and seeking advice on ways to word requisitions so that the lowest bidder, with an inferior product, would not be able to win the bid (National Archives, WPA, Record Group 69, Box 10, folder 3).

79 NGA/GA, Jensen Talk, 1985, 13.

80 NGA/GA, Index Manual 1938, 15.

81 Paper conservator Marian Dirda is preserving Index renderings under a Save America's Treasures grant from the United States Department of the Interior, National Park Service. Much of my discussion of materials in this essay derives from observations Dirda has made in the course of her work and has generously shared with me.

82 "The Index artists employed with the Pennsylvania branch of the Federal Art Program at Philadelphia...used Strathmore water color paper on which to make their drawings. Strathmore paper has 100% cotton fibre content. The sheet size is 20 by 30 inches. Five different weights, or thicknesses, are available; and may be had in a smooth or a medium grain 'kid' finish...first the paper was soaked in water evenly on both sides placed between two blotters to absorb superfluous water then put on the drawing board. In this damp state, gummed paper tape was applied to the edges all the way around to secure it firmly to the board. After the paper completely dried it was ready for use," NGA/GA, Davison 1982, 1.

83 For its Whatman watercolor board, the W. and R. Balston Company placed an intermediate layer of paper between the mounting board and the watercolor paper. This inside stratum of paper, along with the layers of glue on each side, helped keep the acidity of the board from reaching the watercolor paper, adding greatly to its permanence. Favor, Ruhl and Company boards are also common in the Index, but this supplier mounted English watercolor papers directly on board without the benefit of an intermediate layer. Although the artists in the Philadelphia area generally used Strathmore paper, they employed other supports when particular renderings had special requirements. For example, Elmer G. Anderson used mounted drawing board (of fairly poor quality) for his rendering of Uree C. Fell's sampler (cat. 42). He probably decided on mounted board for the sampler rendering because he was going to use gouache with watercolor. Gouache, when applied thickly, requires a stiff support to prevent cracking and paint loss.

84 "They tested pigments for fading, and mixing.... And they came up with a palette for us to use on these drawings of colors which they found pure and permanent." NGA/GA, Jensen Talk 1985, 13.

85 NGA/GA, Index Manual 1938, 16. On materials and techniques, see also NGA/GA, Angus to Fukui 1982. See also NGA/GA, Jensen to Weitzenkorn 1984.

86 See NGA/GA, Davison 1982, 2; NGA/GA, Kottcamp Interview 1985, 9 and 11; NGA/GA, Angus to Fukui, IV; NGA/GA, Chabot Interview 1986, 3; and NGA/GA, Jensen to Weitzenkorn 1984.

87 NGA/GA, Index Manual 1938, 15.

88 NGA/GA, Glassgold to Christensen 1947, 3–4.

89 NGA/GA, Glassgold to Christensen 1946, 5.

90 Jones 1971, 715.

91 Rothschild in O'Connor 1972, 191. Jonathan Harris reached the puzzling conclusion that the Index as a whole "prescribed antimodernist representation practice and ideology" (Harris 1995, 86). Perhaps this basic misunderstanding derived from the fact that the renderings themselves were not abstracted images, and from a lack of recognition of the purpose of the Index as an attempt to support the development of American modernism. Harris also mistakenly believes that "fidelity to the appearance of the object" is "profoundly antimodernist," a criterion that would leave artists like Charles Sheeler—as well as many later artists—out of the modernist canon.

92 On Chapman, see Appendix I.

93 NGA/GA, Chapman Interview 1986, 1.

94 "In Tribute to Suzanne E. Chapman," n.p.

95 This meeting is described in a memo from Nina Collier to Cahill and Reeves, 22 February 1936 (AAA, Cahill Papers, reel 1107, frame 1021).

96 The third manual for the Index that Adolph C. Glassgold compiled in 1938 included a section titled "Suggestions on Rendering," based on Chapman's techniques (NGA/GA, Index Manual 1938, 15–27). An earlier document, "General Rules for All Drawings" (AAA, Cahill Papers, reel 1107, frames 1134–1142), gave only basic directions regarding layout and materials.

97 On techniques of instruction, see NGA/GA, Jensen Interview 1986, 5–6; NGA/GA, Loper Interview 1985, 15–17; NGA/GA, Kottcamp Interview 1985, 4, 9–10; NGA/GA, Gauthier Interview 1985, 4–9; NGA/GA, Ellinger Interview 1985, 19.

98 NGA/GA, Index Manual 1938, 15.

99 Harris 1995, 93.

100 NGA/GA, Index Manual 1938, 22.

101 NGA/GA, Index Manual 1938, 19.

102 NGA/GA, Glassgold to Christensen 1947, 2–3.

103 On artists traveling from state to state to train other artists, see NGA/GA, Glassgold to Christensen 1947, 2.

104 The Index had forty research workers in 1937. On the efforts to compile excellent research materials, see AAA, Glassgold 1939, 7. For instructions on completing data sheets, see NGA/GA, Index Manual 1938, 27–29. See also McDonald 1969, 448.

105 Rothschild in O'Connor 1972, 181–182. The National Gallery archives has preserved boxes with card files of information gathered by Index research workers.

106 The line the Index supervisor signed was labeled "Director," but it was usually the supervisor who signed the sheets.

107 On the portfolios, see NGA/GA, Index Manual 1938, 8–9.

108 The Index staff wrote many memoranda about the portfolios. For a list of the documents in the National Archives relating to the portfolios, see NGA/GA, Crockett 1996, 30–32. A prospectus for the publication of the Index was sent to Mrs. Franklin D. Roosevelt in October 1941 (AAA, Cahill Papers, reel 1107, frames 982–985). It called the Index an "endeavor to recover a usable past in the decorative and fine arts of our country" and offered a plan for publishing it. On the portfolios, see also Allyn 1982, 37–38.

109 McDonald 1969, 442–443n. Another government-funded art project in New Mexico employed Native American craftsmen to make rugs, pottery, and jewelry for display in Indian service buildings in hopes of stimulating increased production of native crafts (*New York Times*, 21 January 1934, 6[E]).

110 Glassgold recognized that "even if these [the portfolios] should prove too costly or inexpedient, for one reason or another, we will still have gathered a vast collection of superb plates which, when housed in leading museums or libraries, will form a permanent, valuable and accessible body of material for artists, designers, manufacturers, students

and the layman interested in American culture," AAA, Glassgold 1937, 5. In 1939 the Index received a grant of $1,500 from the American Council of Learned Societies to produce one hundred color microfilm strips of the renderings, each with forty frames. These were to be accompanied by lecture handbooks. "Due to a series of unfortunate WPA Administrative complications," however, the work was stopped and the $1,200 remaining returned to the ACLS (NGA/GA, Glassgold to Christensen 1946, 8–9). Lecture notes were prepared for the filmstrips and are still preserved (AAA; Cahill Papers, NDA reel 6, frames 12–32).

111 The organizers of the Index of American Design were very pleased to present Index exhibitions in department stores. The earliest and most avid proponents of modern design also favored staging exhibitions in department stores, and some believed that department stores should actually replace museums because only the stores were serving the public by presenting modern design. Museum professionals helped organize department store exhibitions and contributed to their catalogues, and the art press reviewed these shows as important events. Robert W. De Forest, president of the Metropolitan Museum of Art in New York, helped organize department store exhibitions and wrote the preface to the catalogue for an exhibition at Macy's in 1928. For a review of an exhibition at Lord and Taylor, see Helen Appleton Read, "Modern Decorative Art," The Arts 13 (February 1928), 120.

112 Glassgold in O'Connor 1975, 169.

113 On the Congressional Allocations for 1937, see McDonald 1969, 179–181, 223–229.

114 On the Reorganization Act of 1939, see McDonald 1969, 309–315.

115 McKinzie 1973, 138–141, offers the best review of events surrounding the termination of the Index project.

116 Cahill 1957, 394.

117 "[Hopkins] said, 'Where do you want it to go?' I said, 'I want it to go to the National Gallery.' Well, of course, this flattered Harry to beat the band, because the National Gallery was a very distinguished institution, and the idea that this small project that he had run at one time could allocate what it had produced to the National Gallery was terrific. He said, 'Do you think you can do it?' I said, 'I think I can. I think I can talk David Finley into it, because I happen to know that decorative art is one of the fields…that he's very much conversant with,' which is true. He took it right away." Cahill 1957, 526–527.

118 This brochure was based on her excellent 1982 master's thesis; Allyn 1982.

119 Hornung 1972.

120 www.nga.gov.

121 Mumford 1926, 55–81; Brooks 1908.

122 On the impact of primitive art on modernism, see Goldwater 1986; William Rubin, ed., "Primitivism" in Twentieth-Century Art: Affinity of the Tribal and the Modern, 2 vols. [exh. cat., The Museum of Modern Art] (New York, 1984); Charles Harrison, Francis Frascina, and Gill Perry, Primitivism, Cubism, Abstraction: The Early Twentieth Century (New Haven, 1993); Colin Rhodes, Primitivism and Modern Art (New York, 1994).

123 This concept, discussed below, 23, is what Wanda M. Corn called the "new paradigm" in Corn 1999, 334–337.

124 Quoted in Allyn 1982, 32.

125 Rourke in O'Connor 1975, 166.

126 Rubin 1990, 202.

127 Rourke 1935, 397. On regionalist painter Thomas Hart Benton, see Doss 1991.

128 Rourke 1935, 390–400.

129 Van Wyck Brooks notes Rourke's intellectual alliance with anthropology in his preface to Rourke 1942, vii.

130 See Rourke 1935, 390–392. Cahill agreed with this appraisal of the Puritans' contribution to American art. Three years earlier he had written: "The Puritans had no such aversion to art as is commonly ascribed to them. They were wedded to an austere and simple way of living, but austerity and simplicity have never been a bar to art," exh. cat. New York 1932, 3. In 1936 he wrote: "One of the most familiar cliches of art criticism in our time is that art in America has been a comparatively barren plant, and that Puritanism is to blame for this lamentable condition. There is no question that Puritanism affected early American art in the direction of simplicity and austerity. But these qualities are very excellent in art," exh. cat. Newark 1936, 13.

131 "Pioneer experience was extraordinarily full of subtle preoccupations for the eye and hand…and the typical pioneer or frontiersman was master of those daily and primitive arts that have often afforded an ancestry for the fine arts," Rourke 1935, 392. In an article she wrote on the Index in 1937, Rourke explained that although aesthetic criticism had disregarded such humble crafts as ceramics and glass, consigning them to the dusty chambers of historical societies rather than art museums, these objects were "touchstones, revealing widespread and instinctive uses of form [that] may help to fill gaps in our difficult aesthetic history" (Rourke 1937, 207–208).

132 Brooks in Rourke 1942, x.

133 Rourke 1938.

134 Rourke 1935, 401; on Ogunquit, see Elizabeth Stillinger's essay in this catalogue, 52–53.

135 For more on the Whitney exhibition, see Corn 1999, 321–322, and Avis Berman, Rebels on Eighth Street: Juliana Force and the Whitney Museum of Art (New York, 1990), 201–202. I am grateful to Elizabeth Stillinger for calling my attention to Berman's book.

136 Quoted by Rumsford in Quimby and Swank 1980, 19. A review in the New York Times observed: "the strange thing is that most of these very old fashioned pictures give one vividly the sense of exactly the thing our most modern painters [are trying to do]" (quoted in Corn 1999, 322).

137 On Cahill, see Cahill 1957, Vlach 1985, Jeffers 1991, Jeffers 1995, and below, Stillinger's essay, 55–57.

138 "The first that I did publicity for the Society of Independent Artists, I think I doubled or trebled the attendance. I did that by putting a story about a ghost affair, a woman artist whose work mysteriously appeared in the show" (Cahill 1957, 78).

139 In the summer of 1921 Cahill also went to Sweden as a journalist for the Swedish American News Exchange (Cahill 1957, 78).

140 In 1926, the Newark Museum received a gift of $10,000 with which to buy Italian art, but Dana convinced the donor that the museum instead should be permitted to acquire modern American art. Cahill and a museum trustee purchased works by Max Weber, John Sloan, Robert Henri, and other contemporary artists, including Samuel Halpert. Dana did not personally like the work of these artists, but his belief in democracy persuaded him that he should purchase and display the art of his own time and place, and allow the public to judge for itself the merits of that art (Cahill, 1957, 166–167).

141 Exh. cat. New York 1932, 3.

142 Exh. cat. New York 1932, 26–27.

143 Cahill 1932, 1–4.

144 Tepfer 1989, 174–175.

145 Exh. cat. New York 1932, 8.

146 On the earlier Spanish colonial portfolio, see above, 18.

147 Letter from Thomas M. Stell Jr. to Holger Cahill, attention of C. Adolph Glassgold, 15 June 1939 (National Archives, WPA, Record Group 69, Box 2642, file 3152).

148 On Halpert and Cahill and the American Folk Art Gallery, see Stillinger's essay in this catalogue, below 54–55. See also Tepfer 1989, 48–49, 163–181; exh. cat. Lexington 1988, 141–166.

149 I am grateful to Elizabeth Stillinger for sharing research for a forthcoming book to clarify exactly when the partnership ended.

150 Tepfer 1989, 163–186; Corn 1999, 323–324. Abby Aldrich Rockefeller, who had previously purchased American modern art from Halpert, became their major client for folk art. Halpert had convinced her to complete her collection of modern art by providing to her the art of the modernists' aesthetic forebears (Tepfer 1989, 171–175).

151 Tepfer quotes the press release for the first *Ancestors* show in Tepfer 1989, 163–164.

152 Tepfer 1989, 221–225.

153 Corn 1999, 334–347.

154 Corn 1999, 293–337; see also Mandeles 1995, 47–51.

155 On Sheeler's paintings, drawings, and photographs of Americana, see Troyen in exh. cat. Boston 1987b, 21–26.

156 Cahill in Christensen 1950, xxiv.

157 Rothschild in O'Connor 1972, 191.

158 Rourke 1937, 210.

159 AAA, Drozdoff. David Ellinger remembered instructions by his supervisor, Francis Lichten: "'Now, that flower pot that I showed you,' she said, 'your two hands must get in back of this, David.' And she put her hands in back of the pot after she set it up for me to draw, and she said, 'you must be able to stick your hand down into it, and everything must not just look like it, it must be exactly like it,'" NGA/GA, Ellinger Interview 1985, 5.

160 Corn 1999, 301–302. Index artist Austin Davison recalled that Glassgold instructed the project's artists not to represent cast shadows, in order to give the objects in the renderings a "suspended-in-air appearance." NGA/GA, Davison to Ritchie 1985, 24.

161 See memorandum from Cahill to Bruce McClure, "Concerning Project Proposed by Ruth Reeves," dated 27 August 1935 (AAA, Cahill Papers, reel DC 53, frame 162). In another memorandum from Reeves to Cahill and Glassgold, dated 17 June 1936, Reeves wrote: "the meeting with Sheeler was fine, only I couldn't help wishing Dick and I should have gone down to see him two months ago when I wanted to see if he would by any odd chance be prevailed to paint and photograph the Shaker collection.... His photographs of Williamsburg were remarkable.... I practically cried to think what he could do with the Shaker interiors and the furniture" (National Archives, WPA, Record Group 69, Box 4, Ruth Reeves folder, 2).

162 Exh. cat. Newark 1944, 38.

163 Kirstein 1938; rev. ed. 1975, 192. On Evans, see exh. cat. New York 1991, 9–31.

164 Memo from Cahill to Kiplinger dated 9 September 1942 (AAA, Cahill Papers, reel 1107, frame 1073). On documentary art of the 1930s, see Stott 1973 and Levine 1988, 15–42.

165 Stott 1973, 29.

166 Corn 1999, 308.

167 Quoted in Mandeles 1995, 51–52.

168 Rourke 1938, 96. The same "nonappearance" of the artist in his work applied to Evans (see exh. cat. New York 1991, 19).

169 AAA, Reeves to Cahill 1949, 2.

170 AAA, Drozdoff, 2.

171 MacLeish 1937a, 103.

172 AAA, Drozdoff, 2–3.

173 Quoted in Alexander 1980, 203–204.

174 Rourke 1937, 209.

175 "The nation's resources in the visual arts are not confined to painting and sculpture and printmaking. They include all the arts of design which express the daily life of a people and which bring order, design, and harmony into [the] environment which their society creates. These will include the whole range of decorative and useful arts from the shaping of a teacup to the building of a city. This view of American art has given direction to the activities of the Index of American Design" (AAA, Cahill 1941, 5).

176 On the relationship of progressivism and the New Deal, see Graham 1967.

177 Cahill presented a speech at the John Dewey Eightieth Birthday Celebration; see Cahill in O'Connor 1975, 33–44. He also referred to Dewey's ideas in AAA, Cahill 1941, 1, 7.

178 These ideals are represented in Thorstein Veblen, *The Instinct of Workmanship and the State of the Industrial Arts* (New York, 1914).

179 On Dana's regard for Veblen, see Cahill 1957, 158. Cahill honored Dana in an introductory essay to an exhibition catalogue of the Newark Museum's collections of American painting and sculpture, exh. cat. Newark 1944, 9–61.

180 Cahill dealt with these issues in 1957: "After the Russian Revolution, I very rapidly became disillusioned with what was going on in Russia. It seemed a very idealistic thing in the beginning. I became very quickly disillusioned with it, and I saw less and less of Mike Gold because he, like other Bolsheviks, became quite partisan.... Anyway, I didn't see much of Mike. He disappeared. He just appeared here and there, and I would see him. During the Federal Art Project, I think his coming to see me was based on the fact that he expected favors from me, not for himself but for Party members, things of that sort. He talked to me about it. As a matter of fact, I began not to like Mike very much, afterward, so I didn't really see much of him" (Cahill 1957, 90, 93).

181 According to Cahill, "an attempt to bridge the gap between the American artist and the American public has governed the entire program of the Federal Art Project," exh. cat. Newark 1936, 9. Cahill also announced that "the importance of an integration between the fine arts and the practical arts has been recognized from the first by the Federal Art Project, as an objective desirable in itself and as a means of drawing together major esthetic forces in the country," exh. cat. New York 1936, 18–19.

182 Exh. cat. New York 1936, 19; also exh. cat. Newark 1936, 7.

183 Meikle 2001, 18.

184 Exh. cat. New York 1932, 3.

185 Exh. cat. New York 1936, 10. See also Cahill's history of American art in Cahill and Barr 1934, 7–62.

186 Veblen 1899.

187 Mumford in Leonard and Glassgold 1930; 1992, 9–10.

188 Meikle describes this prevailing attitude in the preface to Meikle 2001, 3–4.

189 On the arts and crafts movement, see exh. cat. Boston 1987a. On the proliferation of the modernist movements, see exh. cat. London 1995.

190 Stein in exh. cat. London 1995, 70–73.

191 On the history of the Bauhaus and the American perception of its modernity, see Herbert Bayer, Walter Gropius, and Ilse Gropius, eds., *Bauhaus, 1919–1928* (New York, 1959), originally published in 1938 in conjunction with an exhibition at the Museum of Modern Art.

192 See exh. cat. New Haven 1983, 46, and exh. cat. New York 2000, 10, 17–18.

193 Exh. cat. New York 1934. This show was preceded in 1927 by a "Machine-Art Exposition" in an office building on 57th Street in Manhattan (see Johnson in exh. cat. New York 1934, 17–18).

194 See Tepfer 1989, 206–207.

195 On Sheeler's 1930s factory images, see exh. cat. Boston 1987b, 17–21; Susan Fillin-Yeh discusses Sheeler's forays into industrial design and illustrates examples of products he designed in exh. cat. New Haven 1987, 8, 46, 50–59.

196 Meikle 2001, 3–4.

197 Berman 1988, 19.

198 Barr in exh. cat. New York 1934, n.p.

199 Benson 1934, 307–311. Richard F. Bach had already recognized the need for such a school in the United States in 1930. In his essay for *Modern American Design by the American Union of Decorative Artists and Craftsmen*, he wrote: "it is a task for the near future to develop the type of institution which will train designer-craftsmen to lead industry and thus serve the community, to produce the model and so guide the factory," Bach in Leonard and Glassgold 1930; reprint. 1992, 80. See also Pulos 1983, 399, and Votolato 1998, 398–400.

200 See "Field Notes" 1936, 117; and Rohde 1936, 638–643, 686. The Design Lab opened in October 1935, but when funding to the FAP was cut in 1937, government sponsorship ended. The school was so highly regarded among the arts community that an effort was made to operate it as an independent venture, but sufficient funding could not be found and it closed after several years (McDonald 1969, 462).

201 Ruth Reeves' memorandum to Holger Cahill and Cook [Adolph] Glassgold, 17 June 1936 (National Archives, WPA, Record Group 69, Box 4, Ruth Reeves folder).

202 AAA, Cahill Papers, NDA, reel 15, frames 379–385. On the Index and the Design Laboratory, see also another, undated letter to Brock; AAA, Cahill papers, reels 1108, frames 1076–1077.

203 On the AUDAC, see Byars in Leonard and Glassgold 1930; reprint. 1992, v–xxvi.

204 Glassgold 1931, 440.

205 Frankl in Leonard and Glassgold 1930; reprint. 1992, 27.

206 Bach in Leonard and Glassgold 1930; reprint. 1992, 79.

207 On Reeves, see Carlano and Shilliam 1993, 39–41.

208 Berman 1988, 375.

209 Glassgold 1928, 231. See also his book review of Paul Frankl's *New Dimensions in The Arts* 14 (September 1928), 167–168; "The Decorative Arts," *The Arts* 14 (October and November 1928), 215–216, 279–281; "The Decorative Arts," *The Arts* 15 (April 1929), 269; "Modern American Industrial Design," *Arts and Decoration* 35 (July 1931), 30–31; and "Toward the Future," *Creative Arts* 9 (August 1931), 97–98.

210 Glassgold in Leonard and Glassgold 1930; reprint. 1992, 174–175.

211 Carlano and Shilliam 1993, 40. In March 1936, *Design* magazine singled out her work for special praise. The article quoted a review by Lewis Mumford in the *New Yorker* of Reeves' 1935 exhibition of textiles made after her return from a trip to Guatemala. Mumford particularly commended her modern designs for being inspired by—but never copied from—other cultures (Anderson 1936, 26). See also Allyn 1982, 20.

212 "It is the furthest thing from the intention of the Index that the past should be imitated no matter how sincere and honest its design may have been. On the contrary, our interest argues that we recognize its appropriateness of design to its time; that we acknowledge the common basis of good design in the old and new; and that we demand of our time as satisfactory a type of design" (from a lecture Glassgold presented prior to the opening on 3 January 1937 of an Index of American Design show circulated by the American Merchandising Corporation [AAA, Cahill Papers, reel 1107, frame 1310], 6).

213 Cahill and Wellman 1938, 15.

214 Tepfer 1989, 57–58. Stores like Wanamaker's had become important venues for innovative design shows, and some critics of the day claimed that department stores should replace museums, since they were better serving the public in advancing modern American art. On department store shows and modern design, see above, note 111.

215 Glassgold 1928, 228.

216 Dana 1926, 11.

217 On these shows, see "An Apostle of Applied Art in the Home," *The Literary Digest* 98 (July–September 1928), 22–23. A photograph of an installation case for the *Ten Cent* exhibition is reproduced in Peniston 1999, 224.

218 Dana 1929, 40.

219 The lecture became the introduction to exh. cat. Newark 1936. In the preface to this catalogue Beatrice Winser, who succeeded Dana as director of the Newark Museum, specifically cited the Index of American Design as "one of the most significant contributions yet made to the appreciation of American art as defined by John Cotton Dana," 2.

220 See Meikle 2001, 75, and Pulos 1983, 358.

221 AAA, Reeves to Collier 1950, 3.

222 The public affairs office at *Time* provided the circulation figure of 800,000; as this office pointed out, the actual readership number is higher, as a single copy of the magazine is often read by more than one person.

223 "In the Business District," *Time: The Weekly Newsmagazine* 32, no. 10 (5 September 1938), 38.

224 See above, 19; Lewis Mumford, "Letter to the President," *The New Republic* (30 December 1936), 265.

225 E. M. Benson, "Art on Parole," *The American Magazine of Art* 29 (November 1936), 770.

226 See exh. cat. Boston 1987b, cats. 57–62.

227 "It [the WPA Federal Project Number One] has produced...a greater human response than anything the government has done for generations. In the first fifteen months... 50,000 people, not counting radio listeners, heard WPA concerts. In the first year of the WPA Theatre project, approximately sixteen millions in thirty states saw performances.... In the first few months of the Federal Painters Project [the FAP] twenty-eight federal galleries and art centers were established...where art galleries had never existed before. And by the end of the year more than a million people had attended classes in these galleries or listened to lectures or come in to look at traveling exhibits. What the government's experiment in music, painting, and the theatre actually did, even in their first year, was to work a sort of cultural revolution in America." MacLeish 1937a, 111–112. Cahill identified MacLeish as the author of the article in his speech at the John Dewey Eightieth Birthday Celebration (Cahill in O'Connor 1975, 39).

228 MacLeish 1937a, 117.

229 MacLeish 1937b, 103.

230 MacLeish 1937b, 103.

231 Joan Didion, "At the Dam," *The White Album* (New York, 1979), 199.

232 Kaplan in exh. cat. London 1995, 44.

233 See Alexander 1980, 242–245.

234 H. W. Janson in "A Symposium: The State of American Art," *Magazine of Art* 42 (March 1949), 96.

235 Holger Cahill in "A Symposium: The State of American Art," 88. A few years earlier he remarked that "the younger artists of today... tend toward an internationalist position more in harmony with postwar ideas" ("In Our Time," *Magazine of Art* 39 [November 1946], 312).

236 H. W. Janson, "Benton and Wood, Champions of Regionalism," *Magazine of Art* 39 (May 1946), 184. Janson's real target in this article was the regionalist movement, as discussed in Doss 1991, 363–364.

237 Janson 1946, 200.

238 Alfred H. Barr Jr. in "A Symposium: The State of American Art," 85. Dwight Macdonald agreed: "the U.S.S.R. is even more a land of Mass Culture than is the U.S.A. This is less easily recognizable because their Mass Culture is *in form* just the opposite of ours, being one of propaganda and pedagogy rather than entertainment." Macdonald in Rosenberg and White 1957, 60.

239 Greenberg in Rosenberg and White 1957, 102. "It is also true that Mass Culture is to some extent a continuation of the old Folk Art" (Macdonald in Rosenberg and White, 1957, 60); "folk and popular art have much in common; they are easy to understand, they are romantic, patriotic, conventionally moral, and they are held in deep affection by those who are suspicious of the great arts" (Seldes in Rosenberg and White, 1957, 79).

240 Rosenberg in Rosenberg and White 1957, 9.

241 Exh. cat. New Haven 1983, 48.

242 In 1954 Cahill wrote: "a thing to be remembered about the projects is that the mandate from Congress was not for creating works of art. Congress passed the appropriations for the purpose of putting the unemployed to work. That was my primary directive. Quality was a thing that supervened." Cahill 1954, 22.

243 McDonald 1969, 454.

244 Rosenberg 1959, 13–22; Harold Rosenberg, "The Search for Jackson Pollock," Art News 59 (February 1961), 35.

245 Rosenberg 1959, 19–20.

246 "Barney studied each one intensely, his hand on his chin in a characteristic attitude.... When we were finished, he pointed to the pile with a fling of his hand and said, 'that's it.' He mentioned there was a German art critic coming to interview him the next day and that the critic should see the quilts. It would help him understand something about indigenous American aesthetic attitudes. Barney had understood instantly what we were doing." Holstein 1991, 26.

247 More than ten years before Rosenberg published his "coonskinism" theory, Newman had declared that it was because American artists were "free from the weight of European culture" they were able to make "cathedrals," or art, "out of ourselves, out of our own feelings" (Barnett B. Newman, "The Sublime is Now," The Tiger's Eye 6 [December 1948], 53).

248 Quoted in Holstein 1991, 44. See also Kramer's disgruntled review of the Metropolitan Museum of Art's 1970 exhibition Nineteenth Century America, in which he wrote that "the true genius of the American decorative arts and crafts of the nineteenth century is to be found in its folk expression—in the kitchen pottery, the wool coverlets, the patchwork quilts, and the humble, plain-style furniture that was created to meet the needs of workaday living. None of this folk art is represented" (quoted in Stott 1973, 118).

249 Exh. cat. Washington 1990, 39.

250 "Andy had continually been labeled by critics a 'naif,' a genius whose intuitive magic, rather than studied technical perfection, has produced the classics of our time.... In collecting folk art, Warhol continues in the tradition of a previous generation of American artists—Elie Nadelman, Charles Sheeler, Charles Demuth, William Zorach, and Yasuo Kuniyoshi. Attracted to folk art's bold inventiveness and abstract design, their own work was strongly influenced by their collecting," Sandra Brant and Elissa Cullman, "Introduction," in Andy Warhol's "Folk and Funk" [exh. cat., Museum of American Folk Art] (New York, 1977), 8.

251 Dorothy Gees Seckler, "Folklore of the Banal: An Introduction to the Provocative New Realism," originally published in Art in America, reprinted in Jean Lipman, ed., What Is American in American Art (New York, 1963), 29.

252 Tracy Atkinson, "Introduction," in Pop Art and the American Tradition [exh. cat., Milwaukee Art Center] (Milwaukee, 1965), 9.

253 Lucy Lippard, Pop Art (New York, 1966), 12–13.

254 One artist who seems to have been directly affected by the Index was not a painter, sculptor, or industrial designer, but the poet Louis Zukofsky, who worked as a researcher for the New York City Index project. On Zukofsky and the Index, see Ira B. Nadel, "A Precision of Appeal: Louis Zukofsky and the Index of American Design," in Upper Limit Music: The Writings of Louis Zukofsky, ed. Mark Scroggins (Tuscaloosa, Ala., 1997), 112–126; and in the same volume, Barry Ahearn, "Zukofsky, Marxism, and American Handicraft," 81–93 (National Gallery photographer Lee B. Ewing kindly brought this book to my attention). Zukofsky was already fascinated by American history before he joined the Index project, and he recognized an analogy between poetry and handicraft, comparing the act of writing poetry to cabinetmaking. As Nadel observed (124–125): "The history of American design that Zukofsky wrote provided him not only with a means to repossess a fading American culture but also with a corroborative epistemology that reconfirmed the value of sight over intellect.... The Index completed a decade devoted to exploring the value of sight, detail, particulars, and fact—and the conclusion that it is impossible 'to communicate anything but particulars— historic and contemporary—things.'"

From Attics, Sheds, and Secondhand Shops
Collecting Folk Art in America, 1880–1940

Elizabeth Stillinger

The idea on which the Index of American Design was based—that there was a continuous, identifiable body of specifically American art—evolved in the twentieth century. Although painters, sculptors, and creators of objects in silver, ceramics, and other media were at work from the seventeenth century onward, Americans and Europeans alike considered American creations inferior to European ones and therefore of no particular value except perhaps sentimental. As William Bentley of Salem, Massachusetts, wrote in 1819 of a turkeywork settee that is today considered an icon of seventeenth-century artistry, "All were willing honorably to dispose of to a friend of the family what they feared to destroy & dared not disgrace."[1] The settee had survived because it was inherited from revered ancestors, not because of its artistic, cultural, or historical importance. Such appreciation evolved slowly as a result of forces and ideas that arose in the Western world by the mid-nineteenth century, and it stimulated the journey of folk art from town attics, farm sheds, and secondhand shops to museums, collectors' homes, and modern artists' studios.

The earliest collectors, such as the owners of the turkeywork settee, were motivated by the desire to acquire or retain objects associated with America's founders and heroes—at first the pilgrims and puritans, and later luminaries such as Thomas Jefferson, Benjamin Franklin, and George Washington. Momentous historical events, such as the pilgrims' landing at Plymouth Rock, the signing of the Declaration of Independence, and the American Revolution, also inspired early collectors.

Valuing associational qualities over artistic ones, these collectors assembled miscellaneous objects related only by the circumstance—actual or purported—of their connection to one or more famous person or event. Often such collections included objects that today we classify as folk art.[2]

Beginning in the 1880s, the amorphous movement now called the colonial revival provided many more Americans with a reason for collecting the chests and chairs, pewter, ceramics, and paintings of their forebears.[3] By acquiring the trappings, these collectors hoped to assimilate the taste and gentility of their American ancestors. They usually associated themselves with the elite of preindustrial America and therefore sought formal rather than folk-art objects. The colonial revival, however, in focusing increasing interest on the American past and its remains, elevated the status of everything in that category, including folk art.

The arts and crafts movement appeared in America at about the same time as the colonial revival and also stimulated collecting.[4] The American arts and crafts movement was inspired by its English namesake, which had arisen to protest the poor materials, workmanship, and design of machine-made objects, and to promote the pursuit of good design through honest materials, sound workmanship, and the eschewal of extraneous ornament. Like colonial revivalists, arts and crafts advocates venerated early American furnishings, but they concentrated on the principles of design and construction that characterized such pieces rather than entirely on their acquisition and display.

Nineteenth-century English design-reform pioneers A.W.N. Pugin, John Ruskin, and William Morris were united in the belief, engendered by their study of medieval guilds, that unless modern societies fostered high moral values, their architecture and other material objects would inevitably be inferior. Detached from a specifically medieval context, the association of handwork with high moral and aesthetic values resulted in one of the most important aspects of the arts and crafts movement: its emphasis on the revival and perpetuation of hand-craft techniques and objects. By 1900 American artist-craftsmen worked in many such traditions, from glass, ceramics, and metals to weaving and woodworking, thus prompting widespread interest in handmade objects of all kinds, including folk art. In fact, this activity specifically fostered the appreciation of folk art, for folk objects very often met essential arts and crafts criteria: they were composed of solid, natural materials in simple, unpretentious designs with integral ornament. Pioneer collector Henry Mercer noted in speaking of Pugin, whose precepts he followed: "Decorate construction but never construct decoration."[5]

Information about early objects was virtually nonexistent in the mid-nineteenth century, but it gradually became available during succeeding decades. By about 1900 a few reliable books and articles could be found on specific categories such as furniture, silver, and ceramics—in the field of folk art, for example, a book on Pennsylvania German redware was available as well as an article on fraktur and a number of publications on antiques and collecting in general. From the 1890s onward authors such as Alice Morse Earle, who published eighteen books and more than forty articles on the home and family in early America, and Mary Harrod Northend, who published over 185 articles and books on subjects ranging from old inns and colonial doorways to early American glass, catered to a curious, but amateur, audience. In the 1910s and 1920s, periodicals such as *House and Garden*, *Country Life*, and *House Beautiful* educated their readers about a wide variety of early objects, old houses, and decorating with antiques.

By the 1920s museum and historical-society exhibitions, house museums, antiques shops metamorphosed from junk and secondhand stores, department-store galleries, and auction houses contributed substantially to the growing interest in both folk and formal early American art. Among the first noteworthy auctions of what is now considered folk art were the 1913 Alexander W. Drake sales of, among numerous other items, antique samplers and needlework, pottery, and bandboxes decorated with woodblock-printed American scenes, which Drake was credited with "discovering" about 1900. Other early auctions were the 1921 Lawrence sale of "hook rugs" and the 1922 Temple sale of Pennsylvania German art.[6]

New York City became a major center for the study and purchase of American folk art in the 1920s, but folk-art collecting had begun earlier elsewhere—mainly in New England and Pennsylvania. The earliest collectors were most often motivated by antiquarian or ethnological interests. These "ethnologists" collected or studied preindustrial material for what it revealed about a culture, about the routines and technologies of the people who produced and used the objects. Few early folk-art collectors had ethnological training, but a number focused on the ethnological contexts of objects and their meanings in the cultures that created them.

Among the antiquarians was George Sheldon of Deerfield, Massachusetts, who founded the Pocumtuck Valley Memorial Association (PVMA) in 1870 to commemorate Deerfield's early settlers and "the race which vanished before them." In 1880 the PVMA opened Memorial Hall, a museum for the display of artifacts from both European settlers and Native Americans. Sheldon had collected the museum's contents over the preceding decade by means both fair and foul ("It is said," wrote one longtime Deerfield resident, "that when an older member of the community died one might hear the Hon. George tiptoeing up the attic stairs as the coffin was carried out of the front door"). The remarkable collection Sheldon amassed was displayed in seven exhibition rooms, including a "colonial kitchen" and a "colonial bedroom" said to be the earliest period rooms in America. Among the folk art on display were Hadley chests and other local furniture, trade signs, powder horns, portraits, stoneware, wrought-iron tools and utensils, and samplers, quilts, and other textiles. The exhibition of folk and vernacular objects in a venerable Victorian institution such as Memorial Hall conferred increased status on these categories.[7]

A few miles south of Deerfield a student at Smith College, who had perhaps seen Memorial Hall, began to collect similar objects from the farm families around Northampton, Massachusetts. Edna Hilburn (later Little, then Greenwood) was fascinated by the "old folks," as she called these

New England descendants of colonial settlers. From about 1910 she visited them to hear about their histories and traditions and, when possible, acquired their heirlooms as tangible evidence of life in colonial and early Federal New England. Sometimes she received these objects as gifts, sometimes through barter, and sometimes by purchase at the "vendues," or sales, held at the homes and farms of long-established families who were giving up their struggle with the rocky soil and moving away. At such sales, she said, there were often "things no one could identify. These intrigued me. I bought them to find out what they were."[8] She pursued her research in early books, manuscripts, and treatises, all of which she collected, and through interviews with old-timers and fellow antiquaries.

With her 1925 purchase of Time Stone Farm in Marlborough, Massachusetts, Edna was able to realize her longtime dream: to live in an early New England farmhouse in a manner closely approximating that of the eighteenth century (fig. 1). Shunning plumbing and electricity, she arranged and used her folk and vernacular objects as she believed colonial Americans would have done. A visit to Time Stone Farm, said a friend in 1936, "can truly be described as an adventure in hospitality and the ways of antiquity."[9]

In 1949 Edna Greenwood gave more than two thousand objects to the Smithsonian Institution. Curator C. Malcolm Watkins displayed them in an ethnologically oriented exhibition titled *Everyday Life in Early America*, which opened in 1957. As Watkins wrote, this groundbreaking installation was the first in America in which objects "show the customs and cultural patterns of the [Anglo-Americans] who developed this country."[10] Folk art had taken a big leap forward.

Among the New England objects that Edna Greenwood was one of the first to collect were those made by Shakers. This sect, long feared and reviled by their New England neighbors because of their unconventional lifestyle and odd religious practices, appealed to Edna enormously. Her fascination was shared by only a few others, among them Faith and Edward Deming Andrews of Pittsfield, Massachusetts, who began to collect Shaker material in 1923. The first time they visited the Shaker community at Hancock, Massachusetts, the Andrews were struck by the beauty of the objects surrounding them. They considered a

Fig. 1
The "Old Kitchen" at Edna Greenwood's Time Stone Farm, Marlborough, Massachusetts, 1951, The Magazine Antiques, photograph by Samuel Chamberlain

trestle table, rocking chairs, and built-in cupboards "beautiful in their simplicity."[11] They quickly developed a taste for Shaker crafts, which they ardently collected (cat. 52); a fascination with Shaker beliefs; and affection for the Shakers themselves. Convinced that Shaker culture was important yet little understood and appreciated, they felt immediate action was necessary to gather and preserve a record of it; this task became their mission and their life's work.

"No one had ever collected it," the Andrews said of Shaker furniture. "No one knew the history of their chair industry, nor when and by whom the furnishings of the community dwellings and shops were produced." To discover the answers to these and hundreds of other questions, the Andrews engaged in what Holger Cahill, describing the work of the Index of American Design, later called "a kind of archaeology."[12] Through collecting and studying Shaker objects, talking with Shaker friends, searching through Shaker documents, and observing the routines of the dwindling Shaker communities, they painstakingly uncovered and examined patterns of Shaker life and thought.

Homer Eaton Keyes was immediately enthusiastic when the Andrews showed him a Shaker chair, and he encouraged the couple to write for the *Magazine Antiques*, of which he was the editor. Their first article, "Craftsmanship of an American Religious Sect: Notes on Shaker Furniture," appeared in the August 1928 issue, followed by a long series of articles and books on Shaker beliefs and artifacts that shaped public perception for much of the twentieth century. Although recent scholars have corrected the Andrews' romantic and idealized picture of the Shakers, the couple's enduring contribution is the body of information about many aspects of Shaker life and production that they were the first to identify, synthesize, and present to others through their publications.[13]

Other early collectors of Shaker material include the New York State Museum in Albany, New York, particularly under director Charles C. Adams; and John Williams, who founded the Shaker Museum in Old Chatham, New York. Like the Andrews, both museums worked with Shakers in forming their collections, which therefore contain many outstanding, well-documented objects. Charles Sheeler discovered and began to collect Shaker furniture in the 1920s, and he encouraged Juliana Force, director of the Whitney Museum in New York City, to add Shaker items to her large and varied folk-art collection. In 1935 Force promoted the recognition and appreciation of Shaker craftsmanship by sponsoring *Shaker Handicrafts* at the Whitney. This first major museum exhibition of Shaker objects was organized by the Andrews and not only introduced the genre to a wider audience, but also presented it for the first time as art. Inclusion of numerous Shaker objects in the Index of American Design gave this category even wider exposure.

Edna Greenwood and Faith and Ted Andrews were certainly motivated by romantic antiquarian attitudes, but also to some extent by ethnological ones. During the 1920s, however, the nostalgic antiquarian notion of eighteenth-century America

as a golden age motivated ever more Americans to collect antiques and restore old houses. The increasingly industrialized and impersonalized world around them made these collectors long for a comforting "colonial" retreat. The period room, which achieved instant popularity when the American Wing of the Metropolitan Museum opened in New York City in 1924, was a particular inspiration, for it provided collectors with a framework. Collecting was no longer a process of acquiring possibly unrelated individual objects. It could now be an exciting, ongoing hunt for compatible objects with which to create interiors that radiated the charm of the past. Pieces could be from the same period but of different materials, achieving harmony through form and decorative motif, or they could be of differing periods, materials, and forms, and achieve cohesion through color, texture, and pattern.

Collectors who were outstandingly successful in combining objects into pleasing, artistic interiors include Henry Davis Sleeper of Boston and Gloucester, Massachusetts; Electra Havemeyer Webb of Old Woodbury, New York, and Shelburne, Vermont; and Henry Francis du Pont of Southampton, New York, and Wilmington, Delaware (fig. 2). These gifted collectors expressed their artistry three-dimensionally, in room settings in which their medium was folk-art objects.

Du Pont, Webb, and Sleeper were among the first to treat unpretentious American folk and vernacular objects as worthy of inclusion in rooms used for formal entertaining. Because all three associated with circles of wealth, sophistication, and power, they were important in introducing American folk art to an influential stratum of society. Gifted, intuitive decorators with a sense of color, form, and line and the best interaction with surrounding architecture and objects, they often created in their captivated guests the desire for similar interiors.[14]

Among collectors who gathered folk objects entirely for ethnological reasons was Henry Chapman Mercer of Doylestown, Pennsylvania. Trained as an archaeologist, Mercer turned from ancient to colonial objects after visiting the home of a friend who bought "penny lots" at country sales. There, he said, among the "old wagons, gum-tree saltboxes, flax-brakes, straw beehives, tin dinner horns, rope-machines, spinning wheels—things that I had heard of but never collectively saw before—the idea occurred to me that the history

Fig. 2
*Entrance Hall,
Henry du Pont's
Chestertown House,
Southampton,
New York,* 1927,
The Winterthur
Library, Winterthur
Archives

of Pennsylvania was here profusely illustrated and from a new point of view."[15] If the ancient objects of traditional archaeology were valuable conveyors of information about their era, location, maker, and user, he reasoned, the objects made and used in eighteenth- and early nineteenth-century Pennsylvania were equally significant.

Inspired by this revolutionary insight, Mercer immediately began to comb the Pennsylvania countryside for tools, implements, and other items made in the preindustrial era, gathering the material for his 1897 *Tools of the Nation Maker* exhibitions. In this capacity he "discovered" Pennsylvania German cast-iron stove plates and fraktur. He became aware of fraktur when he acquired "a rude, lidless paint-box, fastened with wooden pegs," that, he said, "long puzzled us." The box was finally identified as that of a teacher at one of Pennsylvania's German schools. The teachers used such boxes, wrote Mercer, "as a receptacle for their home-made pens, brushes and colors... [when they] instructed scholars in the art of Fractur or illuminative handwriting...." A search for fraktur produced by the German-school teachers and their pupils resulted in the discovery of "glowing relics [that were] sometimes falling to pieces through carelessness, sometimes preserved with veneration between the leaves of large Lutheran Bibles" (fig. 3). Subsequent study and research revealed that fraktur had been produced throughout the Pennsylvania German community and that the art had been perpetuated by "deliberate instruction" in the German schools until 1854, when a new law led to the demise of such schools.[16]

When Mercer discovered eighteenth-century iron stove plates cast with decorative scenes and motifs largely taken from the Bible, their original use had been all but forgotten. The stove plates were serving as "makeshift chimney tops, stepping-stones or gutter lids, buried under soot and ashes."[17] Mercer began to collect these plates, which had originally been bolted together to form box-shaped stoves, and to research their origins and history (cat. 16). His pioneering *The Bible in Iron*, which began as a pamphlet in 1897, was published as a book in 1914.

Mercer displayed his stove plates, along with many other folk objects, in the Mercer Museum, which he designed, built, and presented to the Bucks County Historical Society in 1916. Since his approach was ethnological rather than art-

historical, Mercer employed the unusual technique of hanging wagons, boats, baskets, and other utilitarian objects from poles jutting into the museum's seven-story atrium, making them visible from several points of view—from above and below, and at eye level. Small rooms off the balconies on each floor contained the tools to make the hanging objects and myriad other utilitarian items. If visitors did not understand Mercer's point—that viewing these items could summon a mental picture of preindustrial Pennsylvania—they could simply enjoy inspecting some of the thousands of folk and vernacular objects he had assembled.

Although by no means as scientific as Henry Mercer, Albert B. Wells of Southbridge, Massachusetts, shared Mercer's fascination with tools as unique carriers of information about the preindustrial age. Wells' collecting pursuits began one rainy afternoon in 1926 when his golf game was canceled. He went antiquing instead and was captivated by the objects he saw: the tools, implements, and furnishings used in the homes, barns, and workshops of an earlier New England. The antiques he bought that day—two wagonloads, according to family tradition—interested him "not merely [as] antique objects, but rather everything these objects imply—how they were made, how they were used, what the people and conditions of life were that made them necessary and influenced their designs; above all, how virtues and ideals expressed in them can be applied to life and work today."[18] This was

Fig. 3
Elmer G. Anderson (American, active c. 1935), *Birth Certificate*, c. 1936, watercolor over graphite, National Gallery of Art, Washington, Index of American Design (original object The Mercer Museum of the Bucks County Historical Society, Doylestown, Pennsylvania)

a remarkable point of view for the day, when collectors from Maine to Texas were focusing entirely on the flowing lines and patrician lineage of their objects, but it was the logical result of Wells' background and occupation. He was chairman of the American Optical Company, which his father had developed and which he ran with two brothers and his son. The Wells tradition, said Albert Wells' first curator, Malcolm Watkins, "was that of the New England craftsman and the pragmatic manufacturer. The ability to get more out of less in terms of both energy and materials is one of the underlying motivations behind American success."[19]

Wells went on as he had begun: "Somehow or other I can't stop buying," he wrote to a friend in 1932, "Never saw such values."[20] Within two years he added to his house a "great room" whose weathered barn boards created a sympathetic background for his careful arrangements of wood and metal tools and implements: churns, corers, snuffers, locks, lathes, spinning wheels, and innumerable other items. Wells later wrote: "I had been having the time of my life for 10, 15 years...collecting oddities and some primitives. Buying the old things wherever people lived...I crowded our house in Southbridge from the cellar to the garret, about 45 rooms...until finally my wife had to move out."[21] The house became the Wells Historical Museum, opened to the public in 1936 (cats. 27, 68, 69). The size of the collection and the need to continue

to plan for its future led to a family conference, in which it was decided to construct a "living village." Technical processes were as important to Wells as the objects themselves, and it was decided to show craftspeople actually using his tools and implements to perform the tasks for which the tools were originally intended. Within a week, Wells said, he had acquired a farm in nearby Sturbridge, and Old Quinabaug Village began to take shape (the name was changed to Old Sturbridge Village in 1946). Like Mercer's museum, Albert Wells' village focused on the tools for everyday tasks: paring apples, skimming soup, lighting interiors, fastening doors, shoeing horses, or planing boards. It was the first outdoor museum devoted to everyday life in rural New England, a museum that emphasized the lives and accomplishments of American folk.

Another early collector with an ethnological (as well as an art) orientation was Edwin Atlee Barber of the Pennsylvania Museum, now the Philadelphia Museum of Art. Barber's specialty was ceramics—he was the author of the exhaustive *Pottery and Porcelain of the United States* of 1893—and he was elated when he discovered in 1891 that the Pennsylvania Germans had been producing distinctive slip- and sgraffito-decorated redware pottery since the eighteenth century. Barber had become interested in ceramics when, as a member of the team that conducted the U.S. Geological and Geographical Survey of the Territories in 1874–1875, he helped unearth ancient Pueblo pottery in the American Southwest.

Like Mercer, Barber understood that modern cultures could be studied just as profitably as ancient ones through the objects they produced. When he returned to the East to complete his education (he received a Ph.D. in ethnology and philology from Lafayette College in 1893), Barber began to collect and study the ceramics of the European settlers in America. Included in the outstanding collection of pottery and porcelain he created for the Pennsylvania Museum was an exceptional group of locally produced redware (fig. 4). His *Tulip Ware of the Pennsylvania German Potters*, published in 1903, was the first book on the subject. Not surprisingly, Barber's interest in fraktur, which he began to collect for the museum upon discovering his first example in 1897, grew from his interest in ceramics. He called his fraktur "a very interesting old paper 'sampler' made by a Pennsylvania Dutchman," and acquired it because "the designs are exactly similar to those on the old pottery."[22]

Barber recognized that there were many other important products of the Pennsylvania Germans besides their highly decorative fraktur and pottery wares, and he was the first curator in America to display a wide variety of American useful and decorative arts in a major museum. A large proportion of these were donated by Sarah Sagehorn Frishmuth, redoubtable collector of "colonial relics."[23] Included in the collection she gave the museum in 1902 were apparel, lighting and fireplace equipment, farm implements, carpenters' tools, and a great many other preindustrial items. Sarah Frishmuth's particular interest among the decorative arts was textiles, and she presented numerous samplers, quilts, coverlets, and decorated hand and show towels.

Another devotee of textiles and needlework was Titus C. Geesey, who appeared on the Pennsylvania collecting scene in 1925, just as Sarah Frishmuth was departing.[24] A native of York, Pennsylvania, Geesey was intrigued by the artifacts of his German ancestors. He had been a longtime bachelor, marrying late in life, and for many years had spent his spare time hunting folk art in the Pennsylvania countryside. In addition to textiles, he collected painted furniture, chalkware, fraktur, spatterware, toleware, carved and painted toys (cat. 1), wrought iron, Kentucky rifles, and many smaller items, including cookie and butter molds and mechanical toys. Like contemporaries such as Henry du Pont, Geesey was extremely interested in arranging, as well as collecting, his antiques. At Longago, his home in Wilmington, Delaware, he integrated his folk art into harmonious room arrangements and settings. In 1953 he offered "the best of my collection" to the Philadelphia Museum, where it was accepted with delight. The Geesey galleries, designed to re-create the ambiance of "the simple farm dwellings of the Pennsylvania Dutch countryside," opened in 1958.

The Pennsylvania German arts were slow to catch on among collectors outside Pennsylvania, but they achieved increasing respect and popularity within the state during the 1920s. Building on the foundation Edwin Atlee Barber laid from the 1890s to the mid-1910s, the Pennsylvania Museum continued to collect Pennsylvania German artifacts. In 1926, as a result of the enthusiasm and support of trustee J. Stogdell Stokes, the museum acquired two rooms and a staircase from the Lebanon County house of the miller of Millbach.[25] This outstanding example of mid-eighteenth-century Pennsylvania German architecture, furnished with ironwork, pewter, tinware, lighting devices, furniture, and Pennsylvania and English earthenwares that Stokes donated from his own collection, opened to the public in 1929. The Millbach rooms were the first folk-art period rooms installed in an American museum, and they provided, as the American Wing had for formal American decorative arts, a context for the objects displayed.

Besides Geesey and Stokes, George Horace Lorimer, editor of the *Saturday Evening Post*, and Henry du Pont searched for superior Pennsylvania German objects during the 1920s. Pennsylvania dealers paid increasing attention to native wares. One dealer, Hattie Brunner of Reinholds, claimed to be the first to specialize entirely in choice Pennsylvania folk art. According to one veteran in the field, Brunner brought this genre to prominence with her display at the Sesqui-Centennial International Exposition, a world's fair held in Philadelphia in 1926 to celebrate the 150th anniversary of American independence. "Without Hattie," said the collector, "and her endless stock of information and tireless energy in running down wanted items, few of the great collections today would be as great or as complete as they are."[26]

Interest in Pennsylvania German art burgeoned in the 1930s as a result of publications, museum exhibitions, and antiques shows, which grew into a permanent feature of the American cultural scene at the end of the 1920s. In 1934 New York City became the site of the first permanent exhibition of Pennsylvania German objects outside their home state when an exhibition gallery and a room trimmed with woodwork from a Lancaster County farmhouse of about 1761 were opened in the American Wing at the Metropolitan Museum of Art. The exhibition and its contents—furniture, ironwork, textiles, ceramics, and fraktur—were the gift of Emily Johnston de Forest, who had been a serious collector of Pennsylvania German redwares since Barber brought them to her attention in the early 1900s (cats. 30, 34).[27] New Yorkers could also view and purchase Pennsylvania German fraktur, paintings, carvings, and chalkware at the American Folk Art Gallery, which opened in Greenwich Village in 1931. With the advent of the Index of American Design, these vivid and distinctive wares at last received national attention at Index exhibitions

52

held throughout the country.

Modernist artists began to collect folk art in the 1910s for an entirely new reason. Looking for a link to an established American artistic tradition, they believed it could be found in folk paintings and sculpture. The modernist revolution had begun in France in the nineteenth century. The impressionists and their successors concentrated on depicting their responses to the world around them, rather than on physical appearance. They investigated the underlying structure of forms, explored the meanings and uses of color, and otherwise experimented with the formal elements of painting. Emphasis thus shifted from pictorial subjects to line, form, color, texture, and space.

Related to this shift and in some ways resulting from it was an accompanying interest in nontraditional, nonacademic, non-Western art, including the folk and indigenous art of many parts of the globe. American artists who studied in France and Germany absorbed a taste for such works. When they returned to the United States, they found that folk portraits, carved figures, and such domestic items as hooked rugs embodied many of the same qualities they had observed in European collections of folk and primitive art.[28]

The modernist artists settled mainly in the East, and many of them summered along the New England coast. There they found, at least until the arrival of the "antiques mania" of the

mid- to late 1920s, that folk art was fairly plentiful and inexpensive. Other artists settled in the Southwest, in Santa Fe and Taos, and collected the carved and painted santos, painted chests, tinware, and textiles produced by Hispanic-American settlers (fig. 5).[29] Whether Eastern or Western, however, modernist collectors focused almost exclusively on the formal artistic and, particularly in the Southwest, "spiritual" qualities of objects rather than on provenance, historical association, or original context and use.

By the same token, modernist collectors identified not with the original owners, but with the creators of their folk art, for they wanted very much to be part of an American, as opposed to European, artistic tradition. Art critic and museum director Lloyd Goodrich confirmed the importance of this notion: "I think quite deep was the search for national character. Here was art that was entirely out of the soil and out of the people and had very little to do with what was going on in Europe, and this search was a very conscious thing at that time among the younger artists. They were looking for a national identity, a national character too."[30]

It seems probable that from the beginning the artists and their sympathizers stressed that these objects were American, devoid of academic contexts, as much as that they were folk art. To these European-trained artists, it was the simplicity and vitality of the rural American paintings, carvings,

Fig. 5 LEFT Elodora P. Lorenzini (American, 1910–1993), *Saint Acacius*, 1938, watercolor over graphite, National Gallery of Art, Washington, Index of American Design (original object Taylor Museum, Colorado Springs Fine Arts Center)

Fig. 6 RIGHT Unidentified artist, *Portrait of a Baby*, possibly from Dover, New Hampshire, c. 1849, oil on canvas, formerly Robert Laurent collection. Laurent called this painting "Dover Baby" because he found it in Dover, New Hampshire. Abby Aldrich Rockefeller Folk Art Museum, Williamsburg

Drawing on America's Past

weather vanes, ceramics, rugs, chairs, and stools that gave them a uniquely American character.

Perhaps the best-known pioneer modernist collectors are the artists who attended Hamilton Easter Field's Summer School of Graphic Arts in Ogunquit, Maine, begun in 1911.[31] Field's interest seems to have centered largely on furniture and hooked rugs, while that of his protégé, the French-born sculptor Robert Laurent, focused on folk paintings and sculpture (fig. 6). Among the artists who shared these interests were Stefan Hirsch, Yasuo Kuniyoshi, Katherine Schmidt, Dorothy Varian, Wood Gaylor, and Bernard Karfiol, all of whom acquired folk objects to furnish and decorate their homes and studios (fig. 7). Some modernists also endeavored to achieve rapport with earlier artists by mastering the techniques they had used. Kuniyoshi, Marsden Hartley, and Konrad Cramer taught themselves to produce reverse paintings on glass, Marguerite Zorach adopted the techniques of rug hooking and embroidery, and Robert Laurent and William Zorach were among those who employed the folk sculptor's method of carving directly in the wood without preliminary models.

The actual subjects and poses of folk art also sometimes appeared in the work of modernist artists. Kuniyoshi's paintings *Boy Stealing Fruit* and *Child* of 1923 are well-known examples, as is Laurent's sculpture *Flirtation* of 1921.[32] The work of the sculptor Elie Nadelman is often said to have been influenced, if not inspired, by folk-art forms, but Nadelman's son, Jan, feels that his father's intrinsic bias toward abstraction and simplicity of form expressed itself first in his sculpture—in pieces such as *Man in the Open Air* of 1914–1915 and *Woman at the Piano* of 1917—and later in his collection of folk art. Nadelman began to collect in 1919, after his marriage to Viola Flannery, and by the mid-1920s the couple had amassed the largest collection of American and European folk art in America.[33] In 1926 they opened the Museum of Folk and Peasant Arts on the grounds of Alderbrook, their Riverdale, New York, estate. Open by appointment, the museum featured displays that strikingly illustrated the couple's belief in the importance of comparing and contrasting American folk art with its European antecedents. Each of the museum's fourteen galleries showed related objects from different countries and demonstrated how they had originally been used if this seemed necessary—a method perhaps inspired by groupings in European ethnological museums. There were portraits, landscapes, and decorative paintings, including a group of theorems, or paintings on velvet. Several paintings are well-known today, among them the mysterious *Outing on the Hudson* and *The Yellow Coach*, both now at the Abby Aldrich Rockefeller Folk Art Museum; the amusing *Bears and Beeves*, now at the New York State Historical Association; and three of Edward Hicks' engaging didactic scenes,

Fig. 7 LEFT Dorothy Varian, *Interior with Stove and Nude*, 1932, oil on canvas. This painting gives a good idea of the kinds of objects Ogunquit artists like Dorothy Varian collected: simple nineteenth-century furnishings such as the rocker, table, shelf clock, and stove; sculptural forms such as decoys and baluster candlestick; and floor coverings of the braided or hooked variety. Newark Museum, Gift of Abby Aldrich Rockefeller

Fig. 8 RIGHT William Stearns (American, active c. 1830/1840), *Bowl of Fruit*, c. 1830/1840, watercolor on velveteen, National Gallery of Art, Washington, Gift of Edgar William and Bernice Chrysler Garbisch

From Attics, Sheds, and Secondhand Shops

Fig. 9
View of Abby
Aldrich Rockefeller's
top-floor art gallery
at 10 West 54th
Street, New York
City. Designed by
Duncan Candler
and Donald Deskey,
the avant-garde
gallery contained
modern works, folk
art, paintings, and
"primitive" African
works; Rockefeller
Archive Center,
photograph by
Samuel Gottscho,
1936

then appreciated by very few collectors. There were also Pennsylvania German chalkware, hooked rugs, toys, dolls, firefighting equipment, and furniture. European furniture, both painted and carved, provided a counterpoint to the American. A gallery devoted to one thousand examples of American and European ceramics contained a special display of the work of eighteenth-century New York stoneware potters. Nadelman was particularly interested in this group and proud of his batter pitcher signed by Clarkson Crolius (cats. 18, 19).

The Nadelmans were forced to sell their collection because of financial losses in the depression, at first parting with individual items but in 1938 selling the whole collection to the New-York Historical Society. With the proceeds, they immediately began a second collection, composed this time entirely of American folk art. After Elie's death in 1946, Viola gradually sold objects to institutions, dealers, and other collectors.

Today remembered by few, but in the 1920s and early 1930s the owner of perhaps the largest collection of American folk paintings, carvings, and weather vanes in America, was Isabel Carleton Wilde of Cambridge, Massachusetts (fig. 8). A knack for buying and remodeling old houses had led Isabel Wilde to an absorption in all early Americana. Of her taste for folk art she said: "I was interested in salvaging these paintings, the animals and figures carved from wood, the rooster weather vanes, and other sculptures, not from the point of view of the antiquarian, but rather as exemplifying the art of a pioneer people, who, with little energy left over after their arduous labors of the day, still expended that little in the effort to create something beautiful."[34]

New Yorkers became acquainted with the Wilde collection when the Whitney Studio presented *An Exhibition of Early American Paintings, the Loan Collection of Isabel Carleton Wilde,* 3–12 February 1927. Like the Nadelmans, the Wildes suffered financial losses during the depression and Isabel was forced to let go of her beloved collection. Many outstanding pieces she owned may now be seen in museum collections, among them the Garbisch collection at the National Gallery of Art and the Abby Aldrich Rockefeller Folk Art Museum in Williamsburg.

Abby Aldrich Rockefeller, Holger Cahill, and Edith Gregor Halpert made up the triumvirate that established folk art firmly as art rather than as history or ethnology. Together, these three—the collector, the theorist, and the promoter—accomplished what none could have achieved alone, creating a folk-art collection that has remained the most important in America. Raised in an old-line Providence family, Abby grew up surrounded by American and European art and antiques. She married John D. Rockefeller Jr. in 1901. Their union was remarkably happy, yet their tastes in art could not have been more different. John preferred—and devoted millions to—Chinese porcelains, medieval tapestries, and similar princely treasures, while Abby loved—and acquired for a comparative pittance—Japanese prints, modern art, and folk art.[35]

Abby encountered folk art through Edith Halpert, from whose Downtown Gallery she purchased modern art. Halpert, from her early teens a passionate devotee of American modern art, was the wife of Samuel Halpert, a modernist who had studied art in Paris and was a member of the New York circle to which the Ogunquit artists also belonged. The couple spent the summers of 1926 and 1927 at Ogunquit, where Edith was not only in constant contact with modern art and artists but was also introduced to folk art.[36]

Holger Cahill, then a publicist and critic in the field of modern art, visited the Halperts at Ogunquit. There he furthered his acquaintance with Edith, particularly, and observed the artists' folk-art-filled studios and living quarters. Cahill had visited folk museums in Sweden, Norway, and Germany in 1922 and was thus familiar with European attitudes toward folk art. He quickly picked up American artists' view of folk art as an indigenous tradition of which they could become a part.

In 1926 Edith Halpert opened the Downtown Gallery on West 13th Street in Greenwich Village. She furnished the space with antiques to achieve, according to a publicity release, a homelike atmosphere in which to exhibit "the work of the best men representing the various tendencies in Contemporary American Art." Edith had done extremely well in the business world for several years before opening the gallery, and she found she had a talent for selling art. In 1929 Holger Cahill became "an informal consultant" to the Downtown Gallery, according to Halpert's biographer Diane Tepfer.[37] When Abby Rockefeller became a client, she and Edith developed a strong rapport.

By 1931 Abby was buying folk as well as modern art (fig. 9). This came about as a result of Halpert's promotion of folk art as the "ancestor" of modern art. According to Dorothy Miller, Holger Cahill's wife, this concept was Cahill's, picked up from his artist friends. Dorothy asserted that her husband had a real struggle to convince Edith Halpert of the importance of folk art as the precursor of modern art.[38] He finally succeeded, however, and she became an enthusiastic convert. In fact, the first exhibition held at Halpert and Cahill's newly formed American Folk Art Gallery (AFAG), in December 1931, consisted of folk portraits entitled *American Ancestors*.

Edgar Holger Cahill, known to his friends as Eddie, was born to Icelandic parents who emigrated to the United States when he was about two years old.[39] He later worked his way east, arriving in New York City in 1913, the year the renowned Armory Show introduced Americans to European modern art. Working as a journalist, taking courses with eminent thinkers such as John Dewey and Thorstein Veblen, and making friends with avant-garde artists, Cahill became vitally interested in modern and folk art. In the 1920s his association with John Cotton Dana, founder and director of the Newark Museum, impressed him with the importance of making ordinary as well as elite objects the focus of museum collections and exhibitions. "Beauty has no relation to price, rarity or age," said Dana, and, "a product of human skill, no matter how much it may be machine-aided, if perfectly adapted to its purpose... is a work of art."[40]

Proof that Cahill assimilated Dana's lessons is provided by the two folk-art exhibitions he produced for the Newark Museum. The first, *American Primitives: An Exhibit of the Paintings of Nineteenth-Century Folk Artists*, which opened 4 November

Fig. 10
Edward Hicks, *Peaceable Kingdom*, 1832–1834, oil on canvas. Included in *The Art of the Common Man*, this was the first of Hicks' *Peaceable Kingdom*s shown in a public exhibition. Abby Aldrich Rockefeller Folk Art Museum, Williamsburg

1930, included eighty-one folk portraits, landscapes, and still lifes. It was the most comprehensive display of American folk paintings assembled up to that time.[41] Cahill, said Edward Alden Jewell in the *New York Times*, "tramped all over the Eastern States to assemble this material."[42] This was true, but Cahill also borrowed a number of paintings from his artist friends, many of whom belonged to the Ogunquit group, such as Wood Gaylor, Robert Laurent, Alexander Brook, Stefan Hirsch, and Elsa Rogo, Hirsch's wife. The Nadelmans and the Zorachs also lent works, as did Isabel Wilde.

Cahill wrote the introduction to the modest catalogue, providing a context to explain these unconventional works. He described the types of craftsmen and amateurs who had created the paintings, why and how they achieved their effects, and how *American Primitives* fit into the total picture of American art. Holger Cahill was the first—and for many years the only—scholar to explain how and for what reasons folk art came into being and to situate it in the continuum of American art.

The following year Cahill once again took to the road to search out folk art and produced *American Folk Sculpture: The Work of Eighteenth and Nineteenth Century Craftsmen*, which opened at the Newark Museum on 20 October 1931. Among the categories included were ships' figureheads, shop figures such as cigar-store Indians, portrait sculptures, weather vanes, bird and animal carvings, toys, and firemarks. The show was notable not only for presenting the first thoughtful, comprehensive exhibition of this material, but also for calling public attention to virtually unknown categories such as iron stove plates, chalkware figures, and carved gravestones (which were shown in photographs).[43] Like *American Primitives*, this exhibition was extremely well received.

With *American Folk Art: The Art of the Common Man in America, 1750–1900*, which opened at the Museum of Modern Art on 30 November 1932, Cahill introduced folk art to the entire nation. The exhibition was made up of 175 oil paintings, pastels, watercolors, paintings on velvet and glass, sculpture, and chalkware, and all but one item was borrowed from Abby Rockefeller's newly formed collection (fig. 10), much of which Cahill had discovered and acquired for the American Folk Art Gallery. The show received nationwide attention both when it opened in New York and during stops in six other American cities.[44] Cahill's introduction, expanding on those he had written for the two Newark exhibitions, listed the categories included, explained how each type was made and by whom, and its place in the community in which it was made; it also defined folk art, and compared and contrasted it with academic art. In closing, Cahill stated: "There is no doubt that these works have many technical deficiencies...but with the artists who made them realism was a passion and not merely a technique...folk artists tried to set down not so much what they saw as what they knew and what they felt. Their art mirrors the sense and the sentiment of a community, and is an authentic expression of American experience."[45]

The *Common Man* exhibition and its catalogue established American folk art as a respectable, collectible category. The most thorough and thoughtful treatment of American folk art to appear up to that date, the catalogue remained a classic for most of the twentieth century and is a valuable reference to the present day.

In 1935 Abby Rockefeller lent more than 250 folk objects to Colonial Williamsburg, whose restoration was funded by her husband. That same year she commissioned Cahill to take an eighteen-month journey through the South looking for folk art to add to her collection. Cahill discovered many fine objects, including face jugs made by African American potters, fraktur by German immigrants to North Carolina, and carvings, needlework, ironwork, furniture, and paintings. His most exciting find was *The Old Plantation*, a rare and unusual watercolor depicting a group of African Americans in a plantation landscape. "I practically fainted when I saw that picture," Cahill recalled. He struggled to contain his jubilation in order to get the best price, and he was successful, acquiring the work for $20.[46]

Upon his return, Cahill helped with preparations for exhibiting the Rockefeller collection at the Ludwell-Paradise House in Williamsburg, which opened March 1935. Cahill's active involvement with searching out and buying folk art ceased at this point and he returned to New York with the intention of devoting himself to the fiction- and playwriting he loved. By the end of the summer, however, he had been persuaded to take on the position of director of the Federal Art Project (FAP). It was in this capacity that he presided over the founding and implementation of the Index of American Design.

According to *Time* magazine, Cahill's goals for the FAP were: "1) to clarify, by research, 'the native background of the arts,' and 2) to break up the big city monopoly on Art by getting people all over the U.S. interested in art as an everyday part of living and working."[47] The idea of an Index of American Design appealed to him enormously as an ideal way to accomplish his first goal. Not only would its participants engage in what Cahill called "a kind of archaeology" by finding and illustrating forgotten or unappreciated examples of American craftsmanship, but also these excavated artifacts would be available to all Americans in a national picture archive. Cahill could thus carry out John Cotton Dana's belief, "That in a democracy such as ours art should not be a luxury product of a minor order intended only for the select few [but] that art should be, and could be interwoven with the very stuff and texture of our national life."[48] The Index of American Design administrators functioned as the ultimate folk-art collectors in identifying, recording, and displaying folk art from many sections of America. The Index prospered, said Cahill, in New England and the Middle Atlantic states, where there was a great deal of material to record and many extremely competent artists to do the work. Some states in the South and West lacked both material and the artists to record it, but there were at least a few treasures in most regions.

The process of finding objects to record seems to have been somewhat hit and miss, depending on whom regional Index administrators knew or could find out about. In addition, when the Index began many people were suspicious of government projects. Nevertheless, according to Cahill, museums were "won over when they became convinced of the sound purpose of the Index, the quality of its drawings and its careful research methods. Dealers and collectors followed."[49] Among those who believed in the Index and helped its administrators convince skeptical collectors, dealers, and museum professionals to make objects available for copying were cultural historian and folk-art scholar Constance Rourke, who was for a period national editor of the Index; Homer Eaton Keyes, founder and editor of the *Magazine Antiques*; and curator Charles O. Cornelius of the American Wing. Among Index workers who came to prominence later were glass scholar Helen McKearin, New England folk-art expert William Warren, and Pennsylvania artist and folk-art specialist Frances

Lichten. Of the collectors discussed in this essay, Faith and Edward Deming Andrews, Henry Chapman Mercer, Elie and Viola Nadelman, Isabel Carleton Wilde, and, of course, Abby Rockefeller, Edith Halpert, and Holger Cahill, lent objects for Index artists to record. In addition to the American Folk Art Gallery (cats. 3, 5, 56, 57), the New York City shop of Helena Penrose and J. H. Edgette was a major source of folk objects for Index artists to copy (cats. 10, 26, 29, 59–61, 67). Penrose was known for her Americana, particularly her large stock of cigar-store Indians, ships' figureheads, carved eagles, weather vanes, decoys, and other folk-art items. Collector-dealer Adele Earnest recalled that Penrose seldom went down into the "dark, unkempt basement" where she kept her folk sculpture, preferring to preside "upstairs in a little alcove in the company of an electric heater and a bottle of gin."[50]

Lectures, radio programs, and exhibitions introduced the American public to the Index of American Design, educating both existing and potential collectors. The exhibitions were particularly effective in illustrating regional styles such as those of the Pennsylvania Germans, the Shakers, the Zoarites, and the creators of Spanish-colonial, pioneer, and cowboy arts. Little-known categories such as stoneware and painted tinware, and particularly wonderful items such as the Caswell carpet, were also brought to the attention of the American public. In recording and exhibiting these and thousands of other specimens of American folk and vernacular art, the Index engendered knowledge, inspired pride in American achievement, and spurred collecting throughout the country.

Notes

1 Quoted and discussed in Benno M. Forman, *American Seating Furniture 1630–1730* (New York and London, 1988), 212; Elizabeth Stillinger, *The Antiquers* (New York, 1980), 18; and Robert F. Trent, "A History for the Essex Institute Turkey Work Couch," *Essex Institute Historical Collections* 113, no. 1 (January 1977), 29–37.

2 See Cahill in Christensen 1959 for the source of the title and for collecting history; and Elizabeth Stillinger, "'A Kind of Archaeology': Collecting American Folk Art 1876–1976," forthcoming.

3 See William B. Rhoads, *The Colonial Revival* (New York, 1977); Alan Axelrod, ed., *The Colonial Revival in America* (Winterthur and New York, 1985); Karal Ann Marling, *George Washington Slept Here: Colonial Revivals and American Culture 1876–1986* (Cambridge, Mass., and London, 1988); and Stillinger 1980 for more on the colonial revival.

4 See exh. cat. Boston 1987a for a thorough treatment of the movement.

5 Quoted in Bucks County Historical Society, *The Mercer Mile: The Story of Dr. Henry Chapman Mercer and His Concrete Buildings* (Doylestown, Pa., 1972), 16.

6 "Famous Collections formed by Mr. A. W. Drake," American Art Association, 10–12 March 1913; "C. E. Lawrence Collection," American Art Galleries, 19 May 1921; "The Jacob Paxson Temple Collection of Early American Furniture and Objects of Art," Anderson Galleries, New York, 23–28 January 1922.

7 See Suzanne L. Flynt, Susan McGowan, and Amelia F. Miller, *Gathered and Preserved* (Deerfield, Mass., 1991), for an excellent brief history of George Sheldon, the PVMA, and Memorial Hall. The quotation is from Margery Burnham Howe, *Deerfield Embroidery*, 2d ed. (Deerfield, Mass., 1993), 14.

8 "Edna Who Only in Name Was Little," Edward F. Little, ed. (privately published, n.d.), 28. See also Elizabeth Stillinger, "Edna Greenwood and Everyday Life in Early New England," *The Magazine Antiques* (August 2002).

9 Alexander J. Wall, "Time Stone Farm, the Old Deacon Goodale Homestead at Marlborough, Massachusetts, Its History and the Story of Its Preservation by Edna and Arthur Greenwood," *New-York Historical Society Quarterly Bulletin* (April 1936), 12.

10 Undated, unsigned two-page memorandum almost certainly written by Malcolm Watkins (Collection Record Office, NMAH,SI), record no. 182022, .247.

11 Edward Deming Andrews and Faith Andrews, *Fruits of the Shaker Tree of Life: Memoirs of Fifty Years of Collecting and Research* (Stockbridge, Mass., 1975), 21.

12 Andrews and Andrews 1975, 21. The Cahill quote is from Cahill in Christensen 1959, xv.

13 *The Magazine Antiques* 14, no. 2, 132–136. See Stephen J. Stein, *The Shaker Experience in America, A History of the United Society of Believers* (New Haven and London, 1992), 381; see also 373–380, 382, and 395–397 for a current scholar's assessment of the Andrews and the "Shaker myth" they promulgated.

14 Henry Sleeper's summer home, Beauport, now belongs to the Society for the Preservation of New England Antiquities and may be visited from mid-May through mid-September; Electra Webb's Shelburne Museum is open to the public from mid-April through early December; and Henry du Pont's Winterthur Museum is open to the public all year. Du Pont is well known for his collections of formal American decorative arts, but the folk art he gathered—his Southampton home, Chestertown House, was furnished largely with Pennsylvania German and other folk objects, and the Winterthur Museum also contains quantities of folk art—warrants his inclusion here.

15 Henry C. Mercer, "The Survival of the Mediaeval Art of Illuminative Writing among Pennsylvania Germans," 1897, reprinted in Cary M. Amsler, ed., *Bucks County Fraktur* (Doylestown and Kutztown, Pa., 1999), 5. See also Helen H. Gemmill, *Pioneering Americana: A Mercer Museum Centennial* (Doylestown, Pa., n.d.).

16 Mercer in Amsler 1999, 6. See Amsler 1999 for much new information about the German schools, Pennsylvania German fraktur, and fraktur artists.

17 Mercer 1961, 1.

18 "Old Quinabaug Village" (1941), 2, booklet prepared by A. B. and J. Cheney Wells for the visit of the Walpole Society, a collectors' group.

19 Typescript of C. Malcolm Watkins, "Old Sturbridge Village: Beginnings, 1936 to 1948, a talk delivered at Antique Collectors' Weekend 10/29/1971," 10, Old Sturbridge Village archives.

20 Quoted in David M. Simmons, "The Wells Family and the Development of Old Sturbridge Village," 7, typescript of an oral presentation, 28 September 1996, Old Sturbridge Village archives.

21 Letter from A. B. Wells to Mrs. Arthur Shurcliffe, 2 December 1948, Old Sturbridge Village archives. A. B. Wells' collection became a family concern in the mid-1930s: his brother J. Cheney Wells, his son, George, and eventually George's wife, Ruth, were very much involved in planning for the transition from private collection to public museum and in developing museum policy.

22 Barber is quoted in Jean Sutherland Boggs, "Foreword," Beatrice B. Garvan, *The Pennsylvania German Collection* (Philadelphia, 1982), x.

23 I am indebted to Jack Lindsey, curator of American decorative arts at the Philadelphia Museum, for telling me about Frishmuth and directing me to the Frishmuth papers in the museum's archives.

24 Sarah Frishmuth died in 1926; Barber, who had become curator of the museum in 1901 and director in 1907, had died in 1916.

25 See Garvan 1982, 6–7, for information about the Millbach rooms.

26 Earl F. Robacker, *Touch of the Dutchland* (New York, 1965), 21. Arthur J. Sussel of Philadelphia was another important dealer and collector of Pennsylvania German objects during the 1920s.

27 See Alice Cooney Frelinghuysen, "Emily Johnston de Forest," *The Magazine Antiques* 157, no. 1 (January 2000), 192–199, for more about De Forest's extensive collecting activities.

28 Largely as a result of modern artists' perception of a disparate group of paintings, sculptures, and various domestic, farm, and commercial items as "folk art," this category came, in the United States, to be a catchall embracing folk, popular, and utilitarian objects. In the 1970s folklorists challenged this use of the term "folk art," maintaining that this country had no true folk in the European sense, that many objects classified as "folk" fell outside the definition of European folk art, and that objects made for specific utilitarian purposes should not be divorced from their original contexts and presented simply as art. See David Park Curry, "Rose-colored Glasses: Looking for 'Good Design' in American Folk Art," in *An American Sampler: Folk Art from the Shelburne Museum* [exh. cat., National Gallery of Art] (Washington, 1987), 24–41, for an excellent discussion of all sides of this issue. See also Stillinger forthcoming.

29 See Charles C. Eldredge, Julie Schimmel, and William H. Truettner, *Art in New Mexico, 1900–1945: Paths to Taos and Santa Fe* (Washington and New York, 1986), 108–143, and Lonn Taylor and Dessa Bokides, *New Mexican Furniture 1600–1940: The Origins, Survival, and Revival of Furniture Making in the Hispanic Southwest* (Santa Fe, 1987), 213–288, for information about folk-art collectors in the Southwest.

30 Transcript of Lloyd Goodrich interviews with Harlan Phillips, 1962–1963, Archives of American Art, reel 3197, 225.

31 See Doreen Bolger, "Hamilton Easter Field and His Contribution to American Modernism," *The American Art Journal* 20, no. 2 (1988), 79–107, for a review of Field's life and accomplishments, and Louise Tragard, Patricia A. Hart, and W. L. Copithorne, *A Century of Color, 1886–1986* (Ogunquit, Maine, 1987) for a history of Field's and Laurent's participation in the Ogunquit art colony.

32 See Jane Myers and Tom Wolf, *The Shores of a Dream: Yasuo Kuniyoshi's Early Work in America* (Fort Worth, 1996), for more on Kuniyoshi; and Hirschl & Adler Folk, *Source and Inspiration: A Continuing Tradition* (New York, 1988), for more on the influence of folk art on American modern artists.

33 See Christine I. Oaklander, "Pioneers in Folk Art Collecting: Elie and Viola Nadelman," *Folk Art* 17, no. 3 (Fall 1992), 48–55; and Elizabeth Stillinger, "Elie and Viola Nadelman's Unprecedented Museum of Folk Arts," *The Magazine Antiques* 146, no. 4 (October 1994), 515–525, for more extended discussions of the Nadelmans' lives and folk-art collection. I am indebted to Jan Nadelman and his daughter, Cynthia Nadelman, for access to the Nadelman papers and for many valuable discussions about the collection.

34 Quoted in Alice Lawton, "Early American Folk Art, Paintings and Sculptures, Entertaining Display at Harley Perkins' Gallery," *Boston Sunday Post*, 27 May 1936, A-8. I am indebted to Wilde's granddaughters, Ellen Doughty Graves and Frances Doughty, for access to the Isabel Carleton Wilde papers and for their family recollections.

35 Bernice Kert, *Abby Aldrich Rockefeller, the Woman in the Family* (New York, 1993), is the most recent—and very thorough—biography of Abby Rockefeller.

36 See Tepfer 1989 for a detailed discussion of Halpert's life and work.

37 Tepfer 1989, 43, 48.

38 Typescript of Dorothy Miller interview with Paul Cummings, Archives of American Art, 1970, reel 4210, 29.

39 See Jeffers 1995, 326–335; and Jeffers 1991, 2–11.

40 Letter from John Cotton Dana to Richard D. Jenkinson, 15 April 1925, Newark Museum Archives, quoted in Barbara Lipton, *John Cotton Dana and the Newark Museum* (Newark, 1979), 50; and Dana, Introduction to "A Weston Electrical Instrument," quoted in Lipton 1979, 42.

41 Smaller exhibitions had taken place in New York City during the 1920s: *Early American Art*, organized by Henry Schnackenberg for the Whitney Studio Club, contained forty-five folk paintings, sculptures, and miscellaneous objects borrowed from other members of the club, which included several Ogunquit artists as well as Charles Sheeler, Charles Demuth, and club director Juliana Force. The exhibition was on view at the club from 9–24 February 1924. *Early American Portraits & Landscapes*, a show held at the Dudensing Galleries in December 1924, consisted of sixteen folk portraits and eight landscapes, hooked rugs, and early furniture, some of which were for sale. Valentine Dudensing was Robert Laurent's dealer, and Laurent helped organize the show, lending at least six portraits and securing others from his friends. I am indebted to Charlotte Emans Moore for identifying the artists and current locations of several works in the show.

42 "A Venture in Homespun/Fascinating Display at Newark, within Tubing Distance of Fifty-seventh Street," 9 November 1930.

43 Gravestones had first been shown as folk art the previous year at the Harvard Society for Contemporary Art's *Exhibition of American Folk Painting in Connection with the Massachusetts Tercentenary*. Cahill may have borrowed the photographs the society commissioned at that time.

44 The exhibition itinerary included the Pennsylvania Museum of Art, Philadelphia (4 February–4 March 1933); Rhode Island School of Design, Providence (1–30 April 1933); Museum of Fine Arts, Boston (10 October–5 November 1933); Nelson Gallery, Kansas City (1 February–1 March 1934); Greenwich (Connecticut) Public Library (26 May–19 June 1934); and Westchester County Center, White Plains, New York (25 June–9 July 1934).

45 Cahill 1932, 28.

46 Cahill 1957, 264.

47 *Time* (5 September 1938), 36.

48 Typescript of "Mr. Cahill's speech at opening of Newark show, November 6, 1936," Archives of American Art, unmicrofilmed Cahill papers, box 1, "speeches and lectures" folder, 1.

49 Cahill in Christensen 1959, xiii.

50 Adele Earnest, *Folk Art in America: A Personal View* (Exton, Pa., 1984), 136.

American Folk Art's "Distinctive Character"

The Index of American Design and New Deal Notions of Cultural Nationalism

Erika Doss

In the opening paragraph of her 1936 essay "What Is American Design?" cultural historian and critic Constance Rourke asserted: "American design has many ancestries, but this circumstance does not exclude the possibility of a distinctive character." Rourke wrote prolifically on American folklore, publishing her classic book *American Humor: A Study of the National Character* in 1931, producing biographies on American pioneers and artists such as Davy Crockett (1933), John Audubon (1936), and Charles Sheeler (1938), and working for three decades on a projected three-volume history of America's "esthetic tradition" titled *The Roots of American Culture*. From 1936 to 1937, Rourke served as field editor of the Index of American Design, a New Deal project aimed at an extensive pictorial record of the decorative, folk, and popular American arts from the colonial era to about 1900 (fig. 1). As her remarks on American design suggest, Rourke recognized the inherent diversity of the nation's many material cultures but also believed that, collectively, these local and regional folk cultures embodied a larger common culture, and national identity, of "distinctive character."[1]

Throughout the interwar era of the 1920s and 1930s, Rourke and other American intellectuals, historians, artists, museum curators, art dealers, and politicians became intensely preoccupied with issues of cultural nationalism, with determining the links between American national identity and American art and material culture. Prickling anxieties about European cultural superiority and perceptions of the shallow provinciality of American art had rankled many for years. But in the wake of World War I, with European cultural capitals in ruin and unprecedented prosperity and a rapid rise to global economic leadership in the United States, many came to believe that the time was ripe for a corresponding ascendancy of America's visual arts. "We have been sponging on Europe for direction instead of developing our own," lamented critic Paul Rosenfeld in *Port of New York* (1924), a collection of essays on modern American artists and writers. Rosenfeld optimistically sensed "a new spirit dawning in American life," a veritable cultural and intellectual renaissance centered on specifically American forms of art and literature.[2]

Such notions of a unique American culture and character burgeoned during the interwar years, when critics and artists alike machinated a kind of "cultural boosterism" to define and direct this "new spirit" of American aesthetic exceptionalism. "There is an American art," New York art dealer Robert Coady boldly stated in his short-lived magazine *The Soil* in 1916–1917. It was "young, robust, energetic, naive, immature, daring, and big spirited," and it was especially, said Coady, an American *material* culture of everything from "the Panama Canal, the Sky-scraper and Colonial Architecture" to beadwork, crazy quilts, cigar-store Indians, electric signs, and commercial posters. American art was not, Coady concluded, "an illustration to a theory" but "an expression of life—a complicated life—American life.... It has grown out of the soil and through the race and will continue to grow. It will grow and mature and add a new unit to Art."[3]

Other interwar critics were similarly nationalistic about American art. Coining the term "usable past" in a 1918 issue of the literary journal *The Dial*, Van Wyck Brooks urged artists to look to distinctive American forms and traditions as they forged a "new Americanism." Likewise, in his 1925

Fig. 1
Index of American
Design poster,
National Gallery
of Art, Washington,
Gallery archives

book *In the American Grain*, poet William Carlos Williams extolled the rich cultural resources of the nation's "peculiar and discoverable ground" as Americans self-consciously searched for the moral and aesthetic roots of national character and identity. "There is a source," said Williams, "IN AMERICA for everything we think or do." Artist Stuart Davis wrote in his journal in March 1922: "Starting now I will begin a series of paintings that shall be rigorously, logically American, not French. America has had her scientists, her inventors, now she shall have her artists."[4]

Even when the economy collapsed in 1929 and the nation was beset by a tumultuous decade of social and political disaffection during the Great Depression, widespread assumptions of a uniquely American aesthetic persisted. Historian Warren Susman remarked that during the 1930s phrases such as "the American Dream" and an "American way of life" became common as "Americans then began thinking in terms of patterns of behavior and belief, values and life-styles, symbols and meanings" that alluded to "something shared collectively by all Americans." In 1931 Congress officially designated the "Star Spangled Banner" the national

anthem; in the late 1930s, Kate Smith's version of "God Bless America" (written by Irving Berlin in 1918, revised 1938) pervaded the airwaves. From 1939 to 1940, the New York World's Fair displayed a towering statue of George Washington designed by James Earle Fraser (whose similarly iconic sculpture of a defeated American Indian, *End of the Trail*, was first seen at the 1915 Panama-Pacific Exposition in San Francisco).[5] New York's fair also featured the futuristic Trylon and Perisphere, two dazzling-white monuments that spoke to the nation's coming technological prospects. These depression-era symbols of American collectivity and unity, and of the country's historical past and future promise, became further linked with New Deal notions of nationalism: the particular beliefs, traditions, and values that mold an ethnically and racially diverse society into a nation.

A nation is an "imagined community, a cultural artifact," anthropologist Benedict Anderson argued in his influential 1983 case study of the making of modern Indonesia. Stemming from a confluence of capitalism and print technology, the concept of the nation-state first emerged in the eighteenth century, gaining credence and sustenance in the modern era through the devices of mass media (such as magazines, movies, radio, and advertising) that helped shape and regulate social attitudes and behaviors. However constructed (or "invented," as Ernest Gellner argued), national communities are distinguished, Anderson further explained, "by the style in which they are imagined."[6] During the Great Depression, the United States government played a central role in shaping and directing the "style" of American cultural nationalism, particularly by becoming the nation's primary patron of the arts and by supplying emergency labor relief for the country's artists through New Deal incentives such as the Works Progress Administration (WPA), the Resettlement Agency, which became the Farm Security Administration (FSA), the Civilian Conservation Corps (CCC), and other so-called alphabet soup agencies.

The Index of American Design was part of the New Deal's larger investment in national culture, which included the WPA's Federal Project Number One and its four arms: the Federal Art Project, Federal Theater Project, Federal Music Project, and Federal Writers' Project. It also included art projects sponsored by government units such as the Department of the Treasury and the Department of Agriculture. The Treasury's Section of Painting and Sculpture (the "Section"), for example, created some 3,350 murals in post offices and other public buildings across the country. Artists employed by the Department of Agriculture's FSA, including Walker Evans, Dorothea Lange, and Ben Shahn, produced thousands of documentary photographs (fig. 2). The FSA also oversaw the production of a number of extraordinary documentary films, including Pare Lorentz' *The Plow That Broke the Plains* (1936) and *The River* (1937), both about the ill effects of poor land management (soil erosion and floods) and the beneficence of New Deal agricultural policies. Lorentz' 1939 documentary, *The City*, tackled the problems of urban squalor and overcrowding and portrayed solutions in "new" towns such as Greenbelt, Maryland, a government-planned and financed suburban settlement—complete with a community center, school, shopping center, fire station, movie theater, restaurant, hotel, parks, and well-designed streets for easy automobile access—located between Baltimore and Washington, DC.

The Federal Art Project (FAP) was particularly wide-ranging: sponsoring an additional 2,500 public murals; operating more than one hundred community art centers; organizing handicrafts programs that employed about 35,000 people in bookbinding, textile-block printing, weaving, doll-making, costumery, and furniture design; and overseeing the production of an estimated 108,000 easel paintings, 17,700 sculptures, 250,000 prints, two million posters, and the vast pictorial record of the Index of American Design. The 10,000 writers employed under the Federal Writers' Project (FWP) surveyed each state and major city in the *American Guide Series*, producing more than four hundred volumes. Under another federally funded writers' project, the Historical Records Survey catalogued everything from cemetery gravestone epitaphs to newspaper obituaries, nationwide. The Federal Music Project (FMP) supported orchestras, chamber groups, choirs, and bands, sponsored some 225,000 performances (reaching an estimated audience of 150 million Americans), and presented new works by American composers such as Aaron Copland and William Schuman; the FMP also collected folk songs, as did the FWP, offered music classes, and repaired musical instruments. The Federal Theater Project (FTP) underwrote hundreds of stage productions, from traditional Shakespearean plays to the

Fig. 2
Dorothea Lange, *Along the Highway near Bakersfield, California, Dustbowl Refugees, November 1935*, photograph FSA/OWI Photo Collection, Prints and Photos Division

avant-garde "Living Newspapers," experimental performances that dramatized sociopolitical conditions and issues concerning slums, rural electrification, venereal disease, and working-class labor relations.[7] By employing thousands of artists, writers, actors, and musicians, and with expenditures reaching more than $35 million during an eight-year foray into arts patronage (largely abandoned by 1943 or diverted to military defense efforts), the policies of the New Deal helped legitimate an unmistakably American culture and spurred a renaissance in American art, old and new.

Begun at the end of 1935, the FAP's Index of American Design aimed at reacquainting modern, twentieth-century Americans with their folk and decorative art traditions. It aspired to further encourage a rebirth of uniquely American artistic patterns and styles in the applied arts, to serve as both a record of the past and a sourcebook for contemporary designers. By extension, the Index was predicated on elevating American taste, in abandoning prevailing sentiments of cultural insecurity and enlightening audiences, including modern artists and consumers, about the historical character and quality of the nation's material culture. Original plans included publishing the Index plates in a series of portfolios on American design, but unfortunately, high costs, along with other problems, halted this endeavor. Still, many of the illustrations intended for the Index were reproduced in post–World War II picture books such as Erwin O. Christensen's *The Index of American Design* (1950) and Clarence P. Hornung's *Treasury of American Design* (1972).[8]

As editor of the Index, Constance Rourke was assigned the task of finding examples of this material culture, experience she gained from judging folk art shows in Grand Rapids, Michigan (her hometown), and helping to organize the National Folk Festival in Saint Louis in 1934. During 1936 and 1937 she traveled the Eastern and Midwestern states pursuing "living research": talking with local craftspeople, visiting regional museums and private collections, meeting the few surviving members of the Shaker colonies, as well as locating artifacts and information to be included in the Index. The intended design portfolios were to be "a pioneering force" in a newly self-conscious America, Rourke wrote in 1937, "directing attention in many parts of the country to the field of our early native designs and to its unmistakable richness." The Index's vast pictorial materials would offer "an education of the eye…which may result in the development of taste and a genuine consciousness of our rich national heritage."[9]

Instigated as a work-relief project and mainly serving commercial illustrators who had not found employment elsewhere with the FAP, the Index was also set up to assuage widespread fears that America did not have a folk-art tradition. There was concern among many Americans at this time that whatever folk traditions the United States had once possessed had become diminished or had entirely disappeared because of mass production technologies and modern industrialization. As artist Thomas Hart Benton bemoaned in his 1937 autobiography, *An Artist in America*: "The arts of our pioneers were simple arts perhaps, but they were genuine and they were assiduously cultivated…. [But] under the influence of mercantile persuasion, the fine old patchwork quilts and hooked rugs of the grandmothers and the solid hickory chairs and benches of the grandfathers were thrown out of home after home in favor of cheap, jerry-made, but showy manufactures. The new became synonymous with the better." During the late 1920s and the 1930s, Benton crisscrossed "the back countries of America by foot, bus, and train, searching out American subject matter" for his regionalist paintings, his version of a uniquely American modern art grounded in the nation's historical traditions and sensibilities.[10]

During the 1930s American industry was celebrated for the kind of creativity and modernity seen in the "geometrical beauty" of the Wear-Ever aluminum tea kettles, Steuben glass ashtrays, and Thonet Brothers tubular steel chairs (designed by Le Corbusier and Marcel Breuer). The Museum of Modern Art highlighted a selection of such well-designed American goods in its 1934 exhibition *Machine Art*.[11] The Index similarly challenged contemporary industrial designers and manufacturers to find inspiration for modernity in native design idioms, to create quintessentially American forms of modern material culture equivalent to the streamlined "art moderne" style of much contemporary European industrial design, from French art deco to German Bauhaus sensibilities. Although the Index focused on applied arts dating before the officially "modern" twentieth century and determined that American design was rooted in handmade wood and stoneware goods specifically from the American past—not in the European-influenced present—it was not an antiquarian project. Rather, the Index encouraged the formation of distinctively "American" modern design products, suitable for manufacture, which stemmed from, and enriched, the nation's folk traditions and popular arts.

To a degree, the Index was founded on assumptions of an apparent vacuity of modern American arts and crafts: its mandated pre-1900 chronology required the exclusion of early twentieth-century Rookwood, Cowan, and Van Briggle art pottery, and the textiles and ceramics produced at the Cranbrook Academy of Art (Bloomfield Hills, Michigan). Index staff certainly knew of such material—indeed, several had been leading members of the modernist American Union of Decorative Artists and Craftsmen—yet perhaps found it too romantic, or, more likely, too inflected by European design sensibilities. Likewise, Index administrators assumed that the nation's older arts and crafts were innately American, and yet the easy exchange of designs and technologies within such a national, and international, economy raises questions about the purity of any specifically American (or British, French, or German) style. Moreover, putting commercial artists to work rendering and revitalizing the creative designs of an earlier, supposedly preindustrial, premodern era, was similarly inconsistent. Without exaggerating the substance of these ironies, Index staff were motivated by other concerns: in particular, the project's larger symbolic construction of national cultural identity. As Lincoln Rothschild, who directed the Index project in New York City from 1937 to 1941, later recalled: "Potentially the greatest intangible value of this program lay in the possibility of enriching American culture by illuminating its past. The program of the Index would clearly reveal the existence of an ingenious and highly respectable tradition of genuine, spontaneous creativity early in our history."[12]

Index artists (numbering 372 by 1937) undertook a far-reaching survey of indigenous American design, a pictorial record of hand-produced crafts and domestic goods including toys, quilts, weather vanes, cigar-store Indians, tavern signs, baptismal fonts, Pennsylvania German spoons, wallpaper, fabric samples, ceramics, clothes, and shoes (fig. 3). Also included were some manufactured objects, such as toy locomotives and mechanical banks (cats. 60, 62). The project originated in New York City, where several hundred artists drew extensively from the folk art collections of local cultural institutions such as the Metropolitan Museum of Art, the Museum of the City of New York, the New-York Historical Society, and the Brooklyn Museum. Soon, however, the Index became a nationwide endeavor as a unit of the FAP and its central office located in Washington, DC. It eventually grew to include artists in thirty-four states and the District of Columbia, along with state project staffs, who searched their local art and history museums as well as private collections to find the best examples of American design and folk art. These objects were documented (and in some cases, conserved), and then reproduced in watercolor; by the time the Index shut down in 1942, about 18,000 individual plates had been produced (7,000 by the Index's New York branch).[13] In many ways, the Index's project characterized a primary New Deal ideal: that the nation's soul could be found, or "imagined," in American material and visual arts.

New Deal arts patronage was not exclusively concerned with providing work relief, of course, but rested on mainstream political desires to engender national unity and restore national confidence in American forms of capitalism and democracy, both sorely tested by the exigencies of the Great Depression. Many of the art projects supported by the New Deal were documentary in nature, focused both on recording and preserving American culture and history and on illustrating the larger public need for federal assistance. As FSA photographer Arthur

Fig. 3
Unidentified artist at work, Dayton Art Institute, Dayton, Ohio, 24 November 1936, National Gallery of Art, Washington, Gallery archives

Rothstein remarked, "It was our job to document the problems of the Depression so that we could justify the New Deal legislation that was designed to alleviate them."[14] Rothstein, Lange, and other New Deal photographers captured the American folk much as the Index's artists recorded the artifacts of America's folk life. Although physically worn, the plain people shown in FSA photographs and the humble objects depicted in the Index were vital, resilient, and indisputably worthy of preservation—like the nation itself.

Documentary intentions similarly directed the *American Guide Series*, which constituted an exhaustive effort by the Federal Writers' Project (FWP) from 1935 to 1941 to map the American landscape, road by road, state by state.[15] Challenging the cultural stereotypes and European biases in Karl Baedeker's slim one-volume guide to the United States (first published in 1893), the *American Guide Series* aimed at proving the country's cultural legitimacy, historical roots, and national character. *Idaho: A Guide in Word and Picture* was the first book published in the series (in 1937), followed by volumes for the forty-seven other states, such as *North Carolina: A Guide to the Old North State* (1939), *Kansas: A Guide to the Sunflower State* (1939), *The Ohio Guide* (1940), *New York: A Guide to the Empire State* (1940), *Wisconsin: A Guide to the Badger State* (1941), and *Colorado: A Guide to the Highest State* (1941). The series also included multiple volumes on select cities, such as *The WPA Guide to New York City* (1939), or *San Francisco:*

The Bay and Its Cities (1940), and three books on America's roads: *U.S. One: Maine to Florida* (1938), *The Ocean Highway: New Brunswick, New Jersey to Jacksonville, Florida* (1938), and *The Oregon Trail: The Missouri River to the Pacific Ocean* (1939).

The affordable books were travel guides and regional encyclopedias intended to educate middle-class Americans about America. That education was grounded in notions of national collectivity and citizenship, in imagining all-America as a confident country of diverse and discrete communities, regions, and states ("the Badger State," "the Empire State," and so forth). The publication, for example, of the final volume in the series—*Oklahoma: A Guide to the Sooner State*—coincided with President Franklin D. Roosevelt's declaration of "American Guide Week" (10–16 November 1941), which took as its slogan "Take Pride in Your Country." As Roosevelt remarked, the FWP's *American Guide Series* offered "for the first time in our history a series of volumes that ably illustrate our national way of life, yet at the same time portray the variants in local patterns of living and regional development.... I am sure that this shelf of books... will serve to deepen our understanding of ourselves as a people, and hence promote national unity."[16]

The Federal Music Project took an analogous ethnographic-nationalist approach, recording Hungarian Gypsy bands in Detroit, Hawaiian trios in California, and Pawnee chants in Oklahoma, and arguing that all these diverse folk-music traditions represented national cultural identity. While many FMP staff believed that the project's primary objective was to generate jobs for unemployed professional musicians, thereby creating symphonies and chamber groups, others were persuaded to support folk festivals and to "preserve and promote the nation's folk music." In 1936 the FMP partially funded the Ashland Folk Festival in Kentucky, during which staff collected folk songs and tall tales; in 1938 composer Charles Seeger joined the FMP and began administering its folk and social music division.[17]

This preoccupation with the American "folk" as an essential symbol of cultural nationalism mirrored a general populist shift in much 1930s culture. During the depression, for example, many Hollywood movies shifted from the literary English of the stage to "real" (or "street") speech, the everyday patois of the American folk, and of such heroes of popular culture as satirist and "cracker-barrel philosopher" Will Rogers. One of the most popular radio and movie stars of the era, Rogers was a Cherokee Indian who chastised the rich, praised the common man, and delighted in telling audiences, "I have a different slant on things...for my ancestors did not come over on the Mayflower. They met the boat." Depression-era movies and movie theaters alike reflected more egalitarian sensibilities: rejecting the grandiose, exotic styles popular in the 1920s, movie theaters became plainer, smaller, and more attuned to the specific tastes of their local and regional audiences. Similarly, a new national vision of a folkish and more democratic "Americanism" also became a dominant theme in many 1930s movies, including *Judge Priest* (1934), *Showboat* (1936), *Young Mr. Lincoln* (1939), and *Mr. Smith Goes to Washington* (1939), many featuring new "homespun" stars such as Rogers, Henry Fonda, and Jimmy Stewart.[18]

That national vision further informed the Archive of Folk Culture, founded at the Library of Congress in 1928 as a repository for American folk music. Throughout the depression, the Archive collected folk songs and invited musicians including Leadbelly, Josh White, Jelly Roll Morton, and the Almanac Singers to recording sessions at the Library of Congress. In 1940 radical folklorist Alan Lomax arranged for Woody Guthrie's recording of "This Land Is Your Land," a song the "dust bowl balladeer" intended as his version of the national anthem in response to the "passive optimism" of Irving Berlin's "God Bless America."[19] The urge to document and champion the folk as national symbols was strong among both the leftists of the Popular Front (including Lomax and Guthrie) and the mainstream liberals of the New Deal.

Shaping a collective cultural nationalism from a diverse body of American folk traditions, the New Deal's "documentary imagination" was obviously ideological and reformist.[20] In contrast to contemporaneous government arts patronage in Nazi Germany, fascist Italy, and communist Russia, New Deal notions of cultural nationalism focused on affirming aesthetic pluralism and championed local, regional cultures; if there was an obvious proclivity for documentary strategies and representational styles, there was never a particularly official version of New Deal art. Instead, the lure of the local was used as the currency of cultural nationalism, a project that involved blending

America's multiple cultures and art forms (or "ancestries," as Rourke put it) into a larger national picture of unity.

That is not to argue that this New Deal picture of American unity was an uncomplicated, seamless, or even complete celebration of American cultural diversity and democracy. Indeed, local and regional social, political, ethnic, racial, and religious identities and differences were regulated within the WPA/FAP, as in the New Deal in general, and fitted into a federally designed national blueprint focused on cultural commonality and consensus. Most of the objects catalogued in the Index of American Design, for example, were predominantly rooted in Western European ancestries. Early in the project, FAP head Holger Cahill recounted, Native American culture was excluded from the Index because "it was felt that Indian Arts should be left to the ethnologists who had been making pictorial records in that field."[21] Despite this, some Native American art was represented in the Index, including select examples of California Indian basketry.

African American folk art and crafts were included in the Index, but sparingly, perhaps because a number of Southern states (such as Georgia, Mississippi, and Florida) were barely represented; decorative arts such as the appliquéd quilts of slaves and former slaves (such as those made by Harriet Powers in the 1890s), carved walking sticks, and coiled grass baskets were largely absent in the Index. The Index did represent the alkaline-glazed stoneware of nineteenth-century black craftsmen such as the slave known as Dave the Potter, who worked in the Edgefield District of west-central South Carolina, and stoneware face vessels typically made by nineteenth-century African American artisans.

As much as the New Deal strove for a "national-popular" aesthetic through its federal art projects, that aesthetic was limited by a reluctance, however unconscious, to accommodate cultural differences on their own terms and within their own histories.[22] Yet by the same token, those local objects and examples of folk art and design that were included in the Index were conferred with a national, official status largely dissociated from their specific origins and contexts. Consideration of the particular ideologies that guided the making of the Index of American Design further reveals the tensions and limitations that surrounded the production of cultural nationalism in New Deal America.

Self-consciousness regarding the connections between American cultural identity and the "folk" predated the New Deal, and some aspects of the Index's cultural nationalism may be found in the ideology of the arts and crafts movement at the turn of the century. As design historian Wendy Kaplan argues, "the adaptation of folk and other indigenous cultures to express a country's identity," a style now called romantic nationalism, was common throughout Europe by the late nineteenth century. Britain, Ireland, Finland, Norway, France, Germany, and Russia all pursued variants of a national design vocabulary couched in regional folk art and traditions as they reformed or constructed specific national identities. Eliel Saarinen's organic architecture and *ryijy* rug designs, for example, were key components in forming Finland's cultural identity in the early twentieth century.[23]

Likewise, American architects Louis Sullivan and Frank Lloyd Wright shared the conviction that the United States lacked, and needed, a national style of architecture. Romantic nationalism further influenced the design philosophy of American arts and crafts practitioners in the progressive era. The craftsman movement, wrote designer, publisher, and businessman Gustav Stickley in 1913, "stands not only for simple, well made furniture" but "strives for a form of art which shall express the spirit of the American people." Indeed, the clean and unadorned lines of Stickley's mission-style oak chairs and tables (fig. 4) were framed by

Fig. 4
Gustav Stickley, *Armchair and Sidechair*, 1905–1909, mahogany and (replaced) upholstery, Max Palevsky and Jodie Evans Collection, Los Angeles County Museum of Art

moted the revival of medieval designs and the guild system as alternatives to the woes of Victorian-era industrialization and materialism, and also as stabilizing indicators of a purely native British national identity, Stickley similarly linked America's pre-industrial arts and crafts with the nation's "spirit." Articles on Navajo blankets from New Mexico, Pequot rugs from Connecticut, patchwork quilts made in the Appalachian Mountains, and woven baskets from California often appeared in *The Craftsman.* Stickley's archetypal arts and crafts room, remarks one historian, "combined motifs from the medieval, folk, and colonial American traditions to evoke simplicity and stand as a counterpoint to the over civilized stuffed urban dwelling."[26]

With the advent of World War I, Stickley's version of the American arts and crafts movement largely evaporated: the war defined the modern era of the twentieth century as a machine-oriented industrial age dominated by steel, concrete, and plastic rather than hand-worked wood. Still, widespread discomfort with this emergent modern age led many on a search for reassurance and stability in America's "usable past." The appropriation of indigenous craft traditions and folk arts, and their utility as signs of cultural nationalism, became increasingly widespread in the interwar years; as art historian Wanda Corn remarks, "The 1920s raised the curtain on the study of the country's material culture."[27] American art museums proliferated during the decade: by 1930, the nation boasted 167 art museums, 56 percent more than in 1920. Swept up in the rising tide of cultural nationalism, many of these were oriented toward American art; in 1919 the Butler Institute was incorporated in Youngstown, Ohio, the first American art museum dedicated specifically to American art. Other museums began to celebrate American decorative arts. In 1924 the American Wing of the Metropolitan Museum of Art opened, showcasing the museum's vast collection of eighteenth- and nineteenth-century American furnishings in sixteen period rooms. Following this lead, museums in Philadelphia, Boston, Baltimore, and Saint Louis soon opened their own American period rooms.[28]

a particular moral agenda that he and other early twentieth-century arts and crafts revivalists shared: to develop aesthetic and cultural strategies that would restore the economic individualism, political democracy, and national identity they felt had been lost to modern-era industrialization.[24]

Stickley, challenging mass production and its undesirable by-products of worker alienation and poorly made goods, viewed the rehabilitation of American handicrafts as a key factor in a restored national morality. Mission-style furniture designs (and house plans) were regularly featured in his journal *The Craftsman* (published monthly from 1901 to 1916), and readers were encouraged to become artisans, to be both the producers and consumers of simple and useful handmade domestic objects. "Better art, better work, and a better and more reasonable way of living," Stickley declared in 1906, although his fumed white oak furniture was more typically made in small factories, which made full use of both modern machines and the principles of efficiency and organization developed by scientific management expert Frederick Winslow Taylor; it was also most often purchased by middle-class consumers from trade catalogues.[25]

Indebted to English arts and crafts reformers such as John Ruskin and William Morris, who pro-

Wealthy industrialist Henry Francis du Pont began collecting mid-seventeenth- to mid-nineteenth-century American decorative arts in the 1920s, eventually amassing the collection of 85,000 objects now displayed in 175 period rooms at Winterthur, the Du Pont family estate near Wilmington,

Delaware. Henry Ford further institutionalized America's past material culture at Greenfield Village, a 252-acre site near Dearborn, Michigan, whose buildings, grounds, and collections replicated a "typical" mid-nineteenth-century Midwestern rural community. Similarly, John D. Rockefeller Jr. began funding the restoration of the colonial capital of Williamsburg, Virginia, in the late 1920s, to recreate a living community from the eighteenth century by featuring craftsmen (blacksmiths, weavers, coopers) at their trades and hostesses dressed in period costumes. In 1926 Rockefeller founded Santa Fe's Laboratory of Anthropology, whose collections were intended to revitalize Navajo silver crafts "through assembling a representative collection" and supporting their continued production.[29] Certainly, much of this elite patronage was pursued "to invent a tradition that would explain and justify the fact of the family's wealth." Art historian Terry Smith argues that Ford "conjured a precapitalist paradise" at Greenfield Village to elide the realities of the mass-production industry located just a few miles away at his River Rouge Plant, the largest factory in interwar America.[30]

Yet for Rourke, Benton, and African American writer and folklorist Zora Neale Hurston, America's vernacular traditions were to be preserved and appropriated as the stuff of a vital new modern American art. Hurston "collected" the folk tales, slave songs, spirituals, dances, jokes, games, conjure legends, and hoodoo spells of her small hometown (Eatonville, Florida, an all-black community near Orlando) and rewrote them in essays for interwar New Negro journals such as *Opportunity* (the organ of the National Urban League) and the *Journal of American Folklore*, and her books *Mules and Men* (1935) and *Their Eyes Were Watching God* (1937). In 1938 she became an editor with the Federal Writers' Project in Florida, where she concentrated on collecting materials for a projected volume titled *The Florida Negro*.[31] For Hurston, Florida's local folk traditions were creative signs of America's cultural uniqueness.

Others collected American arts and crafts to help explicate and encourage the formation of an American culture in the present. Modern American artists including Bernard Karfiol, Robert Laurent, Charles Sheeler, and Elie Nadelman began collecting folk art in the late 1910s (Karfiol and Laurent summered together at the Ogunquit School of Painting and Sculpture in Maine).[32] Sheeler outfitted

Fig. 6
Charles Sheeler,
American Interior,
1934, oil on canvas,
Yale University Art
Gallery, New Haven

his homes in Bucks County, Pennsylvania, and South Salem, New York, with Shaker chairs, rag rugs, and other nineteenth-century "plain style" American arts and crafts; in the 1930s some of Sheeler's pieces of Shaker furniture would be catalogued and represented in the Index of American Design. From 1926 to 1937 Nadelman's extensive collection of 15,000 objects (including children's toys, sleighs, polychromed wood figures, wrought iron works, fraktur drawings, and more) was open to the public at the Riverdale-on-Hudson estate that he and his wealthy wife shared. Fascination with folk art changed the direction of the Polish-born sculptor's work, from classically figured marbles to the polychromed cherry-wood figures he began making in 1917 (fig. 5). Like other American moderns, Nadelman primarily viewed American folk art on aesthetic terms: the abstract design sensibilities of nineteenth-century braided rugs and iron weather vanes mirrored his own interest in reductive, highly patterned, and precise works of modern sculpture and painting (fig. 6).[33]

Art dealer Edith Halpert, founder and director of New York's Downtown Gallery, and Holger Cahill, then employed at the Newark Museum, "got the folk art fever" at Ogunquit in the mid-1920s. In 1931 Halpert and Cahill opened the American Folk Art

Gallery on the second floor of her Greenwich Village gallery, where, as she explained, objects were selected "not because of antiquity, historical association, utilitarian value, or the fame of their makers, but because of their aesthetic quality and because of their definite relation to vital elements in contemporary American art."[34] Like the modern painters she represented in the Downtown Gallery (including Sheeler, Stuart Davis, and Georgia O'Keeffe), Halpert championed American folk art as a vital source for contemporary American art and artists. Cahill was more expansive, viewing the art of America's historical past as a prime indicator of contemporary cultural identity and nationalism. Prior to his FAP appointment in 1935, he mounted folk art exhibitions at the Newark Museum (1930, 1931) and the Museum of Modern Art (MoMA) (1932).

MoMA's show, titled *American Folk Art: The Art of the Common Man in America, 1750-1900*, consisted almost entirely of objects from Abby Rockefeller's collection, which Halpert and Cahill had helped her form (and which Rockefeller donated to Colonial Williamsburg in 1939, where it is now housed at the Abby Aldrich Rockefeller Folk Art Center). Featuring trade signs, lawn ornaments, plaster candleholders, fraktur birth certificates, and oil paintings by anonymous and known American folk artists (such as Edward Hicks), MoMA's exhibition elevated these arts to museum status and implied that modern cultural institutions were now, in the early years of the Great Depression, keenly interested in the artifacts and essence of the common American.

Cahill's early folk art exhibitions and essays advanced ideas about American art and national identity, including notions of regulation and consensus that he brought to the FAP and the Index of American Design in the mid-1930s. As he stated in the 1932 MoMA catalogue, the social commonality of American art (or what he included as American art) was its most important characteristic: "The pictures and sculptures [in this exhibition] are the work of craftsmen and amateurs of the eighteenth and nineteenth centuries who supplied a popular demand for art.... It is a varied art, influenced from diverse sources, often frankly derivative, often fresh and original, and at its best an honest and straightforward expression of the spirit of a people.... [It] mirrors the sense and the sentiment of a community, and is an authentic expression of American experience." Compare Cahill's comments on folk art with those he provided about New Deal murals in 1936: "Mural art is not a studio art; by its very nature it is social. In its great periods it has always been associated with the expression of social meanings, the experience, history, ideas and beliefs of a community."[35]

The idea that American art, whether nineteenth-century weather vanes or New Deal post office murals, broadly embodied American "experience" and national "spirit" especially resounded during the interwar era. Coady's assertions regarding American art, Brooks' paeans to a "usable past," and Rourke's discussion of the "distinctive character" of American culture grounded this national identity specifically in materialism. "No ideas but in things," William Carlos Williams would state in his book-length poem "Paterson" (1927); no focus except that on the tangible, surface realities of artifacts and objects, including all the stuff of America's many material cultures.[36] Precisionism did exactly this, and the hard-edged, static, and precisely painted pictures of Sheeler and Gerald Murphy addressed both America's longstanding culture of materialism and the interwar era's particular flood of consumer goods (figs. 6, 7).

In *Charles Sheeler: Artist in the American Tradition* (1938), Rourke praised the precisionist artists' "fresh and original use of the American subject" and their attentiveness to the *Urformen* or vernacular "forms that were basic in American creative experience." Minimizing the ambivalent, and often anxious, manner in which Sheeler and other precisionists painted American subjects of contemporary industry and commercialism, Rourke set out to explain Sheeler's art in terms of America's "fundamental traditions and resources." His "purity of outline" and "sense of order, function, and design," she argued, typified a longstanding American aesthetic based on the plain and practical expression of the nation's things, peoples, and places. Following the intellectual trajectories of her mentor, Van Wyck Brooks, and her friend, anthropologist Ruth Benedict, Rourke's critical project throughout the New Deal years was to determine the specific patterns and *Urformen* that constituted this aesthetic, as her work at the Index of American Design and numerous essays reveal.[37]

Cahill was similarly impressed with Sheeler's spare formalism and focus on American subjects, which the artist honed in both his precisionist paintings and in his photography. From about 1912 to 1933 Sheeler worked as a freelance photographer for advertising agencies, among them N. W. Ayer, photographing spark plugs, cars, soft drinks, sinks, and the River Rouge Plant for clients such as Lincoln, Canada Dry, Koehler plumbing, and the Ford Motor Company; from 1923 to 1929 he also did studio portraiture for Condé Nast (publisher of *Vogue* and *Vanity Fair*). Abby Aldrich Rockefeller was so enamored with Sheeler's work that she commissioned him to depict Colonial Wiliamsburg's domestic interiors and folk art. In 1935, when Cahill began staffing the Index of American Design, he wrote: "We would have to get people who know the field thoroughly, who love it, and who are experts.... I would like to put to work at once on this idea such photographers as Ed Steichen, Charles Sheeler, Walker Evans and all those who are deeply interested and have done a lot of work in this field."[38]

Cahill's initial sense that the objects of American design would be documented via photography is telling. Photography played a key role in 1930s cultural engineering, largely because of contemporaneous assumptions of its seemingly straightforward, informational nature and because so many New Deal projects relied on a documentary aesthetic to visibly prove the need and official sponsorship of the federal government. The Index was certainly imagined on documentary terms: its folk and decorative arts were understood as being discovered (or rediscovered), rather than newly created, perceptions that "effectively naturalized their very

selected and interested representations."[39] The majority of Index images were rendered in watercolor, and most followed a "meticulous photographic-cum-archeological type of illumination."[40]

Employing an aesthetic akin to documentary photography (many Index plates are extraordinarily photographic), the Index's focus on information gathering and recording, as well as data classification, further meshed with the New Deal's larger bureaucratization of modern American culture and society. From following representational strategies prescribed in an agency manual to adhering to the directives of supervisors and editors centralized in the FAP's main offices in Washington, DC, the Index of American Design was very much part of the "modern cultural apparatus" by which the New Deal constructed national identity.[41]

When the United States became embroiled in World War II, the Index's impulses toward documenting and classifying America's usable past were enlisted in the service of wartime propaganda. As Holger Cahill stated in the catalogue essay for *Emblems of Unity and Freedom* (1942), a small exhibition of Index plates and American folk art incorporating national symbols such as the eagle, the liberty cap, and Uncle Sam: "It is a responsibility of the artists who are placing their skills at the service of the national war effort to familiarize themselves with this traditional material, to study its sources in the life of the people, and to know the popular symbols which have been created to express and transmit the historic meanings of democracy."[42] By the early 1940s America's applied arts and designs were no longer simply evidence of a unique, historically grounded national aesthetic, but material documents that defended cultural democracy. The "distinctive character" of the country's folk cultures was muted in favor of its thorough assimilation as a symbol of cultural nationalism.

Notes

1   Rourke in O'Connor 1975, 165-166; on Rourke's life and writings see Rubin 1980. Brooks collected and edited fragments of Rourke's multivolume study; see *The Roots of American Culture*, Van Wyck Brooks, ed. (New York, 1942), which was published posthumously.

2   Paul Rosenfeld, *Port of New York: Essays on Fourteen American Moderns* (New York, 1924), 281-295.

3   Wanda Corn discusses "cultural boosterism" in Corn 1999, 4. Robert Coady published his thoughts on American art in the first two issues of *The Soil*; see Robert Coady, "American Art," *The Soil* 1 (December 1916), 3, and "American Art," *The Soil* 1 (January 1917), 1. For further discussion of these articles, see Dickran Tashjian, *Skyscraper Primitives: Dada and the American Avant-Garde, 1910-1925* (Middletown, Ohio, 1975), 72-79.

4   See Brooks 1918, 337-341; William Carlos Williams, *In the American Grain* (New York, 1925), 109; Stuart Davis, *Journal*, 68, as noted in Matthew Baigell, "American Art and National Identity: The 1920s," *Arts Magazine* 61, no. 6 (February 1987), 48-55. It should be noted that not all interwar critics, intellectuals, and artists shared in this "boosterism." Writer H. L. Mencken, for example, complained that "the demand for a restoration of what is called the American tradition in letters is nothing more or less, at bottom, than a demand for supine and nonsensical conformity"; see Richard Ruland, *The Rediscovery of American Literature* (Cambridge, Mass., 1967), 155. Other Americans sought refuge in Europe, including writers Ernest Hemingway, John Dos Passos, and F. Scott Fitzgerald; painters Gerald Murphy and Louis Lozowick; and African American artists including dancer Josephine Baker, writer Langston Hughes, and painters Hale Woodruff and Palmer Hayden.

5   Warren Susman, *Culture as History: The Transformation of American Society in the Twentieth-Century* (New York, 1984), 154. The phrase "the American Dream" was popularized in historian James Truslow Adams' best-selling book *The Epic of America* (Boston, 1931). On Fraser, see Robert L. McGrath, "The Endless Trail of the *End of the Trail*," *Journal of the West* 40, no. 4 (Fall 2001), 8-15.

6   Benedict Anderson, *Imagined Communities: Reflections on the Origin and Spread of Nationalism* (New York, 1983), 15; Ernest Gellner, *Thought and Change* (London, 1964), quoted in Anderson 1983, 6; see also Gellner, *Nations and Nationalism* (Ithaca, N.Y., 1983).

7   For more information see, for example, Bustard 1997; O'Connor 1975; McKinzie 1973; Christine Bold, *The WPA Guides: Mapping America* (Jackson, Miss., 1999); Kenneth J. Bindas, *All of This Music Belongs to the Nation: The WPA's Federal Music Project and American Society* (Knoxville, 1995); Christopher Denoon, *Posters of the WPA* (Los Angeles, 1987); Marlene Park and Gerald E. Markowitz, *Democratic Vistas: Post Offices and Public Art in the New Deal* (Philadelphia, 1984); Karal Ann Marling, *Wall-to-Wall America: A Cultural History of Post Office Murals in the Great Depression* (Minneapolis, 1982); and Barbara Melosh, *Engendering Culture: Manhood and Womanhood in New Deal Public Art and Theater* (Washington, 1991).

8   The National Gallery of Art acquired the Index plates in 1943. Postwar books incorporating and discussing the plates also include Erwin O. Christensen, *Early American Wood Carving* (Cleveland and New York, 1952).

9   Samuel I. Bellman, *Constance M. Rourke* (Boston, 1981), 20, 28. Recalling a road trip that she and Rourke took in 1938, Margaret Marshall indicates that Rourke, "as usual, was gathering material and noting it on the little blue slips she always carried"; see Bellman 1981, 29. Rourke 1937, 207-211, and quoted by Cahill in Christensen 1950, xvii.

10   Thomas Hart Benton, *An Artist in America*, 4th rev. ed. (Columbia, Mo., 1983), 26, 28, 381; on Benton's aspirations to a uniquely American form of modern art see Doss 1991, 9-145.

11   Exh. cat. New York 1934. See also Janet Kardon, ed., *Craft in the Machine Age, 1920-1945* (New York, 1995).

12   Rothschild in O'Connor 1972, 179.

13   For specific information on the Index, see, for example, Rothschild in O'Connor 1972, 176-196; McKinzie 1973, 135-141; O'Connor 1975, 164-175; McDonald 1969, 441-458; and *Perkins Harnly, from the Index of American Design* (Washington, 1981), which features essays by Virginia Mecklenburg and Lynda Roscoe Hartigan.

14   Arthur Rothstein, *Documentary Photography* (Boston, 1986), 36.

15   See Bold 1999 for an extensive analysis of the *American Guide Series*.

16   Roosevelt quoted in Bold 1999, 189.

17   Bindas 1995, 37, 96-104, 114.

18   On depression-era movies and new understandings of populism and the folk, see especially Lary May, *The Big Tomorrow: Hollywood and the Politics of the American Way* (Chicago, 2000), 13, 64, 102, and so forth.

19   On Guthrie, see, for example, Michael Denning, *The Cultural Front: The Laboring of American Culture in the Twentieth Century* (New York, 1996), 37, 91, 269-270, and Charles J. Shindo, *Dust Bowl Migrants in the American Imagination* (Lawrence, Kans., 1997), 178-179; see also the American Folklife Center's Woody Guthrie Manuscript Collection at the Library of Congress American Memory Web site, *http://memory.loc.gov/ammem/wwghtml*. Guthrie was also commissioned by the United States Department of the Interior in May 1941 to write songs promoting the building of the Bonneville Dam on the Columbia River in Washington state.

20   On the "documentary imagination" of the depression era see Stott 1973.

21   Cahill in Christensen 1950, xii.

22   Harris 1995, 7.

23   Exh. cat. London 1995, 19.

24   Gustav Stickley, "The Craftsman Movement: Its Origins and Growth," *Craftsman* 25 (October 1913), 17, reprinted in Barry Sanders, ed., *The Craftsman: An Anthology* (Santa Barbara, Calif., 1978), 291-292. See also the discussion of Stickley and other American crafts revivalists in T. J. Jackson Lears, *No Place of Grace: Antimodernism and the Transformation of American Culture, 1880-1920* (New York, 1981), 66-96.

25   Gustav Stickley, "Als Ik Kan," *Craftsman* 11 (October 1906), 128-130.

26   Eileen Boris, "'Dreams of Brotherhood and Beauty': The Social Ideals of the Arts and Crafts Movement," in exh. cat. Boston 1987a, 217; for examples of Stickley trade catalogues from 1910, see *Stickley Craftsman Furniture Catalogs* (New York, 1979).

27   Corn 1999, 298.

28   Dianne Pilgrim, "Inherited from the Past: The American Period Room," *American Art Journal* 10 (May 1978), 4-23.

29   Jay E. Cantor, *Winterthur* (New York, 1997). On Greenfield Village see Terry Smith, *Making the Modern: Industry, Art, and Design in America* (Chicago, 1993), 141-155; on Colonial Williamsburg see Warren Susman, "Introduction," in Warren Susman, ed., *Culture and Commitment, 1929-1945* (New York, 1973), 6, and Richard Handler and Eric Gable, *The New History in an Old Museum: Creating the Past at Colonial Williamsburg* (Durham, N.C., 1997), 31-37. On John D. Rockefeller's interests in Santa Fe see William Anthes, *The Laboratory of Anthropology: Navajo Silver and Rockefeller Revivalism* (Master's thesis, University of Colorado, Boulder, 1994).

30 Peter Dobkin Hall, "The Empty Tomb: The Making of Dynastic Identity," in George Marcus, ed., *Lives in Trust: The Fortunes of Dynastic Families in Late Twentieth-Century America* (Boulder, Colo., 1992), 264; Smith 1993, 153.

31 Robert E. Hemenday, *Zora Neale Hurston: A Literary Biography* (Urbana, Ill., 1977), 73, 251–253. Hurston was also employed with the Federal Theater Project from 1935–1936, helping to organize the FTP's special Harlem unit in New York and staging Elmer Rice's production of *Walk Together Chillum*. For further discussion of the similar interests of Rourke, Benton, Hurston, and others see Kammen 1991, 299–527.

32 The school was founded in 1913 by painter and writer Hamilton Easter Field, who moved to Ogunquit in 1910 and was one of the first American artists to collect folk art; see Doreen Bolger, "Hamilton Easter Field and His Contribution to American Modernism," *American Art Journal* 20 (Summer 1988), 78–107. See Rumford in Quimby and Swank 1980, 13–33.

33 Exh. cat. Boston 1987b, 22; Roberta K. Tarbell, "Primitivism, Folk Art, and the Exotic," in Ilene Susan Fort, ed., *The Figure in American Sculpture: A Question of Modernity* [exh. cat., Los Angeles County Museum of Art] (Los Angeles, 1995), 121; Tom Armstrong, "The Innocent Eye: American Folk Sculpture," in *200 Years of American Sculpture* [exh. cat., Whitney Museum of American Art] (New York, 1976), 94, 111; see also Lincoln Kirstein, *Elie Nadelman* (New York, 1973). As Armstrong remarks, the Nadelmans dispersed their collection for financial reasons in 1937, the majority of it going to the New-York Historical Society and the Abby Aldrich Rockefeller Folk Art Collection in Williamsburg. For an extensive discussion of Sheeler's interests in American folk art, see Corn 1999, 293–337.

34 Cahill 1954; Edith Halpert, "Folk Art of America Now Has a Gallery of Its Own," *Art Digest* 6 (1 October 1931), 3.

35 Exh. cat. New York 1932, 3, 28; exh. cat. New York 1936, 32.

36 William Carlos Williams, "Paterson," *The Dial* 82, no. 2 (February 1927), 91–93; see also Dickran Tashjian, *William Carlos Williams and the American Scene, 1920–1940* [exh. cat., Whitney Museum of American Art] (New York, 1978), 59.

37 Rourke 1938, 5, 69, 97, 187. See also Rubin 1990, 191–222. Corn notes that Rourke "quoted at length" from a handwritten autobiography that Sheeler had begun in writing her own book; see Corn 1999, 335. Rourke's numerous 1930s essays and book reviews on American art and culture include Rourke 1935, 390–404; "Traditions for Young People," *The Nation* (20 November 1937), 562–564; and "Have We an American Art?" *The Nation* (11 November 1939), 527–529.

38 On Sheeler's commercial photography see Martin Friedman, *Charles Sheeler* (New York, 1975), 65. Holger Cahill comments noted in Harris 1995, 87.

39 Bold 1999, xv.

40 On the watercolor techniques employed at the Index, see Cahill in Christensen 1950, xii, and McDonald 1969, 449–451.

41 Denning 1996, 48.

42 Cahill quoted in Merle Colby, "Emblems of America," *Magazine of Art* 35 (October 1942), 207.

Catalogue

DC   Deborah Chotner

VTC   Virginia Tuttle Clayton

LR   Louisa Ransom

Yolande Delasser / active c. 1935

1   **Garden of Eden**

1939 / watercolor over graphite / 45.5 x 50.4 cm ($17^{15}/_{16}$ x $19^{7}/_{8}$ in.)

Marian Page / active c. 1935

2 Rooster

1940 / watercolor with white heightening over graphite / 42.2 x 34.6 cm (16⅝ x 13⅝ in.)

Selma Sandler / active c. 1935

3 Poodle

1940 / watercolor over graphite / 32.3 x 49.2 cm ($12^{11}/_{16}$ x $19^{3}/_{8}$ in.)

Attributed to Wilhelm Schimmel
(American, 1817–1890), *Poodle*,
1860–1890, painted wood,
32.4 x 49.5 cm ($12^{3}/_{4}$ x $19^{1}/_{2}$ in.),
Richard Kanter

Carvings

Giacinto Capelli / active c. 1935

4 Squirrel and Eagle

c. 1939 / watercolor over graphite / 40.6 x 35.4 cm (16 x 13¹⁵/₁₆ in.)

Attributed to Wilhelm Schimmel (American, 1817–1890), *Squirrel and Eagle*, 1860–1890, painted wood, 26.7 x 22.9 cm (10½ x 9 in.), Museum of Fine Arts, Boston, Gift of Maxim Karolik

All the objects depicted in these renderings appear to be by the hand of Wilhelm Schimmel (1817–1890), an eccentric, expressive immigrant carver who lived in Pennsylvania's Cumberland Valley during the late nineteenth century. Traveling the roads around Carlisle, he traded his wood figures for food and drink or sold them for a small sum. He was well known among the Pennsylvania Germans, finding shelter at the farms of several families. During his lifetime Schimmel may have made nearly five hundred figures.[1] These were carved with a penknife out of blocks of pine scavenged at the local sawmill or at barn raisings. Born in Darmstadt, Germany, he was undoubtedly familiar with the Black Forest tradition of precise, realistic carving, but his own sculptures were rough-hewn and vibrant. Some, like the *Poodle* and Schimmel's famous eagles, show a distinctive sawtooth incising technique meant to suggest fur or feathers. Others, such as the *Rooster*, had smoother surfaces.[2] In his more elaborate works Schimmel first covered the carving's surface with gesso and then applied paint in the brightest colors that were easily available, usually black or brown with red or yellow ocher accents. Birds and other animals were his most common subjects, but on at least three occasions he also depicted Adam and Eve in a fenced-in Garden of Eden. Schimmel reportedly took great offense when one of these biblical scenes failed to win a prize at the Cumberland County Fair sometime in the 1880s.[3] The works that once casually decorated the shelves of farmhouses and taverns are today prized by folk-art collectors.

DC

1   Milton E. Flower, *Wilhelm Schimmel and Aaron Mountz: Wood Carvers* [exh. cat., Abby Aldrich Rockefeller Folk Art Center] (Williamsburg, Va., 1965), 6.

2   The *Poodle* was in the American Folk Art Gallery in New York and the *Rooster* in a private collection in Cohasset. The *Rooster* has not been located. The *Garden of Eden* was, and still is, in the Philadelphia Museum of Art (Gift of Titus C. Geesey), and the *Squirrel and Eagle* was sold by McKearin's Antiques in Hoosick Falls, New York.

3   Flower 1965, 11.

Elizabeth Moutal / active c. 1935

5 Liberty

1938 / watercolor, gouache, and colored pencil over graphite / 52 x 34.5 cm (20½ x 13⁹/₁₆ in.)

While the majority of the works in the Index document the Anglo-American traditions of the northeastern United States, the collection as a whole demonstrates a surprising recognition of the varied sources of American design. This is exemplified in renderings of the carved and painted *bultos* (devotional sculptures) of Hispanic origin, in the German-influenced furniture of Pennsylvania and Texas, or in idiosyncratic objects such as *Liberty*, which might be derived from the skills and vision that immigrant craftsmen brought to this country.

The maker of this oddly affecting allegorical figure was Eliodoro Patete (1874–1953) of Vastogirari, Italy. Records show that he traveled between the United States and his native country at least twice, but probably three times.[1] The base of *Liberty* is inscribed with the location Anawalt, West Virginia, one of the two American towns (the other being Pocahontas, Virginia) in which Patete lived. The statue's initial purpose is not certain. A letter from President Taft's secretary, dated 17 September 1909, thanks the sculptor for the gift of a woodcarving that is most likely the one represented in Moutal's rendering. All other known carvings by Patete are of religious subjects.[2]

The seated figure of *Liberty* is in essence a secular, patriotic Madonna, with all the color and exuberance of the other saints by the carver. As with other figures by Patete, the proportions in this example are shortened below the waist, and the head is slightly too large and too round. Yet the sculpture has strong emotional appeal. This *Liberty*, although undoubtedly inspired by Frederic Bartholdi's famous statue of *Liberty*, 1886, presides with approachability rather than with grandeur. Her hands are raised in a demonstrative gesture and her lips are barely parted, as if she is about to speak. The symbolism or allegorical meaning of the dog with a book in its mouth at her side is, as yet, unexplained. Is it faithfully guarding the country's freedom and laws?

Patete's *Liberty* made its way from the White House to a Baltimore antiques dealer in the 1930s. When depicted by Moutal, the piece was in the possession of Juliana Force, then director of the Whitney Museum of American Art, New York. By the time

Eliodoro Patete (Italian, 1874–1953), *Liberty*, c. 1909, painted wood and glass, 91.4 cm (36 in.), Shelburne Museum, Shelburne, Vermont

Jean Lipman reproduced it in her 1948 book, it had become one of the best-recognized images in the Index of American Design.[3] In 1953 Edith Halpert arranged the sale of the work from a New York dealer to Electra Webb for her burgeoning museum in Shelburne, Vermont.

DC

1 The research into Patete's life and work was generously shared by William F. Brooks Jr., executive director, Frog Hollow, Vermont State Craft Center, in Middlebury, Vermont, and is the source of nearly all the information listed here; correspondence with Virginia Clayton, 30 March 2002.

2 William Brooks has identified eleven other works; correspondence with Virginia Clayton, 30 March 2002.

3 Jean Lipman, *American Folk Art in Wood, Metal and Stone* (Meriden, Conn., 1948), fig. 153.

Edward DiGennaro / active c. 1935

6 Gate

1940 / watercolor and gouache over graphite / 55.8 x 71 cm (21^{15}/$_{16}$ x 27^{15}/$_{16}$ in.)

Hobart Welton, the creator of this unusual gate, was a man of many talents. Born 1811, the son of a minister, he was raised in Waterbury, Connecticut. He later ran a large farm there, and he also mastered land surveying, acted as the superintendent of public highways for twenty-five years, served as a representative in the state legislature, and was a founder and director of the Waterbury Brass Company.

A history of Waterbury published in 1896, the year after Welton's death, extolls his upright character and business accomplishments, then goes on to say, "Mr. Welton had much skill in mechanical work and the tastes of an artist. As a boy he executed some remarkable wood work with a penknife; chains and temples with balls inside, in the manner of Chinese carving. He was fond of carving both in wood and in stone, and the gateway to his house and the stone work of his farm buildings, with their quaint and ingenious emblems deftly carved in wood and stone, have for many years attracted the attention of passers-by."[1]

This exuberant gate, composed of a yoke, sickle, plow, and other carefully arranged elements, and crowned with a bountiful carved cornucopia, easily captured the Index artist's attention.

DC

1 Joseph Anderson, Sarah Johnson Pritchard, and Anna Lydia Ward, *The Town and City of Waterbury, Connecticut from the Aboriginal Period to the Year Eighteen Hundred and Ninety-five* (New Haven, 1896), 2: 459–460.

Hobart Victory Welton (American, 1811–1895), *Gate*, 1850, painted wood and iron, 99.7 x 108 cm (39 ¼ x 42 ½ in.), Mattatuck Museum, Waterbury, Connecticut

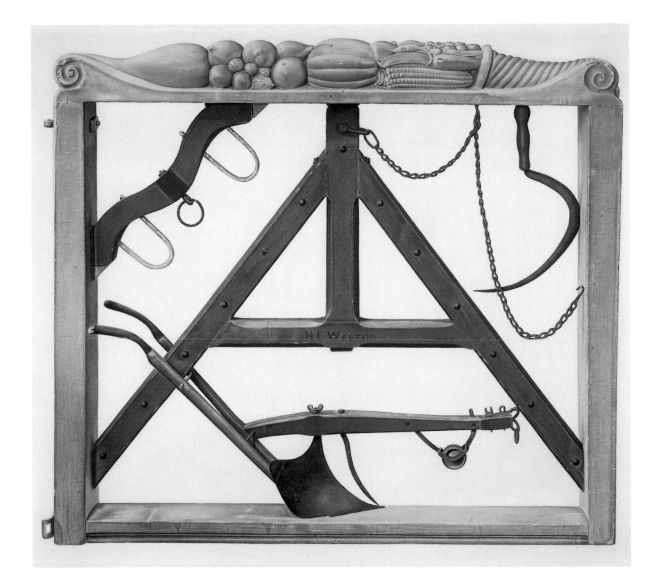

Loungini — aug 29, 1938

Elodora P. Lorenzini / 1910–1993

7 *Bulto* of Saint Isidore

1938 / watercolor with pen and ink over graphite / 55.9 x 40.2 cm (22 x 15 13/16 in.)

Isidore, the patron saint of farmers and protector of crops, was a farm laborer employed by a wealthy landowner near Madrid in the early twelfth century. According to legend, Isidore spent so many hours in prayer that he was in danger of falling behind with his farming chores. As a reward for his exceptional piety, divine intervention dispatched an angel to help Isidore finish his plowing on schedule.[1] This miraculous event is the subject of an eighteenth-century New Mexican devotional sculpture, or *bulto*, rendered for the Index by Elodora P. Lorenzini. It portrays Isidore holding an ox goad in his left hand and raising his right hand in prayer while an angel grips the plough and drives the oxen for him. The diminutive angel was originally equipped with wings, but these delicate appendages have broken off and are now lost. In *bultos,* the most important figure in a composition was also typically represented as the largest, sacred hierarchy triumphing over naturalism. This is why Isidore towers above the angel, who in turn outranks the oxen, surpassing them in scale. The sculpture is twenty-four inches high. It was in the Taylor Museum, now part of the Colorado Springs Fine Arts Center, when Lorenzini rendered it in 1938, and is still preserved as part of that collection. Isidore was canonized in 1622 and the faithful have celebrated his feast day, 15 May, by carrying his image in procession through their fields as they pray for an abundant harvest.

Pious folk artists known as *santeros* carved *bultos* from cottonwood, coated them with gesso, and then painted them with water-soluble pigments. The *santeros* created not only three-dimensional *bultos* but also *retablos*, sacred images painted on flat panels. Jointly referred to as santos, these were placed in both homes and churches to help enlist a saint's intercession on behalf of a prayerful supplicant. This sculpture of Saint Isidore is attributed to a Franciscan friar, Fray Andres Garcia.[2] The Franciscans established missions in New Mexico, the northern frontier of Spanish America, which was first settled at the end of the sixteenth century. This inhospitable territory permitted its Pueblo Indian inhabitants to practice only marginal agriculture. The poverty of the region long isolated New Mexico, and this isolation allowed a distinctive, highly spiritualized art of simple forms to flourish there, barely affected by the art of the outside world.[3] In many ways typified by the Saint Isidore *bulto*, early New Mexican sacred art is more closely akin to ecclesiastical art of the Middle Ages than to that of the eighteenth century in Europe.

Around 1776 Father Francisco Atanasio Dominguez, an ecclesiastical delegate from Mexico, traveled to New Mexico to inventory its churches and their possessions. Among the works of art mentioned in his account were several created by Fray Andres Garcia. The sophisticated Dominguez despised the provincial art of New Mexico. Describing a statue of the Virgin, he wrote: "Father Garcia made the image, and perhaps for the shame of her being so badly made they left the varnish on her face very red."[4] The *bulto* of Saint Isidore was not among the objects tallied by Father Dominguez, but by comparing it stylistically to other *bultos* identified as Garcia's in the inventory, art historians have determined that this sculpture was probably Garcia's work. Since the face of Saint Isidore has been repainted at least once or twice, however, a conclusive attribution is not possible.

VTC

1 On Saint Isidore see E. Boyd, *Saints and Saint Makers of New Mexico* (Santa Fe, 1946), 125–126, and Wroth 1982, 208.

2 Wroth 1982, 65–68, and Sasser 1989, 86: "in the first settlements the duty of carving religious images was given to the missionaries themselves and even to the Indians who, under careful supervision, became *santeros* or carvers of the saints."

3 Wroth 1982, 35–41; Mather 1978, 422–429.

4 Wroth 1982, 65.

Donald Donovan / active c. 1935

8 Carousel Goat

1938 / watercolor over graphite / 35 x 45.7 cm (13³/₄ x 18 in.)

Artists from the Rhode Island project of the Index recorded several of the creatures, including giraffes, a greyhound, panthers, and horses, that graced the Island Park Carousel in Portsmouth, Rhode Island. This carousel was one of about forty built by the Charles I.D. Looff Company. Having arrived in the United States as a skilled artisan (he was born in 1852 in Schleswig-Holstein, Germany), Looff carved his first carousel by 1875 for placement at Coney Island, New York. After this initial success he opened a factory in Brooklyn, followed by another in East Providence (Riverside), Rhode Island, and finally in Long Beach, California. In addition to works produced by his own hand, Looff employed a number of master carvers with their own distinct styles as his business grew.

Goats were not uncommon subjects for carousel figure carvers; the Dentzel company in Philadelphia also made several such examples. The Index artist who recorded this well-proportioned, dynamic animal captures not only details such as the eagle-head saddle cantle, but also the weathered paint finish of the well-used figure.

The Island Park Carousel came about in two stages. The earlier, smaller Looff carousel that was placed there in 1898 consisted of stationary figures, many of them menagerie animals such as the goat, a type Looff created as early as 1885. Some of these creatures were incorporated into a larger carousel, this one with jumping horses, which was installed in 1905/1906. The area of Island Park continued to thrive into the early years of the twentieth century. Many families built small cottages not far from the amusements, but in 1938 a hurricane destroyed most of the area and the park never reopened.[1] The carousel, however, survived and was sold successively to two other amusement parks. By the 1970s the figures showed damage from age and exposure to the elements, but they were purchased and restored by collectors and are now in several private collections.[2] The goat has not been found.

DC

1 For additional information on Island Park see John T. Pierce Sr., *Historical Tracts of the Town of Portsmouth, Rhode Island* (Portsmouth, R.I., 1991), 10–16.

2 This carousel's history was summarized by collector and restorer Marianne S. Stevens, who kindly provided a draft of an article on the Island Park Carousel she wrote for the American Carousel Society; correspondence with the author, June 2001.

Howard Weld / active c. 1935

9 Carousel Rooster

1935/1942 / watercolor and gouache over graphite / 60.8 x 50.2 cm (23^{15}/$_{16}$ x 19^{3}/$_{4}$ in.)

Roosters were a common subject for weather vanes, but they also appeared occasionally as carousel animals.[1] The sight of this robust, more than three-foot-tall fowl must have been impressive to the children awaiting their rides. Privately owned in Pound Ridge, New York, when it was rendered, it is the cherished possession of another private collector today.

Erwin O. Christensen's 1950 book on the Index of American Design reproduced Howard Weld's rendering of this carousel rooster, stating in the caption that it had been made in Saint Johnsbury, Vermont, in the nineteenth century. This information naturally aroused curiosity about the carving among the citizens of this town. In response, the Saint Johnsbury newspaper published an article on the rooster and its creator, Edmund Brown, in 1951.[2] For the article, the *Caledonia Record* reporter interviewed Brown's surviving daughter along with some of the older residents of Saint Johnsbury who still remembered Brown and the traveling carousel he brought to county fairs.

According to the article, the striding rooster, one of a pair, was carved by Brown around 1890. Brown, who also made furniture and other carved decorative items, was born in Nicolet, a town on the Saint Lawrence River in Quebec. As a young man, he moved to Vermont and settled for a number of years in Saint Johnsbury, where he married a local woman. The article in the *Caledonia Record* included a photograph of one of the Browns' five daughters as a child, riding the carousel rooster.[3] The Browns eventually moved to West Hartford, Connecticut, where Edmund Brown died around 1935.

DC and VTC

Edmund Brown (American, 1870–c. 1935), *Carousel Rooster*, c. 1890, painted wood, 95.3 x 111.8 cm (37^{1}/$_{2}$ x 44 in.), Private collection

1 A 1902 example by the Herschell-Spellman company is illustrated in Charlotte Dinger, *Art of the Carousel* (Green Village, N.J., 1983), 88.

2 Partial photocopy in Index file: "Trace Ancestry of Wooden Rooster," *Caledonia Record* (Saint Johnsbury, Vt., 6 August 1951), 1, 4.

3 "Trace Ancestry of Wooden Rooster," 4.

Carvings

Hester Duany / 1891–1964

10 Greater Yellowlegs Decoy

1942 / watercolor with white heightening over graphite / 35.7 x 40.9 cm (14 1/16 x 16 1/8 in.)

Although they were not as common a food source as wildfowl, shorebirds were once avidly hunted. Decoys are known of at least nineteen Atlantic coast species.[1] The birds were easily lured by the simplest of decoys, both flat and three-dimensional, which were secured on sticks driven into the ground.

This example appears to reproduce the greater yellowlegs, a wading bird about fourteen inches in length. Carved from a single block of pine, the decoy shows traces of a stylized feather design. Dark purple glass balls were set into the head for eyes, and a whittled bill, the tip of which has broken off, was mortised into the front of the head. The decoy was found in Hampton Bay, Long Island, and depicted by Duany while it was with the New York dealers Helena Penrose & J. H. Edgette. Its present location is not known.

A bit of old text, unfortunately without attribution on the Index data sheet, provides a colorful description of the type of game the decoy would have attracted: "Yellow-legs are extensively hunted, although their flesh does not rank so high as some others of the Sandpiper family, as for example Woodcock and Upland plovers. They are shot chiefly over wooden models cut out to represent the bird and stuck up in the mud near a shooting blind. To these decoys they often come with little hesitation, especially if to this deception the hunter adds an additional lure by imitating their call with a fair degree of accuracy."

By 1927 the hunting of shorebirds had so reduced their number that they were given protection by federal law. Shorebird decoys produced after this time were not functional but intended for exhibition.[2]

DC

1 Mackey 1965, 35.

2 Webster and Kehoe 1971, 108.

Heller Duany

Max Feinekes
1938

Max Fernekes / 1905–1984

11 # Bufflehead Decoy

1938 / watercolor over graphite / 29.3 x 39.8 cm (11 $^9/_{16}$ x 15 $^{11}/_{16}$ in.)

By the time Fernekes, an artist from the Wisconsin Index project, depicted this carved duck, decoys were beginning to take on a new role. In 1934 Joel Barber, the early collector of decoys, listed three exhibitions (1923, 1924, and 1931), "conducted by and in the interest of sportsmen," and said further that "the next move lay quite outside of sporting circles. In November of 1931 the Newark Museum sponsored an exhibition of so-called American Folk Sculpture and included among the exhibits a group of old decoys. Here, in company of cigar store Indians, figure heads of sailing ships, and other examples of early American craftsmanship, decoy ducks took over the title of 'Primitive Polychrome Sculpture.'"[1]

The heyday of decoy carving in this country was during the second half of the nineteenth century and into the first decades of the twentieth. This example is a factory decoy from the Mason Factory of Detroit, which was active from 1896 to 1924. Large workshops, in which decoys were produced from lathe-turned bodies made on duplicating equipment, sprang up in response to the demands of the commercial hunters. Market gunners supplied game to the tables of the burgeoning population, taking advantage of the increasingly efficient rail system and a seemingly inexhaustible supply of waterfowl. The industry came to a sudden end with the passage of the Migratory Bird Treaty Act in 1918 to prevent further extinction of overhunted species.

The Mason Factory was one of the most important suppliers of factory decoys, offering five different grades that varied in detail and degree of hand-finishing.[2] This example, produced about 1895, is rated a Challenge grade (next to best).[3] The originally fine paint surface had worn considerably over time, but the bird was still recognizable as a bufflehead drake, although slightly longer and less stocky than its living match. The current owner of this decoy has not been identified.

DC

1 Joel Barber, *Wild Fowl Decoys* (New York, 1934), 9, 10.

2 Russ J. Goldberger and Alan G. Haid, *Mason Decoys: A Complete Guide* (Burtonsville, Md., 1993), chap. 2.

3 Identification courtesy Russ Goldberger; correspondence with Virginia Clayton, 5 January 2001. See photograph of bufflehead pair in Goldberger and Haid 1993, 6; the caption notes "the strong Peterson [earlier Detroit decoy maker] influence in the protruding breasts and sleek lines."

Elizabeth Moutal / active c. 1935

Figurehead

1938 / watercolor with white heightening over graphite / 39.6 x 30.5 cm (15 5/8 x 12 in.)

The nostalgic appeal of certain early nautical carvings, like the figurehead of a woman in Elizabeth Moutal's rendering, led a historian of ships' carvings to observe that "perhaps more than any other maritime artifact, figureheads with feminine subjects evoke the romantic age of sailing. Even when removed from their original context, the mermaids, goddesses, and stately ladies who once guided vessels across the seas are poignant reminders of that bygone era."[1] Figureheads had, in fact, already established a secure niche in this country's sentimental imagination by the end of the nineteenth century, when the production and launching of such carvings had all but come to an end.[2]

The practice of adorning ships' prows with carved figures, possibly to serve as apotropaic charms, seems to have originated thousands of years ago. Long before women's effigies found their place at the forefront of American sailing vessels, animals and dragons had taken the lead on Viking boats and other ancient vessels. Until the middle of the eighteenth century, the lion was often favored for English and colonial American ships, but later in the century figureheads represented characters from ancient history and mythology, as well as biblical subjects and allegorical personifications of the ships' home ports. By the end of the eighteenth century, portraits of contemporary personages, including women, gained popularity, although these were generally limited to royalty and other celebrities.[3]

American ship carvers had closely followed British precedents during the seventeenth and most of the eighteenth centuries, but they began to develop an independent artistic identity even before the revolutionary war, under the leadership of a series of great carvers working in Boston, Philadelphia, and New York.[4] Figurehead carvers in the United States often worked directly with the ships' owners rather than builders. From the mid-nineteenth century some kept a selection of stock figures in their shops to furnish craft of lesser importance, designing and carving on commission only works for vessels of exceptional quality.[5] Pine was the preferred wood for figureheads, and sculptors usually cut them from a single block, with the grain running vertically, to ensure greater durability. The completed pieces were coated with a white lead ground in preparation for painting and gilding. The back or base of the figure might be left flat to fit flush against the ship's stem (the timber at the joint where the two sides meet in front), or it was sometimes carved with a mortise to fit over a tenon on the stem. Bolts or metal rods could fasten the figure to the stem under the bowsprit (the spar projecting forward from of the bow).[6] The figurehead was the centerpiece of a program of decorative carving on the ship that literally stretched from stem to stern.

Starting in the late eighteenth century, American carvers added a variety of indigenous subjects to the more traditional European programs. They frequently

depicted American eagles, Native Americans (both historical and fictional characters, such as Pocahontas and Minnehaha), and such national heroes as George Washington and Andrew Jackson. Figureheads on merchant ships sometimes portrayed members of the owners' or captains' families. The relatively small, hardworking whaling ships that sailed out of New Bedford and Nantucket—vessels mainly owned by luxury-averse Quakers—often carried bust portraits of wives and daughters on their prows rather than full-length figures.

It seems likely that the unidentified figurehead in Moutal's rendering was once stationed at the front of one of these early nineteenth-century whaling ships. In both the smoothly simplified contours of her face and the modeling of her facial features, the figure seems comparable to another figurehead that reportedly came from the whaling ship *Marcia*, which sailed from Fairhaven and New Bedford beginning in the late 1820s.[7] The two figures' costumes and hairstyles—typical of the 1820s—are similar, although the woman in the Index figurehead is more simply dressed.[8] The figures are approximately the same size and both are positioned atop the same type of scrolled base.[9] Although it cannot be located today, the bust portrayed by Moutal was in a private collection in Cohasset, Massachusetts, in 1938. Moutal rendered this piece from a photograph and color notes (see above, Clayton, fig. 11).

VTC

1 Tony Lewis, "Her Effigy in Wood: Figureheads with Feminine Subjects," *Antiques* 150 (December 1996), 835.

2 Jane L. Port, "Boston's Nineteenth-Century Ship Carvers," *Antiques* 158 (November 2000), 760.

3 Lewis 1996, 836–838.

4 On these and other American ship carvers, see M. V. Brewington and Pauline A. Pinckney, *American Figureheads and Their Carvers* (New York, 1940); Brewington 1962; Sylvia Leistyna Lahvis, "Icons of American Trade: The Skillin Workshop and the Language of Spectacle," *Winterthur Portfolio* 27 (Winter 1992), 216–233; Ralph Sessions, "Ship Carvers and the New York City Shop Figure Style," *Antiques* 151 (March 1997), 471–477; and Port 2000.

5 Brewington 1962, 77–78.

6 Georgia W. Hamilton, *Silent Pilots: Figureheads in Mystic Seaport Museum* (Mystic, Conn., 1984), 20.

7 The Marcia Allen figurehead, now in the Mariners' Museum in Newport News, Virginia, is illustrated in Lewis 1996, pl. IX.

8 The 1820s costume and hairstyle of the Index figure can also be compared to two half-length figureheads illustrated in Hamilton 1984, figs. 59, 60.

9 The Marcia Allen figurehead is thirty-one-and-one-half inches high and twenty-one inches wide. The Index figurehead was recorded on its data sheet as twenty-five inches high and twenty inches wide.

Elizabeth Moutal / active c. 1935

13 Figurehead: "Commodore Perry"

1938 / watercolor with white heightening over graphite / 48.9 x 36.1 cm (19¼ x 14³⁄₁₆ in.)

Elizabeth Moutal, one of the most accomplished among the very skillful group of Massachusetts Index artists, produced a masterful rendering of this figurehead. Made of white pine and thoroughly weathered through the years, the carving, whose appearance she recorded in 1938, showed only faint traces of paint on its surface.[1] These remnants indicate that the subject once wore a blue jacket and vest, gray collar, and white shirt. His hair had been black, his face flesh-tone, and the drapery base blue. Several inches of the carving's back and a larger area of the base were removed.

The maker of *Commodore Perry* is unknown, but it appears to be by the same hand as a figurehead called *Woman with a Comb* in Mystic Seaport, Connecticut.[2] In 1931 Holger Cahill included the figurehead in his groundbreaking exhibition of American folk sculpture at the Newark Museum.[3] At that time it belonged to Ralph Warren Burnham, who claimed (without providing documentation) that

the piece had come from the packet ship *Commodore Perry*, built by the well-known shipbuilder Donald McKay of East Boston. Part of James Baines' Australian Black Ball Fleet, this merchant ship caught fire in 1869 while carrying coal from Newcastle and beached near Bombay.[4] If the figurehead was actually from this ship, it might have been removed before the ship changed hands in the 1860s, or it could have been salvaged from the ruins of the fire. According to M. V. Brewington, the bust type of figurehead was popular from the mid-1820s until the mid-1850s, particularly on smaller merchant ships. Bust types were less costly to produce and more appropriate in proportion to these vessels than full-length figures.[5]

It is not clear whether the ship *Commodore Perry* was named for Commodore Oliver Hazard Perry or his younger brother, Commodore Matthew Calbraith Perry. Oliver Hazard Perry became a national hero when the fleet he commanded defeated the British at the Battle of Lake Erie on 10 September 1813. He died in 1819. Matthew Calbraith Perry was also an American naval hero. In 1854—the year the ship *Commodore Perry* was built—he succeeded, mainly through intimidation, in negotiating the treaty that first opened the previously isolationist Japan to trade. This treaty was a triumph for the United States, and Commodore Matthew Calbraith Perry was widely celebrated for his successful mission.[6]

DC and VTC

American 19th Century, *Figurehead: "Commodore Perry,"* c. 1854, painted wood, 88.9 x 61 cm (35 x 24 in.), The Mariners' Museum, Newport News, Virginia

1 Moutal must have seen the figurehead while it was still with a Boston antiques dealer, just at the time of its purchase by the Mariners' Museum, Newport News, Virginia.

2 Nearly two dozen figurehead carving establishments were active in nineteenth-century Boston; see Brewington 1962, 42, 43, and 67. See also the appendices in M. V. Brewington and Pauline A. Pinckney, *American Figureheads and Their Carvers* (New York, 1940).

3 Exh. cat. Newark 1931, no. 2.

4 This and related information is summarized in a 1983 report by Carol Olsen, Mariners' Museum files.

5 Brewington 1962, 46, 48.

6 Chief Ranger Gerard T. Altoff, National Park Service, Perry's Victory and International Peace Memorial, Put-in-Bay, Ohio, helped clarify that either brother would have been considered worthy of having a ship named for him in 1854.

Hazel Hyde / active c. 1935

14 Billethead from the Ship *Favorite*

1938 / watercolor with colored pencil and white heightening over graphite / 27.8 x 38.2 cm (10^{15}/$_{16}$ x 15 in.)

An alternative to the figurehead, the billethead was a less elaborate and costly decoration for a ship's bow. Despite its smaller size and lack of nameable subject, carvers often lavished it with considerable attention. The swooping curl of this billethead's central volute, the liveliness of its lush foliate design and scrolls, and the crispness of its carving all bespeak an experienced and talented craftsman.[1] At one time painted (the Index data sheet describes minute traces of black and salmon), its cracked and weather-beaten surface is evidence of its age and history.

According to the records of the Peabody Essex Museum in Salem, Massachusetts, in whose collection the object has been since 1905, this billethead once decorated the ship *Favorite*. Built at Bath, Maine, in 1853, the *Favorite* plied a route between New Orleans and Boston, carrying a cargo of cotton, molasses, and sugar. She was wrecked off Salem harbor 29 January 1855.[2]

DC

1   The figurehead expert Carol Olsen suggests that billethead carving often "draws on standard architectural decoration" such as the scrolled consoles that serve as window supports; e-mail correspondence with the author, 22 October 2001.

2   *Salem Gazette*, 30 January and 1 February 1855, from notes in curatorial files, Peabody Essex Museum.

American 19th Century, *Billethead from the Ship* Favorite, 1853, painted wood, 54.6 x 44.5 cm (22 x 17 ^{1}/$_{2}$ in.), Peabody Essex Museum, Salem, Massachusetts

Alfred Smith / active c. 1935

15 Paddle Wheel Cover from the Steamship *Island Home*

1939 / watercolor with white heightening over graphite / 27.5 x 47.3 cm (10¹³/₁₆ x 18¹⁵/₁₆ in.)

The successful trial run of Robert Fulton's steamboat up the Hudson River from New York City to Albany in 1807 inaugurated a new age of navigation in America, with steam-powered vessels taking command of rivers and coastal bays throughout the country. Nantucket, with its lucrative whaling business, was a busy and prosperous port and its citizens wasted no time in adopting this new means of transportation between their island and Cape Cod. By 1818 the steamer *Eagle* plied the waters between Nantucket and Hyannis, the first regularly scheduled steam navigation on the Atlantic coast.[1] This steamboat service, with railroad connections in Hyannis, provided the modern traveler with astonishing new convenience: "In one hour and a half, we can jump into the cars and whiz away for Boston or New York; breakfasting at Nantucket, dining at Boston, and supping at bed time in that city to which the other cities of the United States are the merest babies."[2]

Because the prow of the modern steam vessel was vertical rather than raking forward like that of the old sailing ship, it did not lend itself as a site for figureheads and billetheads. The box that enclosed the ship's gigantic paddle wheel, however, did offer a suitable place for ornamentation. Such enclosure was essential for both comfort and safety: "the paddle wheels threw much water on the deck and were constant dangers to anything in their vicinity."[3] The box conformed to the half-cylindrical shape of the wheel above water, with a sunburst of open louvers around a central, solid lunette on each side. These lunettes became a new focus for ships' carvings. Patriotic pride in American naval engineering made the image of an eagle displaying the Stars and Stripes—a variation on the Great Seal of the United States—a common decorative insignia on steamboats.

Alfred Smith's rendering for the Index of American Design depicts one of the two carvings from the sides of the paddle wheel box on the steamship *Island Home*. Launched in New York City, the *Island Home* steamed into Nantucket harbor under the command of Captain Thomas Brown on 5 September 1855, ready to replace her immediate predecessor, the *Massachusetts*, for the voyage to Hyannis the next day. Described as the

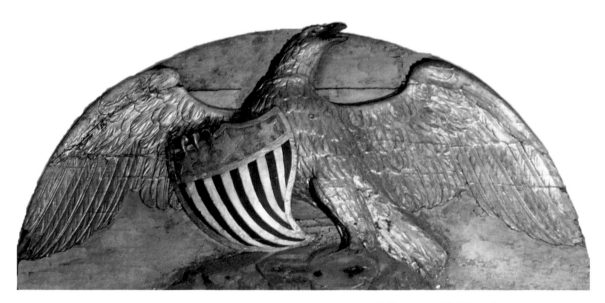

American 19th Century, *Paddle Wheel Cover from the Steamship* Island Home, 1855, painted and gilded wood, 83.8 x 167.6 cm (33 x 66 in.), Nantucket Historical Association

finest ship of her size ever built in New York, the *Island Home* was 184 feet long and weighed 536 tons. The local newspaper described her entry into Nantucket with great enthusiasm: "At 20 minutes past 9 o'clock, the *Island Home* glided into our harbor in beautiful style, and a fine appearance she made, with her flags flying, gracefully skimming over the unruffled water, the bright sun smiling a kindly welcome, and the cannon roaring out its friendly greetings, which were as loudly belched forth on board the boat. She circled round the harbor twice, affording the numerous spectators an excellent opportunity to view her graceful proportions, her swan-like movements, and the very limited space occupied in turning around. In appearance and actions, we have nautical endorsement for saying that she is all that could be desired."[4]

The *Island Home* served Nantucket for forty years, with Captain Nathan H. Manter at the helm during the last thirty. In addition to making regularly scheduled trips to the mainland, the *Island Home* and her crew performed many heroic rescues and towed numerous ships across the bar in Nantucket harbor. She also had a few narrow escapes of her own during winter tempests. In 1872 her route changed from Hyannis to Woods Hole when a branch of the railroad reached the latter town. The two carved lunettes from the *Island Home*'s paddle wheel cover may have been removed in 1895, when the Nantucket steamship line sold the passenger vessel for conversion to a coal barge. They were purchased in 1897 by the Nantucket Historical Association, testimony to the community's profound respect and affection for "our dear old *Island Home*....beloved steamer."[5]

VTC

1   Harry B. Turner, *The Story of the Island Steamers* (Nantucket, 1910), 1–2.

2   Newspaper account of 1855 quoted in Turner 1910, 45.

3   Brewington 1962, 116.

4   Quoted in Turner 1910, 44.

5   Niles Parker, chief curator of the Nantucket Historical Association, kindly sent me a copy of the documents relating to the purchase of the two paddle wheel covers.

Detail cat. 15

Elmer G. Anderson / active c. 1935

16   Stove Plate with Hunting Scene

1936 / black chalk with graphite / 27.9 x 33 cm (11 x 13 in.)

When Henry Mercer wrote his book about "pictured stoves and stove plates of the Pennsylvania Germans," he titled it *The Bible in Iron* because so many stoves and stove plates were decorated with biblical scenes.[1] Pennsylvania German stove plates also displayed stylized floral motifs or arch and lozenge shapes. Landscapes, such as the one depicted here, are rare. The symbolism of this scene remains largely unexplained, although Mercer connects it to the images of misfortune that may have been derived from illustrations of the work of Petrarch.[2]

This stove plate, made for the left side of a five-plate stove (see cat. 17), may have been made in Virginia rather than Pennsylvania. It was purchased from a shop in Harrisonburg in Virginia's Shenandoah Valley, an area settled early on by German immigrants.[3] The last dated five-plate stove from this area is from the year 1773, but the date for the example Anderson illustrated is not known.[4] It has been in the collection of the Bucks County Historical Society since 1927.

Anderson's illustration was made in chalk and graphite, a monochromatic approach more suited to the iron object than the watercolors employed in most Index renderings. The artist used incised lines to create white highlights.

DC

1   Mercer 1961.

2   Mercer 1961, 204.

3   Mercer lists Virginia furnaces, including one called Redwell or Redwil, which operated near Luray. In 1929 the journal kept by this company was in the possession of the Old Mill Stone Antique Shop, Harrisonburg, the same shop from which the stove plate with the hunting scene was sold; Mercer 1961, 119.

4   Mercer 1961, 204.

American 18th Century,
Stove Plate with Hunting Scene,
late eighteenth century, iron,
66.7 x 76.2 cm (26 ¼ x 30 in.),
The Mercer Museum of the
Bucks County Historical Society,
Doylestown, Pennsylvania,
Gift of Henry C. Mercer, 1927

Edward L. Loper / born 1916

17 # Stove Plate with Tulip Decoration

1939 / watercolor with white heightening over graphite / 35.8 x 45.8 cm (14 1/8 x 18 1/16 in.)

Although called a "fireback" on the original Index data
sheet, the cast-iron object illustrated here was not used
to reflect the heat and protect the rear of an open fireplace. Instead it makes up one section, probably the
front, of an early five-plate stove. These were iron boxes
that projected, and thereby radiated heat, into a room.
They were fueled from the other side of the wall by a
fireplace that opened into an adjacent room. Box-shaped
iron stoves were first brought to the colonies by the
Pennsylvania Germans, and local iron makers of British
descent soon answered the demand for this type of
warming device. The stove plate illustrated by Edward
Loper was privately owned in 1939, but its present
location is unknown. It was one of the stove plates cast
at Mary Ann Furnace (many early Pennsylvania forges
bore women's names), probably the first iron-producing
site west of the Susquehanna River. The plate, dated
1763, records the year of the furnace's creation and
the names of its founders, George Ross, George Stevenson, and William Thompson.[1] Because the carver of
the mold from which this plate was made utilized an
earlier design, the lettering of Stevenson's name was
squeezed from the main line into the cartouche above.
The tulip-based design, which is used repeatedly on
stoves after 1750, replaces biblical narratives that were
favored earlier.

DC

1 Mercer 1961, 220.

Detail cat. 17

Yolande Delasser / active c. 1935

Batter Pitcher

1936 / watercolor with white heightening over graphite / 29.1 x 22.8 cm (11 ⁷/₁₆ x 9 in.) /
27.5 x 22.9 cm (10¹³/₁₆ x 9 in.)

So unusual and significant was this early piece of stoneware that it was depicted from three angles. The potter boldly and helpfully inscribed in cobalt on the jug: "New York Feb. 17, 1798 / Flowered by / Mr. Clarkson Crolius." Once owned by the American sculptor and folk-art collector Elie Nadelman and his wife, the jug is now in the collection of the New-York Historical Society.

The pitcher's maker, Clarkson Crolius (1773–1843), was a descendant of Johan Willem Crolius, who came to America from Germany in 1718 and began a dynasty of potters that operated in Manhattan until 1849.[1] The Croliuses were among the earliest and perhaps most important stoneware makers in the

history of this country. By the beginning of the nineteenth century, Crolius wares were becoming widely distributed over several states. In 1809 the company published a price list that offered a variety of products including "spout pots," which may have been the type of jug that is depicted here and was meant to hold and pour batter. The vessel apparently served as a water jug for generations of field-workers on a Wisconsin farm before finding its way into the Nadelman collection.[2]

DC

1 Ketchum 1987, 40, 45–51.

2 Katherine Willis, "Early New York Pottery," *Country Life* 54, no. 5 (September 1928), 78.

Clarkson Crolius (American, 1773–1843),
Batter Pitcher, 1798, stoneware,
27.9 x 21.6 cm (11 ¼ x 8 ½ in.),
The New-York Historical Society

Domestic Artifacts

Isadore Goldberg II and John Tarantino / both active c. 1935

20 Stoneware Jar

1941 / watercolor over graphite / 45.8 x 36.6 cm (18 x 14⁷/₁₆ in.)

Through a truly remarkable technique, several Index artists were able to replicate on paper the illusion of the softly reflective, slightly textured surface of old stoneware. Fired at a high temperature, the dense white clay of this type of pottery vitrifies, becoming extremely hard and nonporous. For reasons of appearance rather than utility, however, the pottery is often glazed. The simple salt glaze, which gives the surface an "orange-peel" texture, was accomplished by the addition of common salt to the kiln at the proper stage of the firing process. The stoneware jar[1] is decorated with a lively, incised drawing, colored with a cobalt slip (a mixture of clay and water), and the interior is glazed with a typical brown "Albany-type" slip.[2]

The jar also bears the stamp W. ROBERTS BINGHAMPTON NY above the number 4. The name refers to the pottery of William Roberts (born 1818, Wales), who immigrated to Utica, New York, in 1827.

He married the daughter of the Utica potter Noah White, and by 1847 or 1848 the couple had moved to Binghampton, a rapidly growing community serviced by both the Chenango Canal and the New York & Erie Railroad. For several years, Roberts' business was combined with that of the White family, but from 1869 to 1882 directories list Roberts alone as a stoneware manufacturer, as is reflected in the stamped mark on this piece.[3]

DC

1 The jar pictured by Goldberg and Tarantino was in the shop of Helena Penrose and J. H. Edgette. It was auctioned at Sotheby's in 1999; its present owner is unknown.

2 For a detailed description of the stoneware-making process see Greer 1981, 14–20, 180–181.

3 Ketchum 1987, 398–401.

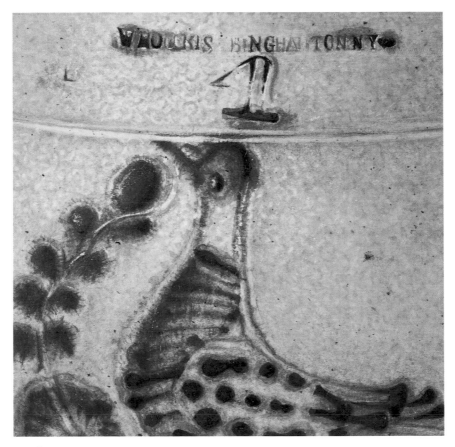

Detail cat. 20

Albert Levone / active c. 1935

21 Plate with Soldier on Horseback

1936 / watercolor over graphite / 52.7 x 38.1 cm (20³/₄ x 15 in.)

When objects from what was then the Pennsylvania Museum (now the Philadelphia Museum of Art) were chosen for the Index project, the appeal of this plate was already long established, for it had been published as an important example by a known maker of Pennsylvania slip-decorated redware as early as 1903.[1]

The plate has been attributed to John Neis, also sometimes known as Johannes Neesz (1785–1867), a potter from Upper Salford Township, Montgomery County, Pennsylvania. It is one of the earliest surviving works attributed to him. Numerous versions of the soldier or horseman design were made by Neis in the first two decades of the nineteenth century, including one of the same date in the collection of the American Folk Art Museum, New York.[2] The jaunty, almost smiling soldier and eager horse shown here belie the morose inscription that runs along its edge: *Ich bin geritten über berg und Dal hob untrei funten üwer ahl Ao 1805* (I have ridden over hill and dale and have found disloyalty everywhere. In the year 1805). The plate is further enlivened by the addition of color, a copper-oxide slip giving the floral design and the rider's jacket a green hue.

DC

1 Barber 1903, 140–142, ill. 48.

2 Exh. cat. New York 2001, cat. 112.

Attributed to John Neis (American, 1785–1867), *Plate*, 1805, matte-lead-glazed earthenware with slip and sgraffito decoration, 32.1 cm (12 ⁵/₈ in.), Philadelphia Museum of Art, John T. Morris Collection

Detail cat. 21

Giacinto Capelli / active c. 1935

22 Plate with Tulip and Two Flowers

1938 / watercolor and gouache over graphite / 45.4 x 37.8 cm (17 ⁷/₈ x 14 ⁷/₈ in.)

Redware or earthenware was generally the most utilitarian and inexpensive pottery produced in America in the eighteenth and nineteenth centuries.[1] Certain decorative or commemorative pieces, however, were created by applying additional time and care. The Pennsylvania Germans, in particular, had a tradition of highly decorated redware, often produced by a method known as sgraffito. In this process the dried earthenware is covered with a light-colored slip. The design is then incised through the light layer to the dark one beneath using a pointed instrument. A limited range of additional colored slip might be painted on areas of the design. The piece was then glazed and fired, the glaze usually giving a yellow cast to the white areas. These objects, scratched with intricate lettering and designs and often presented as gifts, were meant to be enjoyed for their appearance and were probably not intended for practical use.

The simplest and most popular motifs used in sgraffito-ware were floral, often tulips. Early collectors at one point once used the term "tulipware" to describe all decorated Pennsylvania German redware. Variations of the tulip also appear on furniture, fraktur, and even iron stove plates produced in the Pennsylvania German community.[2] The plate depicted here has been attributed to John Neis of Montgomery County, Pennsylvania (see cat. 21), and is now in the American Folk Art Museum, New York, the promised gift of Ralph Esmerian.[3]

DC

1 See Ketchum 1991 for a detailed overview of this craft.

2 "The Tulip in Decoration," in Barber 1903, chap. 7; see also cat. 30.

3 Exh. cat. New York 2001, cat. 113a.

Attributed to John Neis (American, 1785–1867), *Plate with Tulip and Two Flowers*, 1823, glazed red earthenware with slip and sgraffito decoration, 28.4 cm (11 ³/₁₆ in.), American Folk Art Museum, New York, Promised Gift of Ralph Esmerian

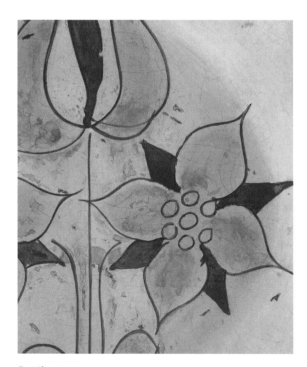

Detail cat. 22

Frank Fumagalli / active c. 1935

23 Face Jug

1936 / watercolor with white heightening over graphite / 22.6 x 29.1 cm (8 7/8 x 11 1/2 in.)

Although the data sheet for this Index rendering reads "Grotesque Jug, Circa 1800," the dating of the piece by Index researchers is incorrect. The African-inspired face jug was not introduced into American pottery design until the time of the Civil War. The only antebellum anthropomorphic jugs were produced by the Remmeys of Philadelphia and New York and were noticeably European in influence. The type of jug reproduced in this rendering was likely created by enslaved potters of the Edgefield district of South Carolina. The term "Grotesque Jug" was coined by ceramic historian Edwin Atlee Barber in 1892 to describe a specific type of alkaline-glazed stoneware produced in Colonel Thomas Davies' Palmetto Fire Brick Works during the Civil War.[1] The jugs created by Davies' slaves share common stylistic devices; the eyebrows, for example, are constructed of rolled pieces of clay adjoining the humped nose and abutted by wide-set eyes. The teeth are exposed through parted lips, painted white, and either incised or left smooth as shown here. Face jugs conveyed the expressive African heritage of their makers and provided storage for food and drink. At the time this face jug was rendered by Frank Fumagalli for the New York project, it was owned by Elie Nadelman and housed in his Museum of Folk and Peasant Arts, Riverdale-on-Hudson, New York. It is now in the New-York Historical Society, along with many other ceramics once owned by Nadelman.

LR

1 Exh. cat. Columbia 2001, 16.

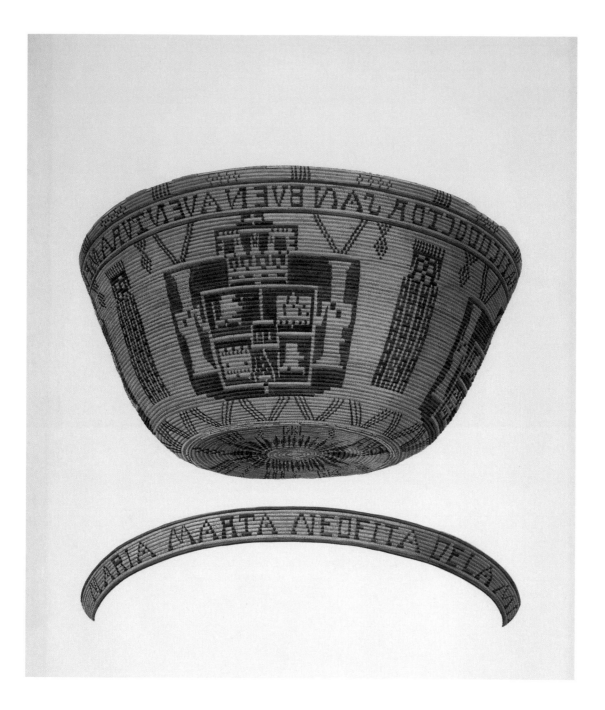

Gordena Jackson / 1900–1993

24 Native American Presentation Basket

1938 / watercolor over graphite / 68.6 x 50.8 cm (27 x 20 in.)

The inscription on this basket, meant to be read from the inside, reports that "Maria Marta, neophyte of the mission of the Seraphic Doctor San Buenaventura, made me in the year...."[1] Apparently there was not enough room to complete the date. Maria Marta, a Chumash Native American whose name had been Zaputimeu before her baptism, was born in 1767 and died in 1830; she became a neophyte at the San Buenaventura Mission in Ventura County, California, in 1788.[2] Her magnificent basket, made of juncus and sumac, is about sixteen inches in diameter and nine and one-half inches deep; each square inch is composed of about 320 weft strands. Maria Marta wove a motif from the coat of arms of the kings of Spain four times around the basket, copying this image from a Spanish colonial coin known as the pillar dollar, or piece of eight.[3] The basket is one of the earliest from California that can be attributed to a specific individual.

The coiled baskets of the Chumash have long been recognized for their extraordinary beauty and the quality of their craftsmanship.[4] Only about three hundred have survived. They were important in nearly every part of Chumash life, including cooking, and were so tightly woven that they could hold water. Before the arrival of Europeans in California, Chumash produced baskets not only for their own domestic purposes but also for trade with other Native American tribes. At the Franciscan missions, Chumash created baskets as presentation objects and for market, to provide revenue for the missions. Apart from the Spanish coin motif, Maria Marta's basket conforms to traditional Chumash basket design in its ornamentation as well as its shape.

Four additional Chumash baskets bearing imagery copied from Spanish colonial coins have survived. At least two of these were made at San Buenaventura, and one has an inscription declaring it was made by Juana Basilia.[5] Maria Marta's and Juana Basilia's baskets were both in the collection of a family in Mexico City from around 1822 until 1895. The inscription on Juana Basilia's basket provides important clues to the shared early history of the two baskets, stating that Juana Basilia made her basket in order to contribute to "the attentions paid by Governor Sola to the Field Marshall Señor Don Jose de la Cruz."[6] Pablo Vincente de Sola was the last Spanish governor of California, serving from 1815 to 1822, and Jose de la Cruz was a general in the Spanish colonial army. Archaeologist Zelia Nuttall, who discovered and purchased Maria Marta's and Juana Basilia's baskets in Mexico City in the 1920s, determined that Governor Sola had presented both baskets to General Jose de la Cruz during a visit Cruz made to California in 1821–1822 and that Cruz had brought the baskets to Mexico City in 1822, shortly before his expulsion from Mexico as a "dangerous personality."[7] Nuttall donated Maria Marta's basket to the Anthropology Museum of the University of California at Berkeley because she recognized its great value in the study of California baskets.

VTC

1   "Maria Marta neofita de la mission de el serafico doctor San Buenaventura me hizo an"; Elsasser 1968, 64. Joan Knudsen, registrar at the Phoebe A. Hearst Museum of Anthropology, University of California, Berkeley, provided a copy of this catalogue; Ira Jacknis, associate research anthropologist at the same institution, was also helpful in sharing information about the basket.

2   Lillian Smith found Maria Marta's name and the date of her baptism, on which she became a neophyte, in the Book of Baptismals of the Mission San Buenaventura (Smith 1982, 67). John Johnson, curator of anthropology at the Santa Barbara Museum of Natural History, later discovered Maria Marta's death date and her correct Native American name; he kindly provided this information by telephone.

3   Smith 1982, 64.

4   On the Chumash and their basketry, see Santa Barbara Museum of Natural History, *California's Chumash Indians* (Santa Barbara, 1986), 49–52; Bruce W. Miller, *Chumash: A Picture of the Their World* (Los Osos, Calif., 1988), 49–58; and Bibby 1996, 9–10.

5   Smith 1987, 12–21. Jan Timbrook, curator at the Santa Barbara Museum of Natural History, informed me during a telephone conversation of the recent discovery of the fifth Chumash presentation basket with a coin motif.

6   This basket is now in the Santa Barbara Museum of Natural History, accession number NA-AC-CII-4F-3. Juana Basilia may not have made the entire basket but only added the inscribed rim to an existing basket (Smith 1982, 66–67).

7   Nuttall 1924, 340–343. I am grateful to Sara Elberg at the California Historical Society for a copy of this article. Cruz was notorious for his "monstrous cruelty, despotism, rapacity, dishonesty, treachery and cowardice" (Nuttall 1924, 342).

Charles Henning / active c. 1935

25 Coffeepot

1940 / watercolor and gouache over graphite / 50.8 x 39.2 cm (20 x 15 7/16 in.)

Wayne White / 1890–1978

26 Coffeepot

1940 / watercolor and gouache over graphite / 38.3 x 28.7 cm (15 1/16 x 11 5/16 in.)

Working in two different states, Index artists coincidentally completed these images at nearly the same time. Henning, in New York, depicted tinware found in Lebanon, Pennsylvania. White, in Chicago, recorded a coffeepot said to have been made in New York State. These objects, identical in function but widely differing in form, help illustrate the prolific creativity of the American tinware artisans.

The tinware (actually tinned sheet-iron) industry in this country began in Connecticut in the mid-eighteenth century.[1] By the early decades of the nineteenth century, tinware peddlers were plying their trade throughout the eastern states.

The most decorative of these wares were painted, a process called japanning that was developed in seventeenth-century England to imitate Oriental lacquer. By 1810 japanning, with varnish as a substitute for lacquer, was widely used in America. The first painted tin surfaces were black, the result of the addition of asphaltum to the varnish, but red and blue backgrounds were introduced within a few years. The wares were often decorated with floral motifs of the type common on pottery. Because many forms of tinware were used up and down the east coast and because shapes persisted over the years, it is difficult to say with certainty when or where these coffeepots were made.[2]

DC

1 For an excellent history of American tinware, see Shirley Spaulding Devoe, "Historical Perspective," in Martin and Tucker 1997, vol. 1. Martin and Tucker's guide thoroughly documents the various makers, shops, and designs from the eighteenth and nineteenth centuries.

2 Jack Lindsay, curator of decorative arts, Philadelphia Museum of Art, indicated that without examining the objects themselves for details such as soldering patterns, it is not possible to determine their origins with any degree of certainty; telephone conversation with the author, 13 February 2002.

American 19th Century, *Coffeepot*,
early nineteenth century, painted tin,
27.3 x 16.5 cm (10 3/4 x 6 1/2 in.),
Chicago Historical Society,
Gift of Mrs. E. C. Chadbourne

WAYNE WHITE

Domestic Artifacts

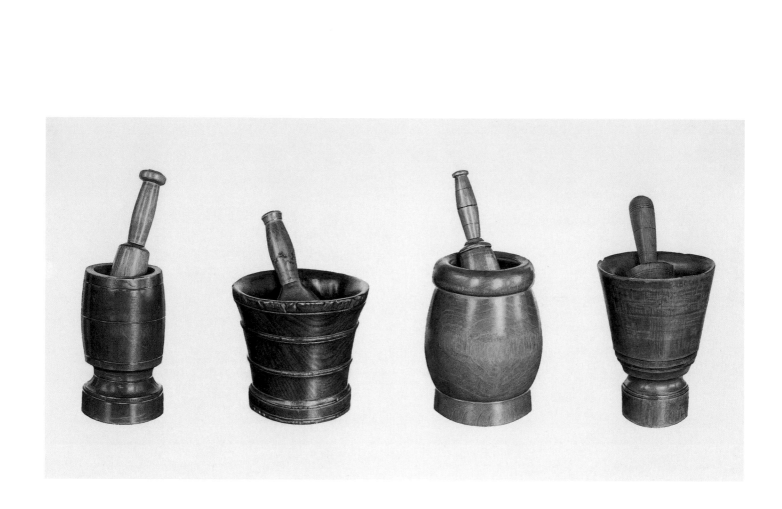

Elizabeth Moutal / active c. 1935

27 Mortars and Pestles

1937 / watercolor with white heightening over graphite / 31.4 x 54.8 cm (12 3/8 x 21 9/16 in.)

With a keen artist's eye, Moutal has carefully arranged the varied bulbous and flared forms of these wooden mortars across the blank sheet. She was required to record the appearance of these chosen objects in straightforward detail, but aesthetic choices within these confines are hers, such as the angle of the pestles (the outer ones are tilted toward the center of the composition like quotation marks), spacing, and sequence.

When documented by the Index, the objects were in the collection of the Wells Historical Museum, Southbridge, Massachusetts, which became the basis for Old Sturbridge Village in Sturbridge, Massachusetts. It is not known whether they were used for domestic or commercial purposes. An apothecary's heavy use of such grinding tools, however, might necessitate that they be fashioned from wear-resistant material such as brass or stone. The brown mortar, second from the left, is made of a tropical hardwood called *lignum vitae*. Very dense and water-resistant, it was often used in making ship accoutrements. The mortars illustrated probably date from the late eighteenth or early nineteenth century.[1]

DC

1 Frank White, curator of mechanical arts, Old Sturbridge Village, kindly provided information on the probable use and dates of the mortars depicted and on the use of *lignum vitae;* telephone conversation with Virginia Clayton, 10 January 2002.

Albert Rudin / active c. 1935

28 Saw and Scabbard

1940 / watercolor over graphite / 42.8 x 58 cm (16⁷⁄₈ x 22¹³⁄₁₆ in.)

Fashioned from hickory wood, with a tempered steel blade, this handsaw and scabbard (case) show the wear and tear of long, hard use. The pistol-grip saw was handmade about 1840, before such tools were industrially manufactured. Later in the century most handsaws were made with broader handles that contained hand holes. The blade's narrow nose indicates that the saw could be used in tight spaces, but its large, ragged teeth suggest that it was intended for rough carpentry rather than cabinetmaking.[1]

The unusual contour of the saw's handle, dipping and pointing like the nose of a dolphin, is echoed in the interior of the scabbard's boomerang shape. This straightforward depiction of a simple tool also emanates a quiet, abstract beauty. The saw and scabbard were in the Chicago Historical Society in 1940 and remain part of that collection.

DC

1 Information courtesy David Shayt, museum specialist, cultural history, NMAH, SI; conversation 12 December 2001.

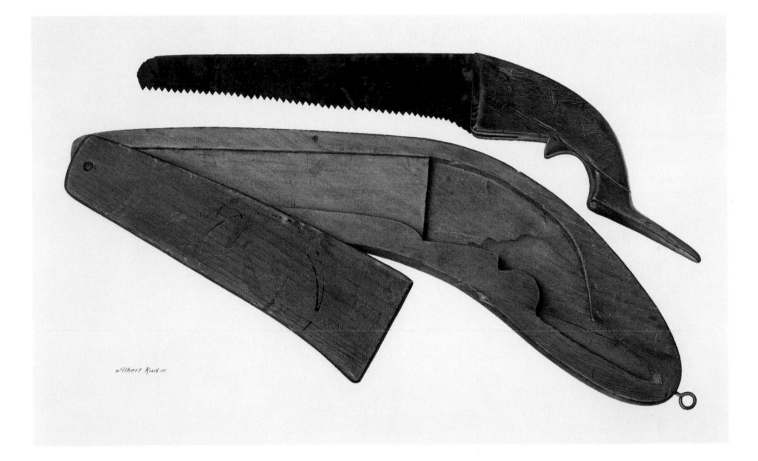

Albert Rudin

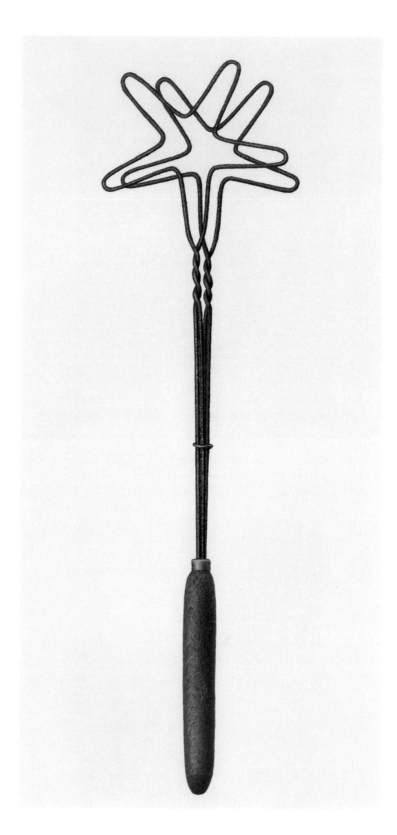

Nicholas Amantea / 1900–1978

29 Toaster

1940 / watercolor over graphite / 47.8 x 30.3 cm (18^{13}/$_{16}$ x 11^{15}/$_{16}$ in.)

Like so many of the objects chosen for depiction by Index artists, this implement does not have special historic interest or an exalted purpose, but it appeals for its unusual form. Made of iron wire, a wooden handle, and a sliding brass ring, the tool is simplicity itself, yet the sprightly star shape on the long handle, repeated twice, almost seems to dance on its point.

Probably made in the late nineteenth century or slightly afterward, this tool was used to toast bread by the fireside.[1] The bread was secured between the two stars by a ring that was pushed up or down the metal stems, pressing them closer or moving them apart.[2] Burned into the handle of the device are the letters and numbers "PAT'D 270." According to the records of the United States Patent Office, however, patent number 270 was for Thomas Peason's blast furnace, 1837, not for a toaster.

DC

1 Carol Bohn kindly provided two references to very similar hand-held toasters that ended in cross-shaped, rather than star-shaped, wires: *Montgomery Ward & Co., Catalogue No. 49* (1891), 116, item no. 43797, and *John Pritzlaff Hardware Co. Catalogue* (Milwaukee, Wis., 1904), 98, bread toaster; correspondence with the author, May 2002.

2 Geoffrey Warren, *Kitchen Bygones: A Collectors Guide* (London, 1984), 74: "Up to the mid-nineteenth century, American toasters are also of the horizontal or standing kind. Later examples, following European custom, consisted of forks on long handles. An American exception is an early twentieth-century toaster consisting of two wire mesh squares in which the slice of bread is held, the squares being attached to a long wooden handle."

M. Rosenshield-von-Paulin / active c. 1935

30 Dough Trough

1940 / watercolor and graphite / 28 x 42.3 cm (11 x 16 5/8 in.)

Pennsylvania German bread makers placed dough inside troughs to protect it from drafts while it rose and possibly kneaded their dough on the trough's flat top. In addition to troughs for tabletop use, such as the one in this rendering, there were larger dough troughs that stood on four legs. Generally simple yet idiosyncratic in design—rarely are two of these objects exactly the same—they are most often made of soft wood such as pine or poplar.[1] The late eighteenth-century example in this rendering was given to the Metropolitan Museum of Art by Mrs. Robert W. de Forest in 1933.[2] Made of poplar, its surface may once have been covered with yellow paint that has now faded. The matching decorative panels each display black vases holding five symmetrically placed tulips, three opened and two closed.

This remarkably handsome dough trough is attributed to Christian Selzer (active c. 1780–1800) or someone closely associated with him, probably one of the four or five members of a school of furniture decorators operating from the 1770s to about 1820 in and around Jonestown, Dauphin County (now Lebanon County), Pennsylvania. This group included Christian Selzer's son John (1774–1845) and members of the Rank family, one of whose daughters was married to John Selzer. It is likely that these decorators constructed as well as painted their furniture. They typically signed and dated nearly all their work, an unusual practice among Pennsylvania German furniture painters, and it is through comparison to their signed pieces that this unsigned dough trough has been attributed to Christian Selzer or some other member of the Jonestown school.[3] Unlike many Pennsylvania German decorators, Christian Selzer appears to have painted his designs freehand.[4]

Such brightly painted and decorated household objects of purely utilitarian purpose were often produced by the Germans who settled in southeastern Pennsylvania. The disasters of war and religious intolerance in central Europe made emigration to William Penn's colony a desperate but necessary choice for many, beginning at the end of the seventeenth century, peaking around 1759, and continuing into the nineteenth century. William Penn himself made two trips to the region to encourage beleaguered farmers and craftspeople to endure the hazardous voyage across the Atlantic and participate in Pennsylvania's "Holy Experiment" of mutual toleration. Many thousands heeded his call; the first United States census in 1790 recorded that one-third of the inhabitants of southeastern Pennsylvania were of Germanic origin. Although these immigrants had been unable to carry many material possessions with them, they imported and long preserved their distinctive culture, including a tradition for painted furnishings.[5]

In the 1930s, studies of Pennsylvania German folk art were dominated by romantic interpretations of the objects' imagery based on a prevailing belief that Pennsylvania German ornament was directly inspired by medieval mysticism.[6] Since at least the early 1970s, however, these interpretations have been largely dismissed.[7] The tulip motif appears to have entered the decorative vocabulary of the Holy Roman Empire, possibly from the Near East, in the mid-sixteenth century, the same time that the actual flower arrived from present-day Turkey. Although it may once have had symbolic significance, by the time the tulip motif had reached Pennsylvania it had long been appreciated solely for its outstanding decorative potential.

VTC

1 John G. Shea, *The Pennsylvania Dutch and Their Furniture* (New York, 1980), 63.

2 See Stillinger, above, 51.

3 Fabian 1978, 64–65.

4 Fabian 1978, 62.

5 On the German settlement of southeastern Pennsylvania and its arts, see Beatrice B. Garvan and Charles F. Hummel, *The Pennsylvania Germans: A Celebration of their Arts, 1683–1850* [exh. cat., Philadelphia Museum of Art and Winterthur Museum] (Philadelphia, 1982); Cynthia Elyce Rubin, "Swiss Folk Art: Celebrating America's Roots," *The Clarion* 16 (Fall 1991), 36–44; exh. cat. New York 2001, 430–431; and Terry A. McNealy, "Bucks County in the Age of Fraktur," in Cory M. Amsler, ed., *Bucks County Fraktur* (Doylestown and Kutztown, Pa., 2001), 63–71.

6 A reference to John Stoudt's *Consider the Lilies and How They Grow*, Pennsylvania German Folklore Society (Allentown, 1937), is on the Index data sheet for the dough trough.

7 By 1961 Donald A. Shelley had already expressed skepticism about such religious interpretations in *The Fraktur-Writings or Illuminated Manuscripts of the Pennsylvania Germans*, Pennsylvania German Folklore Society (Allentown, 1961), 83; writing in 1973 about the same motifs on decorated birth and baptismal certificates, Frederick S. Weiser declared that "the simpler explanation is that they were employed for their inherent beauty and popular appeal" ("Piety and Protocol in Folk Art: Pennsylvania German Fraktur Birth and Baptismal Certificates," *Winterthur Portfolio* 8 [1973], 43).

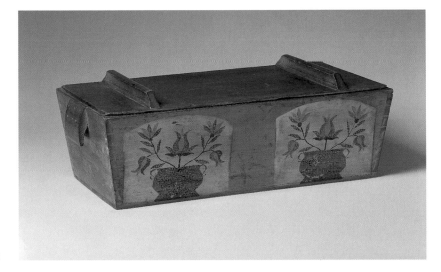

Attributed to Christian Selzer
(American, active c. 1780–1800),
Dough Trough, c. 1775–1820,
painted poplar, 26 x 72.4 x 36.2 cm
(10 ¼ x 28 ½ x 14 ¼ in.), The
Metropolitan Museum of Art, New
York, Gift of Mrs. Robert W. de Forest

Ferdinand Cartier / active c. 1935

31 Hadley Chest

1939 / watercolor over graphite / 45.6 x 51.9 cm (17 $^{15}/_{16}$ x 20 $^{7}/_{16}$ in.)

Although "Hadley chests constitute the largest group of seventeenth-century American furniture with a common vocabulary of ornament," they have not been continually appreciated through the years.[1] Created at substantial effort and expense, they appear to have been prized possessions in the late seventeenth and early eighteenth centuries. Within a few decades, however, their sturdy shapes and busy decoration were already falling out of fashion. The Reverend Clair Franklin Luther provided colorful accounts of the utilitarian use, or disregard, of these pieces in the nineteenth century: one example was sawed apart to make a desk, another was used as a shipping crate.[2]

In the late nineteenth century these antiques elicited new interest. In 1883 the collector Henry Wood Erving (1851–1941) purchased a carved chest from its original home in Hadley, Massachusetts. Referred to thereafter as his "Hadley Chest," the term was popularized among Erving's circle and later became more prevalent.[3] These objects, related in construction, form, and materials, and in their carved and incised motifs, were created between about 1680 and 1740 by joiners working in Hampshire County, Massachusetts, and around the area north of Hartford, Connecticut.

By the time Cartier depicted this piece, Hadley chests, which had been included in important exhibitions of American decorative arts in 1909 and 1929, had become newly popular. This chest was in the Ginsburg and Levy antique shop in New York City in 1939 and now belongs to a private collector. Depicted in Cartier's rendering, the MB chest was "assigned conjecturally" by Luther to Mary Belding, daughter of Samuel Belding and wife of Ichabod Allis. Both men were joiners in Hatfield, Massachusetts.[4] If the chest indeed belonged to Mary Belding, it would likely have been created on the occasion of her marriage in 1698. Painted a brownish red, it was constructed of oak and pine and covered with incised motifs of repeated tulips, leaves, and scrolls, along with diamond, heart, and crossbow shapes—details that were lovingly re-created by the Index artist.

DC

1 Kane 1974b, 81.

2 Luther 1935, 94, 119.

3 See exh. cat. Deerfield 1992 for an extensive history of this type of furniture.

4 Luther 1935, 72, cat. 13.

Amos C. Brinton / 1888–1982

32 Gateleg Table

1939 / watercolor and gouache over graphite / 34.3 x 51.1 cm ($13^{1}/_{2}$ x $20^{1}/_{8}$ in.)

In colonial days, drop-leaf tables were a practical and ingenious response to the need for dining and working surfaces in a limited area subject to multiple uses. One type of table, the gateleg, had movable sections that could be folded in, making the table quite compact. Swung outward, they supported a large, often oval tabletop, in this case approximately sixty-nine by sixty inches.

The table depicted by Brinton is noted to have been made from walnut, a finer wood than the oak that was predominant earlier.[1] The Index data sheet indicates that the piece belonged to a family in Lewes, Delaware, and that it dates from about 1680 (its present owner is not known). The table was probably made slightly later, however, for "turned-leg, oval, drop-leaf tables were based on English models of the late seventeenth century. Fashionable by 1700, they remained stylish through the first four decades of the eighteenth."[2]

DC

1 The rendering gives the wood grain a prominence and contrast that make it appear to be oak.

2 Jobe and Kaye 1984, 269.

M. Rothschild-von-Paulin

M. Rosenshield-von-Paulin / active c. 1935

33 Candle Stand

1940 / watercolor and gouache over graphite / 57.7 x 36.6 cm (22$^{11}/_{16}$ x 14$^{7}/_{16}$ in.)

There are many renderings in the Index that depict some of the most refined and elegant furniture made in America, yet a good number also record distinctly modest objects. These artifacts were chosen, one suspects, because they reveal a sense of age, use, and connection to the everyday life of ordinary people.

Such is the case with the candle stand represented by M. Rosenshield-von-Paulin. The utilitarian object appears to have been roughly cobbled together from a turned baluster and a few other pieces of pine. The chamfered feet provide an effective, tip-resistant base, and the rectangular top serves as a proper platform for a candlestick or lamp. There is a highly visible crack through the cleat which, the Index data sheet notes, is "mortised through the shaft, secured with a transverse dowel, and nailed to top with hand-wrought nails."[1] The artist has done a remarkable job of re-creating the soft sheen of the worn reddish varnish or paint surface, bringing to life once again this well-used, well-loved object.

DC

1 In response to the author's inquiry, Wendy A. Cooper, the Lois F. and Henry S. McNeil Senior Curator of Furniture at Winterthur, provided images of somewhat similar, simple cross base stands in *Connecticut Furniture: Seventeenth and Eighteenth Centuries* [exh. cat., Wadsworth Atheneum] (Hartford, Conn., 1967), nos. 152, 153. Cooper indicated that the stand depicted in the Index rendering probably dates from the early eighteenth century, although this type was also made in the late seventeenth century. Telephone conversation 7 June 2002.

Charles Henning / active c. 1935

34 Maria Stohlern Dower Chest

1938 / watercolor over graphite / 29.6 x 41.5 cm (11 5/8 x 16 5/16 in.)

Wooden storage chests came to Pennsylvania with the earliest waves of German immigrants. Most extant examples are from the last few decades of the eighteenth century. Until the end of that century, "the chest with a lift-top lid remained the most important item of storage furniture in the rural homes of southeastern Pennsylvania. Only gradually was it replaced by the chest of drawers introduced to America by the English settlers."[1] It appears that both young men and women were given these chests once they were old enough to assume responsibility for their possessions. Boys' chests probably held clothes and miscellaneous belongings, while those for girls contained not only clothing, but also fabrics and linens that were intended for their homes after marriage.

A few Pennsylvania German chests were made of walnut and decorated with inlay, but most are made of painted pine or tulip poplar. Numerous pigments were available through apothecaries in the eighteenth century. The example owned by Maria Stohlern appears to utilize a deep blue-green known as verdigris. Some types of this pigment turn black, or almost black, over time (thus explaining the difference in color between the fifty-year-old Index rendering and the object's appearance today). Both the central heart and stylized pomegranates are frequently seen in Pennsylvania German decoration.

When Charles Henning of the New York City project of the Index recorded the chest, it was in the collection of the Metropolitan Museum of Art. It was subsequently deaccessioned and is now privately owned.

DC

1 Fabian 1978, 26.

American 18th Century,
Maria Stohlern Dower Chest,
1788, painted wood,
67.3 x 135.9 x 57.8 cm
(26 1/2 x 53 1/2 x 22 3/4 in.),
Mr. and Mrs. Byron H. LeCates

Harry Eisman / active c. 1935

35 Slat-back Armchair

1940 / watercolor and colored pencil over graphite / 43.3 x 34.6 cm (17^{1}/$_{16}$ x 13^{5}/$_{8}$ in.)

This chair is one of a set of seven, consisting of one armchair and six side chairs, that has been in the collection of the Brooklyn Museum of Art since 1935. Once thought to have come from Philadelphia, its origins are now believed to be the Delaware Valley or Bergen County, New Jersey, about 1750–1800.[1] Certain elements, such as the "slats arched at both top and bottom edges, pointed bulb finials, plain tapered stiles, ball-and-double-vase turned front stretchers, and ball-and-reel feet" are characteristic of examples from Philadelphia and the Delaware River Valley and set this chair apart from similar furniture crafted in New England.[2] With its stretcher turned in the double-ball-and-disc shape and its flattened, serpentine, undercut arms, the chair seems to display additional elements of the region.[3] Slat-back chairs were used throughout the eighteenth century and into the nineteenth.

It was not uncommon for Index artists in one state to make renderings of objects that originated in another, as demonstrated in this example by a New York artist.

DC

American 18th Century, *Slat-back Armchair*, c. 1750–1800, maple, pine, ash, and rush, 130 x 58 cm (51^{3}/$_{16}$ x 22^{13}/$_{16}$ in.), Brooklyn Museum of Art

1 Telephone conversation with Barry Harwood, Brooklyn Museum, 23 January 2002. According to their records, the attribution to Bergen County was suggested by Barbara Trent at the Henry Francis du Pont Winterthur Museum, Winterthur, Delaware; the dating, revised from the Index data sheet of 1725–1750, was suggested by John Bacon, Winterthur Museum.

2 Kane 1974a, 44.

3 See examples in Kane 1974a, 45–46.

Detail cat. 35

Edward L. Loper / born 1916

36 Painted Chair

1937 / watercolor over graphite / 45.9 x 36 cm (18 $^{1}/_{16}$ x 14 $^{3}/_{16}$ in.)

This tablet-top Windsor side chair was in a private collection in Odessa, Delaware, when Loper depicted it; its present location is unknown. The pattern was popular in eastern and central Pennsylvania during the 1830s, although the exuberant, multicolored decoration of fruit and flowers (handpainted rather than stenciled) and the bold, blue striping of this chair specifically indicate that it was made in a Pennsylvania German craft shop. The white example recorded by Loper probably dates from around 1830.[1] Sometimes chairs were ornamented by the same furniture maker who had constructed them, but often they were sold plain and passed on to a painter or decorator who worked full-time or part-time in the shop.

Nancy Goyne Evans, an authority on Windsor chairs, comments:

> Typical of Pennsylvania work in this period is the serpentine-sided plank seat of rounded front edge terminated abruptly. The ring-turned front legs with their prominent vertical stripes are a signature of Pennsylvania work produced during the early nineteenth century. The tablet-top crest, a large, laterally-curved board mounted on top of the back posts, was borrowed from early nineteenth-century Baltimore work, as were the plain, slim rear legs tapered top to bottom. The most common function of the Windsor side chair from the post-revolutionary period until the mid-nineteenth century was as seating around a dining table. Scuffed surfaces could be renewed with a fresh coat of paint, and the wooden seat did not require frequent replacement, as was the case with rush-bottomed chairs.[2]

DC

1 In form the chair somewhat resembles a "late two-slat windsor type," c. 1838; see Lea 1960, 109, or compare 141, fig. 3, tablet-top Windsor side chair, Philadelphia, c. 1828–1835, light olive-green ground with gilt, New-York Historical Society, in Evans 1996.

2 Nancy Goyne Evans graciously responded to a request for expertise; e-mail correspondence with the author, 4 May 2002.

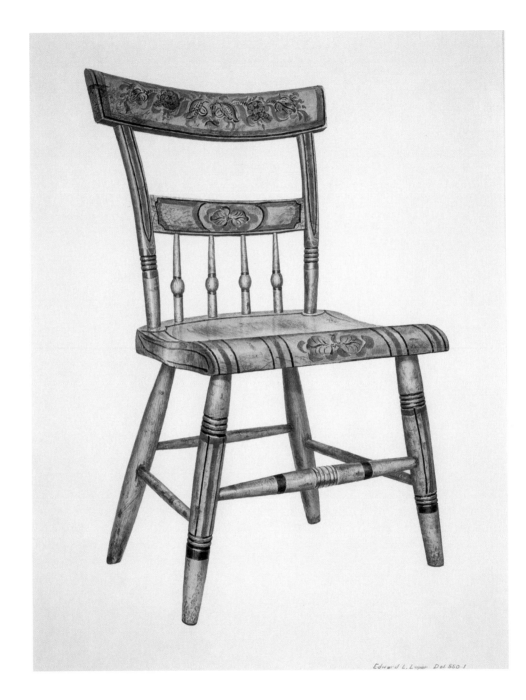

Edward L. Loper Del 550-1

Rosa Rivero / 1905–1998

37 Texas German Chair

1940 / watercolor over graphite / 35.4 x 23.9 cm (13^{15}/₁₆ x 9^{7}/₁₆ in.)

At the inception of the Texas Index project it was decided to seek out "the most abundant sources of highly desirable material in this region (San Antonio)."[1] This meant that Index artists would turn first to the artifacts of the nineteenth-century pioneer communities.

One of the largest of these was made up of the German immigrant population, which began settling several areas of the state in the 1830s. Founding the German-speaking towns of New Braunfels and Fredericksburg in the Western Texas Hill Country, they also settled in the Brazos-Colorado region, became merchants in Galveston, and were an important influence in San Antonio.[2]

The form of this simple, weathered pine chair is German (a *Brettstuhl*), with rounded legs doweled through the plank seat.[3] This type of side chair could be found in other German settlements in America, especially in eighteenth-century Pennsylvania.[4] The Index data sheet assigns the object a date of about 1864, unfortunately without further explanation. At the time of its depiction by Rosa Rivero, the side chair was in the collection of Jean Pinckney, Austin, Texas, one of the earliest collectors of Texas furniture.[5]

DC

1 Correspondence between Thomas M. Stell, supervisor, Index of American Design, and Holger Cahill, director, Federal Art Project, 15 June 1939 (National Archives, WPA, Record Group 69, Box 2642, file 315a).

2 Taylor and Warren 1975, 6–7.

3 See example of 1885, no. 4.25 in Taylor and Warren 1975.

4 See example of Moravian side chairs with rounded tops and heart-shaped decorative cut-outs in Hornung 1972, 692–693.

5 Foreword by Ima Hogg, Taylor and Warren 1975, ix. The chair's present location is unknown.

Rosa Rivero / 1905–1998

38 Texas Corner Cupboard

1941 / watercolor and colored pencil over graphite / 50.7 x 40.6 cm (19¹⁵/₁₆ x 16 in.)

Now in the collection of the Strecker/Mayborn Museum Complex of Baylor University in Waco, Texas, the cupboard in this rendering was originally made for the college's founder, R.E.B. Baylor, to furnish his home at Gay Hill, Texas. Robert Emmett Bledsoe Baylor (1793–1873) was born in Lincoln County, Kentucky, and practiced law in that state and in Alabama. At the age of forty-six he was ordained a Baptist minister and moved to Texas, where he served as a judge and helped write the first state constitution. He was one of the three men who prepared the petition that led to the establishment of Baylor University in 1845. When Rosa Rivero, one of the talented Texas Index artists, depicted the corner cupboard, its location was recorded as the town of Independence in Washington County, the first site of the college.

According to the records of the Strecker/Mayborn Museum Complex, this piece, as well as a related wardrobe and bed, is thought to have been constructed by slaves.[1] It is equally likely, however, that it was made by one of the many professional cabinetmakers working in that area around mid-century. Its appearance suggests that it could have been made anywhere in the South from the 1840s to 1850s.[2] The cupboard seems to have been made from cedar.

It was depicted with one door propped open to reveal the interior and thereby demonstrate its triangular shape. This placement lends this inanimate object a gesture of sorts—almost that of an arm flung open in invitation to the darkened space within.

DC

1 Information courtesy Paige Davis, collections assistant, Strecker/Mayborn Museum Complex, Baylor University; e-mail correspondence with Virginia Clayton, 19 April 2002.

2 Telephone conversation with Lonn Taylor, historian, NMAH, SI, and authority on Texas furniture, 25 April 2002. According to Taylor it is often assumed that these early pieces, which may lack documentation, were made by slaves rather than by the numerous cabinetmakers working in that era.

Rosa Rivers

Suzanne Chapman / 1904–1990

39   Valance

1936/1937 / watercolor over graphite / 33 x 54.8 cm (13 x 21 9/16 in.)

The administrators of the Index of American Design recognized early that the textile collection at the Museum of Fine Arts, Boston, would be an excellent source of fine decorative arts to include in their compendium of Americana. The collection was outstanding and Gertrude Townsend, its curator, was a formidable authority on the New England crewelwork in which the museum's holdings were especially rich. Many of these embroideries had been donated by the descendants of the women who had made them. After initial reluctance, Townsend warmed to the idea of the project and the Index gained entry to a remarkable treasury of early American crewelwork.[1]

The term "crewel" refers to any embroidery that is worked with crewel yarn. Also known as "worsted," crewel yarn consists of multiple strands of wool loosely twisted together. This material was widely available in England by the seventeenth century, when favorable agricultural conditions produced robust sheep capable of growing the longer strands of wool required for worsted yarn.[2] Coastal New England was the center

of crewelwork activity on this side of the Atlantic. The needlewomen of New England purchased their yarn, as well as the fabric on which they embroidered, from England and generally followed the needlework styles of that nation. It seems that they were able to purchase, both locally and from England, cloth on which embroidery designs had already been drawn.[3]

Bed hangings and petticoat borders, like those in Chapman's renderings (cats. 39, 40, 41), were among the objects often lavishly and colorfully embroidered by New England women.[4] There was apparently a hierarchy among such objects, with petticoat borders somewhat further down the scale than bed hangings.[5] Needlework scholars have determined that inexpert hands often embroidered petticoat borders and that these objects of personal adornment might have been the work of young women still learning or others simply less gifted at the art of embroidery. Bed hangings, however, were at the pinnacle of importance and their production was more likely undertaken by women with advanced needle skills. In addition

American 18th Century, *Valance* (detail), 1714, linen plain-weave, embroidered with wool and silk, 26.7 x 206.4 cm (10 ½ x 81 ¼ in.), Museum of Fine Arts, Boston, Helen and Alice Colburn Fund

to bedspreads and the long curtains that closed to make snug chambers inside eighteenth-century canopy beds, bed hangings included short, decorative valances that were attached to the tester stretched across the top of the canopy.

The date 1714 is embroidered on the valance (cats. 39, 40), making it one of the earliest documented examples of New England crewel embroidery in which a typically American self-couching stitch on plain linen was used.[6] This stitch, in which the yarn is crossed on the front side of the fabric, makes thrifty use of materials by squandering very little yarn on the back. Decorated with alternating fruit trees and floral sprays, the valance is more fanciful and lightly worked, with more empty space allowed between the embroidered details, than the Jacobean-style crewelwork made in America at this time. It is a very early example of an American embroidered bed hanging in the eighteenth-century style and somewhat livelier than most English work of this type.[7]

The influence of exotic fabric design is evident in the valance. Painted cloth from India reached England during the seventeenth century in ships used for the East Indian spice trade. Although the fabrics aroused curiosity, they were generally not very attractive to English consumers who preferred the Chinese designs with which they were more familiar. In the second half of the seventeenth century, English merchants began to ship samples of popular English patterns—including chinoiserie—to India for cloth painters to copy, hoping to improve the marketability of their wares. The Indians attempted to follow English patterns but, not fully understanding the images, translated the plants, birds, and beasts into designs that, when shipped back to England, seemed appealingly exotic to their costumers. These imported cloths became the source for many of the bizarre foliage and landscape forms in English and American crewel embroidery. In the 1714 valance, the influence of Indian fabrics is discernible in the trees that sprout enormous, outlandish foliage and flowers, and in the strangely striated, unnatural undulations of the ground plane.[8]

The crewel petticoat border in cat. 41 belongs to a group of very similar petticoat borders dated between 1740 and 1760 and worked with flat, running, satin, and stem stitches.[9] All display the same abundant variety of decorative motifs and attest to the more naturalistic style that characterized such

Fig. 1
Phyllis Dorr (American, active c. 1935), *Needlework Picture*, c. 1937, watercolor over graphite, 58 x 44.3 cm (22 13/16 x 17 7/16 in.), National Gallery of Art, Washington, Index of American Design

Suzanne Chapman / 1904–1990

40 Valance: Demonstration Drawing

1936/1937 / watercolor over graphite / 23 x 21.4 cm (9 $\frac{1}{16}$ x 8 $\frac{7}{16}$ in.)

In this rendering, Chapman repeated a detail
from cat. 39 to demonstrate her watercolor
technique, working from top to bottom

Suzanne Chapman / 1904–1990

41 Petticoat Border

1936 / watercolor over graphite / 24.1 x 33.5 cm (9 ½ x 13 ³/₁₆ in.)

needlework in the mid-eighteenth century. There are panting hounds in pursuit of fleeing deer, darting insects and birds, parrots and squirrels perched on branches and eating nuts, pairs of rabbits, and country houses—some, like the one in Chapman's rendering, with smoking chimneys. It is a charming fantasy of bucolic life ornamented with diminutive trees and gigantic flowers. Despite some discrepancies of scale, this crewelwork panorama is a few steps closer to nature than that of the 1714 valance.

The lively repertoire of creatures and plants in the petticoat borders derives from tent-stitched pictures on canvas made in both England and New England. In these pictures flora and fauna are typically set within a complex scene whose ground plane is tipped up to display more of the landscape and activity (fig. 1). The petticoat borders and other related embroideries show details from the tent-stitched pictures, rearranged along a shallow and laterally extended ground plane. Evidence discovered in printed advertisements of the day suggests that shops and schools in the Boston area were responsible for the dissemination of these patterns.[10]

VTC

1 See Clayton, above, 14.

2 Ronald Rees, *Interior Landscapes: Gardens and the Domestic Environment* (Baltimore, 1993), 82.

3 Rowe 1973, 112. On crewel work, see also Susan Burrows Swan, *Plain & Fancy: American Women and Their Needlework, 1650–1850*, rev. ed. (Austin, Tex., 1995), 107–129.

4 Elizabeth Ann Coleman, David and Roberta Logie Curator of Textiles and Fashion Arts, Museum of Fine Arts, Boston, graciously explained some of the intricacies of crewelwork and its history to the author.

5 Rowe 1973, 102.

6 Rowe 1973, 121–122. The stitch is diagrammed in Rowe 1973, 119.

7 Rowe 1973, 122.

8 Rees 1993, 77–83.

9 Elizabeth Ann Coleman kindly identified these stitches for me. The flat stitch, like the self-couching, is common in American embroidery and uses very little wool on the reverse side. It is diagrammed in Rowe 1973, 119. The running, stem, and satin stitches are diagrammed in the *Anchor Manual of Needlework*, new ed. (Loveland, Colo., 1990), 53, 52, and 66.

10 Rowe 1973, 131–133.

American 18th Century, *Petticoat Border* (detail), eighteenth century, linen plain-weave, embroidered with wool, 21.6 x 193 cm (8 ½ x 76 in.), Museum of Fine Arts, Boston, John Wheelock Elliott Fund

Elmer G. Anderson / active c. 1935

42 Uree C. Fell Sampler

1935/1942 / watercolor, graphite, and gouache / 55.9 x 55.3 cm (22 x 21³/₄ in.)

Samplers are the needlework displays once created by young women to illustrate their command of fine stitchery; they often show the alphabet or inspirational verse. The practice was brought to America from Europe and may have originated, according to Betty Ring, "during the early Renaissance, possibly in a nunnery or at court [as part of] the formal education of women."[1] Samplers were produced in major colonial towns, such as Boston, during the seventeenth century and were widespread throughout the eighteenth and early nineteenth centuries, as they represented an element of the "accomplishments" that were the primary emphasis in the education of girls. The fine handwork of so many of these examples, even those made by relatively young girls, reflects the importance of the teachers under whose careful direction the samplers were produced. The research of Betty Ring has helped to bring about an understanding not only of regional currents in needlework, but also of the specific female academies (and often their instructresses) that favored certain subjects and motifs in their students' work.

By the 1830s and 1840s, samplers were no longer made in much of America, although this was not the case in Pennsylvania. The example now in the Mercer Museum of the Bucks County Historical Society was completed in 1846 by Uree C. Fell, a woman from Buckingham, Pennsylvania, when she was thirty years old.[2] It is of a late type, made from a soft, brightly colored wool thread known as Berlin yarn.[3] Variations of its floral motifs are found in earlier nineteenth-century samplers, many of Quaker origin.[4] Index artist Elmer Anderson chose to replicate the sampler's appearance by an unusual means, drawing white lines on a dark field to provide the illusion of the woven cotton background.

DC

Uree C. Fell (American, 1816–1883), *Sampler*, 1846, wool on cotton, 55.9 x 55.3 cm (22 x 21³/₄ in.), The Mercer Museum of the Bucks County Historical Society, Doylestown, Pennsylvania, Gift of Mrs. William F. Geil

1 Ring 1993, 1:8.

2 According to the genealogy of the Fell family (in the Spruance Library of the Bucks County Historical Society), Uree C. Fell was born on 28 December 1816 and died 24 June 1883. She married Abraham Geil in 1862; they had no children. It may seem surprising that she made a sampler when she was thirty years old, but Fell, who did not marry until she was forty-six, was probably considered a "spinster aunt" at the age of thirty and may have worked this embroidery as a teaching aid for a niece. Alternately, Fell may have been a school teacher who made this sample as a demonstration piece for her students.

3 *"This Work in Hand": Samplers from the Collection of the Bucks County Historical Society* [exh. pamphlet, The Mercer Museum of Bucks County Historical Society] (Spring 1977), no. 27: "Until the mid-19th century, wool, with the exception of the worsted crewel yarns, was rarely used for samplers. Then, technological developments originating in Germany allowed for the production of softer, brilliantly colored wools. These wools, excellent for sampler use, came to be known as Berlin yarn. Uree Fell's decorative work is a good example of the variety of shades and tones available to the needlewoman of the Victorian era."

4 Ring 1993, 290–291 and fig. 314.

·3/4·of·original·size··Elmer·G·Anderson

Martha Elliot / active c. 1935

43 **Adam and Eve**

1938 / watercolor over graphite / 48.9 x 38.1 cm (19 ¼ x 15 in.)

The subject of this embroidery was popular in both English and American needlework. Some of the earliest such samplers were from the Boston area and were based on British models that showed Adam and Eve facing front and standing on either side of a serpent-encircled tree, with varied creatures in the foreground.[1] These early examples were created in silk on linen.

The image recorded by Martha Elliot was executed several decades later. The Index data sheet notes that the creator was Mary Sarah Titcomb of the Boston area and that it was made in 1760. Unlike the earlier "Adam and Eve" embroideries, this piece is not a sampler but rather a pictorial needlework, in this case made from crewel, a worsted wool yarn, on linen. Betty Ring noted that "in the 1750s and 1760s, a growing number of women offered instruction in every variety of needlework. They produced a fascinating wealth of fishing lady pictures, embroideries on silk, and elegant coats of arms."[2] The Index example is one of a multitude of subjects that interested young needlewomen. It may have been based on a pattern book or print source, but its relative simplicity and the obvious familiarity of the story suggests it could just as easily have been created from the maker's imagination, although perhaps based on observed or remembered prototypes.

Adam and Eve was purchased by the Wadsworth Atheneum from a descendant of Mary Sarah Titcomb in 1934.

DC

1 Ring 1993, figs. 33–38.

2 Ring 1993, 53.

Mary Sarah Titcomb (born c. 1750), *Adam and Eve*, 1760, colored crewel on linen, 33 x 22.2 cm (13 x 8 ¾ in.), Wadsworth Atheneum Museum of Art, Hartford, Connecticut, Purchased from the Carrie Ida Pierce Fund and J. J. Goodwin Fund

Mae A. Clarke / active c. 1935

44 Quilt: "Birds in Air," or "Old Maid's Ramble"

1938 / watercolor, gouache, and graphite / 61.8 x 52.1 cm (24⁵/₁₆ x 20¹/₂ in.)

A nostalgic myth of remarkable endurance maintains that quilt-making began in America with colonial women frugally scavenging scraps of fabric to make inexpensive bed coverings. In fact, quilts were highly prized luxury items in this early period when cloth was so scarce that most people considered themselves fortunate to own more than one change of clothing. Blankets and bed-rugs were more commonplace household articles than quilted bed coverings, which were fairly rare and expensive. Only about fifteen documented American bed quilts from the eighteenth century survive today.[1] Quilts continued to rank as valuable chattels in the late eighteenth and early nineteenth centuries, when some quilters cut the animal, plant, and bird motifs from costly, imported chintz—possibly using worn curtains and bed hangings—and appliquéd them onto white backgrounds to create particularly sumptuous quilt tops.

It was the industrial revolution that democratized quilt-making as cotton became readily available and easily affordable. By 1814 the first textile mill had begun weaving cotton by machine, and by the 1820s and 1830s printed calicos were mass-produced in America, in addition to being imported.[2] As the nineteenth century progressed and the production of textiles expanded, quilters had ever-increasing choices of color schemes and, with less expensive cloth, enjoyed greater freedom to experiment in developing new patterns. Many women purchased cotton specifically to make their quilts rather than using leftover scraps. Since designing and sewing the quilt top and then stitching it to its backing demanded prolonged, exacting effort as well as great skill and artistry, quilts were still considered more valuable than blankets and woven coverlets. Often a woman would piece or appliqué a quilt top herself and then enlist friends and family to help with the actual quilting, which consists of sewing through the quilt top and its backing in order to join them, along with the batting that might be sandwiched between the two layers for added warmth. The delicacy and artistic qualities of this final stitching contribute greatly to a quilt's aesthetic value.

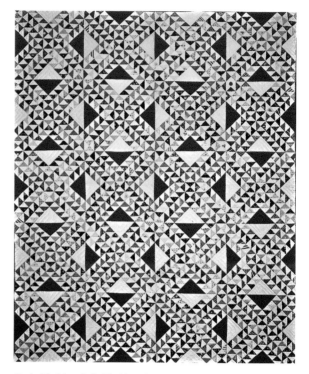

Probably Mrs. J. C. Ely (American, active c. 1865), *Quilt: "Birds in Air,"* or *"Old Maid's Ramble,"* 1865, printed cotton and cotton batting, 222.3 x 179.1 cm (87 ½ x 70 ½ in.), Brooklyn Museum of Art, Gift of Margaret S. Bedell

We can rarely be certain of the descriptive names early quilters may have given their patterns.[3] Often the names by which we refer to such designs were first published in late nineteenth-century women's periodicals. Today we may call the quilt in Mae A. Clarke's rendering "Birds in Air" or "Old Maid's Ramble," yet Mrs. J. C. Ely, probably the creator of the quilt, may have named it something else entirely.[4] Patterns like this one, which consists of many small triangles pieced together, date back to the eighteenth century and persist in popularity to this day.[5] Toward the middle of the nineteenth century this type of overall design without a central focus became most common.

Dating a quilt can be very difficult if the year of its creation is not actually inscribed on it. Ely stamped her name in ink on all four corners of the quilt's back, a standard practice in the nineteenth century, but her stamp did not include a date. When the name of a quilt's maker is known, genealogical research may help determine the quilt's date. Sometimes colors and fabrics help establish a range of years in which a quilt was likely made. The combination of Turkey red, indigo, and madder brown fabrics seems to appear frequently—but not exclusively—in quilts made during the 1830s to the 1860s, such as that of Caroline Lusk illustrated in cat. 45. In the case of Ely's quilt, curatorial files at the Brooklyn Museum indicate a date of 1865, although the reason for this date is not documented. Both Ely's and Lusk's quilts, along with about twenty others, were given to the Brooklyn Museum of Art in 1925 by Margaret S. Bedell of Catskill, New York.

VTC

1 Brackman 1989, 13–16.

2 On the effects of technology on the art of quilting, see Kiracofe 1993, 74–75.

3 See Barbara Brackman, "What's in a Name? Quilt Patterns from 1830 to the Present," in Lasansky 1988, 107–114.

4 See Barbara Brackman, *Encyclopedia of Pieced Quilt Patterns* (Paducah, Ky., 1993), 294–295.

5 Brackman 1989, 125.

Detail cat. 44

Jenny Almgren / 1881–1962

45 Caroline A. Lusk's Album Quilt

1938 / watercolor and gouache over graphite / 50.2 x 42 cm (19³/₄ x 16⁹/₁₆ in.)

During the 1840s many American quilters began to make a new type of quilt, one composed of multiple blocks with spaces provided for signatures of the friends, relatives, or fellow church members of either the quilt's maker or its recipient. This fashion coincided with the popularity of bound autograph albums—books in which friends would inscribe their names on blank pages, perhaps along with a bit of verse. As one quilt historian has observed, signed quilts were "literally album books in cloth."[1] Today these handsome bed coverings are known as single-pattern album or friendship quilts if the blocks have the same design, and as sampler album quilts if the designs differ.[2] In some cases they were made by a single quilter who, when her work was finished, would solicit the appropriate signatures for their designated spaces; in other instances the individual blocks were each made by a different quilter and later joined together.[3] The "album-quilt craze" apparently began in the mid-Atlantic region and soon worked its way south and then west. One of the most popular designs for album or friendship quilts throughout the United States was "Chimney Sweep," the pattern of the quilt rendered by Jenny Almgren for the Index of American Design.[4]

Three cultural developments in mid-nineteenth-century America are credited with fostering the popularity of album quilts: "the separation of American society along gender lines, America's westward expansion, and the rise of evangelical Protestantism."[5] The strong personal relationships that developed among women who were increasingly confined to the domestic realm, and their anguish over losing personal contact with friends and family migrating westward, were often expressed on album quilts in terms of the powerful religious sentiments of the day. These quilts reaffirmed precious but fragile communities.

The quilt in Almgren's rendering is clearly inscribed on its center block: "Miss / Caroline A. Lusk's Album Quilt / New Baltimore / Green County / New York / Pieced in the year 1847 / June 20th." The quilt may have been made by Lusk, or it may have been made by a friend or a group of friends and presented to her. All the blocks bear names; one is signed "Father 1847." Lusk's home town of New Baltimore is on the west bank of the Hudson River, not far north of Catskill, home to Margaret Bedell, the donor who presented this quilt to the Brooklyn Museum in 1925.

VTC

Possibly Caroline A. Lusk (American, active c. 1847), *Album Quilt*, 1847, printed cotton and cotton batting, 205.7 x 237.5 cm (81 x 93½ in.), Brooklyn Museum of Art, Gift of Margaret S. Bedell

1 Jane Bentley Kolter, *Forget Me Not: A Gallery of Friendship and Album Quilts* (Pittstown, N.J., 1985), 9.

2 Brackman 1989, 147–150.

3 Ricky Clark, "Mid-19th-Century Album and Friendship Quilts, 1860–1920," in Lasansky 1988, 77.

4 Kolter 1985, 15. For illustrations of this pattern in quilts from several states, see Kolter 1985, figs. 66, 68, 69, 75, 85.

5 Clark in Lasansky 1988, 79.

JENNYALMGREN

Textiles

CHARLOTTE ANGUS

Charlotte Angus / 1911–1989

46 Appliqué Sampler Quilt Top

1940 / watercolor over graphite / 42.7 x 50.6 cm (16^{13}/$_{16}$ x 19^{15}/$_{16}$ in.)

Sometimes many years passed before a quilt top was stitched to additional layers of cloth to complete it as a bed covering, and some quilt tops, for one reason or another, were never joined to their backings. Perhaps these works were abandoned when their quilters became overwhelmed by the many routine chores women performed in the nineteenth century. Charlotte Angus documented one of these unattached quilt tops in 1940. It belonged to her colleague on the Pennsylvania Index project, David Ellinger.[1]

This quilt top is appliquéd. Shapes cut from fabrics in various colors were arranged and sewn onto blocks of solid white cloth to create appealing designs. This technique differs from that used for the quilts illustrated in cats. 44 and 45, in which small pieces of cloth were sewn together to form patterns. These two methods, appliqué and piecing, have coexisted throughout the history of quilt-making in this country, although appliqué enjoyed its greatest popularity from 1840 to 1880. Quilt historian Barbara Brackman states, "if the quilt is the quintessential American folk art, appliqué is the characteristic American quilt."[2]

The quilt top in Angus' rendering was neither signed nor dated, but the brilliant color scheme of green and red with accents of yellow was extremely popular in the mid-nineteenth century, a fashion that seems to have diminished after the Civil War. The design motifs are also typical of this period. Four eagles—two green and two red—appear in the four corner blocks, and wreaths—each one at least slightly different—adorn the remaining twelve squares. It is a sampler quilt: nearly all the blocks have different designs and they are not signed.[3]

VTC

1 In a recent telephone conversation with the author, Ellinger explained that he sold the quilt about sixty years ago and, not surprisingly after so many years, cannot recall to whom. Ellinger is known today both for his own works of art and his antiques business in Pennsylvania.

2 Barbara Brackman, *Encyclopedia of Appliqué: An Illustrated, Numerical Index to Traditional and More Modern Patterns* (McLean, Va., 1993), 11.

3 Brackman 1989, 150.

Detail cat. 46

Arlene Perkins / active c. 1935

47 Appliqué Quilt: Black-Family Album

1941 / watercolor and gouache over graphite / 50.3 x 57.8 cm (19¹³⁄₁₆ x 22¾ in.)

This pictorial quilt is filled with images of plant and animal life, people, and places. Expressive in its detail, the quilt presents a narrative complete with five figures dressed in the delightful fabrics of the second half of the nineteenth century.[1] At first glance these figures, constructed of black cloth, appear to be silhouettes, but closer inspection reveals the embroidered detailing of the clothing and facial features. The figures are in fact African Americans, represented here in what appears to be a "Black-Family Album" quilt. The technique of embroidering physiognomic details on black cloth to portray African Americans is also seen in a quilt dated 1873, in which figures of both races are depicted together.[2] Another quilt, remarkably similar to the one in Perkins' rendering and presumably made by the same quilt-maker or by someone closely related, shares many of the Index quilt's otherwise unique motifs and its distinctive, scalloped border. This other quilt bears the embroidered signature and date, "Sarah Ann Wilson / 1854," and reportedly was made in New York or New Jersey.[3]

The man and woman with interlocking hands on the lower half of the quilt may be a wedding couple, as the flower stemming from their hands is a traditional marital symbol used in quilting. The man has what seems to be a pocket watch, denoted by white embroidery. The window-pane construction of the quilt holds many views of the abundant world the quilter inhabited. Fruit trees sway under the bounty of their harvest, carrying ripened and near-ripe fruit. A bird perches atop an inviting house, and flowers bloom in profusion. This specific and idiosyncratic quilt pays homage to the bounty of an African American family living in the second half of the nineteenth century. In 1941 it belonged to a woman in New York City, but its present location is unknown.

LR

1 Information gained from conversation with Karey Bresenhan, president of Quilts Inc., Houston, Texas, February 2002.

2 Kiracofe 1993, fig. 83.

3 Susanna Pfeffer, *Quilt Masterpieces* (New York, 1988), 56–57.

Esther Molina / 1895–1988

48 Crazy Quilt

1942 / watercolor over graphite / 45.7 x 35.7 cm (18 x 14 $^{1}/_{16}$ in.)

Crazy quilts, the colorful and lively textiles made from irregular patches of fabric artfully pieced together, were tremendously popular in the last decades of the nineteenth century. Sometimes the maker used fabrics of varying texture (such as silk or velvet) as well as a variety of patterns. The quilt pieces were often sewn together with contrasting, decorative stitching. Even though just a small portion of this quilt is illustrated, the Index data sheet provides a good deal of information on the object. Six by six feet (perhaps used as a parlor throw rather than as a bedspread), the quilt was made primarily from patches of silk. Its original owner, and perhaps the maker, was Jennie Hooper of San Antonio, Texas.

Molina's unfinished rendering demonstrates her method of layering watercolor over light pencil to create illusions such as the intricate crocheted or knitted border that decorates the quilt. With extreme delicacy of brushwork, the artist has also uncannily reproduced the threadbare areas of well-worn brown velvet. She appears to have used various means, such as abrasion and coatings, to prepare her paper.

DC

Detail cat. 48

Magnus S. Fossum / 1888–1980

49 Boston Town Coverlet

1941 / watercolor over graphite / 67.3 x 54.2 cm (26 ½ x 21 ⁵/₁₆ in.)

Magnus Fossum captured the complex, detailed weaving of this lively bedcover with a masterful touch. Produced around 1835, this piece reflects the technology invented in France by Joseph-Marie Jacquard (1752–1834) and introduced into this country in the 1820s: "The Jacquard mechanism was attached to the warp. As the weaver's shuttle carrying the crosswise yarns moved across the loom, the designated warp threads were lifted and the pattern began to emerge.... A skilled weaver could finish a coverlet in a day instead of a week, and it was possible to create endless varieties of designs composed of complicated curvilinear patterns...limited only by one's supply of (punched pattern) cards."[1]

A weaver could vary the design by reversing the border pattern cards for those of the central motifs. Cards could be purchased or traded and designs might be shared and transformed. Variations of this example from the Index, utilizing either a similar bird and vase of flowers motif, a border of buildings, or elements of both, have been discovered.[2] The Index data sheet identified the sites depicted around the edge of the "Boston Town" coverlet as well-known landmarks from that city, but one cannot ignore the tropical palm tree in the corner or the inclusion of a Chinese pagoda.

When Fossum depicted the coverlet, it was in the possession of a woman in Coconut Grove, Florida, who reported that it was said to have been made in Massachusetts; its present location is unknown. While the maker has not been identified, it is quite likely that the piece was created in Pennsylvania, rather than in New England or New York. Amelia Peck has noted "the Pennsylvania weaver's delightful use of many different colored wools in a single coverlet....The majority of Pennsylvania coverlets are striped with at least three colors of wool.... Traditional motifs such as stylized pairs of birds flanking a bush, tulips and vases of flowers, all of which are typical in German folk art, also set the coverlets apart."[3]

DC

1 Weissman and Lavitt 1987, 87.

2 See Weissman and Lavitt 1987, 97, for an example that may be from Ohio. See also Eliza Calvert Hall, *A Book of Hand-woven Coverlets* (Boston, 1931), ill. opposite page 177, an example possibly woven by Pennsylvania weaver Gabriel Miller. Yet another related work, from Historic Deerfield in Massachusetts, is illustrated in Ellen Paul Denker, *After the Chinese Taste: China's Influence in America, 1730–1930* (Salem, Mass., 1985), 25. The Winterthur Museum has in its collection a related piece by Lewis Weighly (died c. 1836), also a Pennsylvania weaver.

3 Amelia Peck, *American Quilts and Coverlets* [exh. cat., The Metropolitan Museum of Art] (New York, 1990), 151.

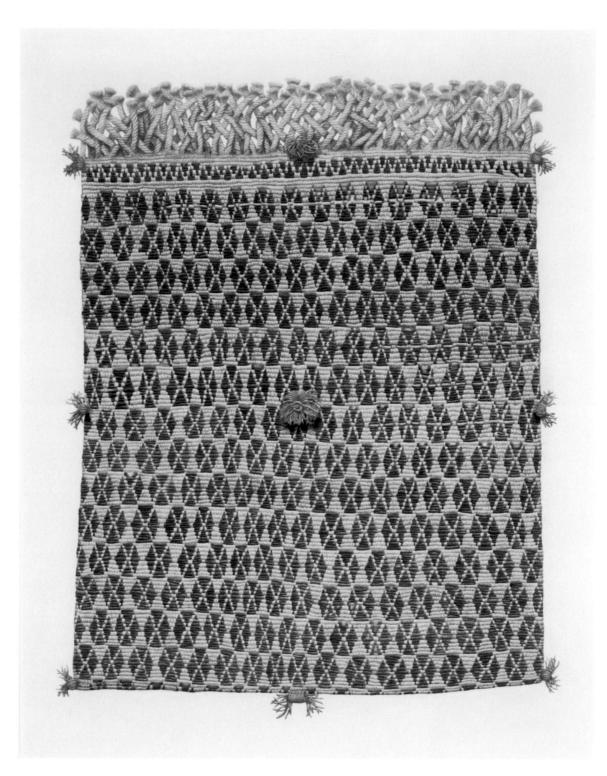

Flora G. Guerra / 1900–1989

50   Money Bag

1940 / watercolor over graphite / 34.9 x 25.5 cm (13³/₄ x 10¹/₁₆ in.)

This bag holds many mysteries. Its function is puzzling, since at a size of nine by twelve and one-half inches it is probably too large to have been a money bag.[1] Although it was at the Frontier Museum in Bandera, Texas, when Flora G. Guerra rendered it in 1940, its present location is unknown. The accompanying data sheet states that it was made by Señora Marcela Pepeda Ramirez in Zapata, Texas, about fifty miles south of Laredo on the Texas side of the Rio Grande. This, at least, seems plausible.[2] The data sheet dates the bag to 1826 and claims that it was made of mohair, but only one of these assertions can be correct.

Mohair-producing angora goats indeed thrive in Texas, as in few other locations in the United States, but they probably did not arrive there until the late nineteenth century. In the mid-nineteenth century, the Ottoman sultan, Abdulmecid I, sent nine angora goats to America as a gesture of gratitude to President James Polk, who had dispatched American agricultural experts to Constantinople to help farmers in present-day Turkey grow cotton more successfully. There is no evidence, however, that the descendants of these animals arrived in Texas for several decades.[3] The Spanish did have mohair before this time, and it is not impossible that some of this material reached Zapata from Spain before Mexico gained independence in 1821. If the bag was made of mohair, however, it is more likely that it was produced much later than 1826; if instead the date is correct, the bag was probably made of wool. Unfortunately, the bag is no longer available for analysis of its fiber content.

Despite all this uncertainty, it is a handsome artifact, beautifully designed and intricately woven, and Guerra's rendering is one of the masterpieces of the Index of American Design.

VTC

1   Cecelia Steinfeldt, curator emeritus at the San Antonio Museum, Texas, observed that the bag was probably too large to lend itself to holding coins; telephone conversation with the author, 2 May 2002.

2   I am grateful for Steinfeldt's verification that the bag could have been made in Zapata.

3   Brian J. May, agriculture department at Angelo State University, San Angelo, Texas, kindly told me about the introduction of mohair into the United States and its arrival in Texas; telephone conversation, 1 May 2002.

Detail cat. 50

Ethel Dougan / 1898–1976

51 Saddle Blanket

1939 / watercolor over graphite / 40.7 x 50.8 cm (16 x 20 in.)

In 1939 the saddle blanket portrayed in this rendering belonged to J. G. Trescony, owner of Rancho San Lucas in Monterey County, California.[1] According to its Index data sheet, the blanket was woven with hand-spun wool colored by native dyes and measured twenty-six by ninety-four inches.[2] Its present location is unknown. Since there was no blanket-weaving tradition among Native Americans in California, it is unlikely that Trescony's blanket was made in this region. It seems most closely related to a hybrid style of blanket-weaving that evolved through overlapping traditions among indigenous peoples and Hispanic settlers in northern New Mexico, along with significant influence from Mexico.[3] Like many other Index objects, this blanket may therefore have traveled far from its place of origin by the time it was rendered in the 1930s.

The Spanish brought sheep farming and wool to New Mexico in the early eighteenth century.[4] Initially it was the Pueblo Indians who learned to weave woolen textiles, but during the eighteenth century the Navajo began to dominate the production of blankets. The Navajo traded blankets not needed for their own purposes with other Native American tribes as well as with Spanish settlers; both groups were eager to acquire these textiles not just for their utility but for the extraordinary beauty of their designs. In the early nineteenth century the Spanish colonial government of New Mexico arranged for professional weavers from Mexico to train local Hispanic weavers, introducing them to complex Mexican textile patterns and generally elevating the quality of their blankets.[5] Following this training, and after Mexico's independence from Spain in 1821, the manufacture and trade of blankets increased in New Mexico, especially among Hispanic weavers whose productivity surpassed that of the Navajo by 1840.

The serrated zig-zag motif seen in Dougan's rendering probably originated in central or northern Mexico in the middle of the nineteenth century. It was one of the patterns used by Hispanic Mexican weavers for an intricately woven, splendidly ornamented garment known as the Saltillo serape. This handsome, dynamic pattern was eagerly appropriated by New Mexican weavers in the mid-nineteenth century.[6] Both Hispanic and Navajo weavers combined zig-zags, as well as other Saltillo patterns, with the bands of plain stripes that had characterized an earlier, simpler blanket style. The design of the saddle blanket in Dougan's rendering may have resulted from this particular pairing of designs. It is relatively simple in ornamentation and may have been intended primarily for utilitarian purposes rather than as an object for display or to serve the tourist trade.

By the late nineteenth century, blanket-weaving had greatly declined among Native American and Hispanic peoples in New Mexico. The effects of annexation by the United States in 1848 gradually began to be felt and inexpensive, factory-produced blankets became readily available. An influx of tourists to the area at this time, however, along with the advent of shrewd curio dealers serving as intermediaries between local weavers and clientele far outside the region, rejuvenated the art of blanket-weaving by creating new markets with demands for new stylistic elements.

VTC

1 Trescony's son, J. M. Trescony, now owns this ranch but does not specifically recall the saddle blanket. He explained that his father and grandfather did not seek to acquire such artifacts as collectors, but that there were nevertheless a number of intriguing objects at the ranch during his youth; telephone conversation, 12 May 2002.

2 Suzanne Baizerman, curator of decorative art, Oakland Museum, Oakland, California, observed that it probably would have been folded in half to arrive at about the customary size for saddle blankets (forty-eight by thirty inches) and that folding for this purpose was not unusual. E-mail, 2 May 2002.

3 The data sheets reported that the blanket had been made by "Avila, an Indian woman," who was described as a "skilled weaver living near the mission of San Antonio" in Jolon, but since such blankets were not woven in California, this information is probably incorrect. The data sheet also dates the saddle blanket to 1890. Archaeologists Robert L. Hoover and Gary Breschini in Monterey County indicate that the Avila family, who owned a ranch in the vicinity of the mission, were descendants of the Salinan tribe indigenous to this part of California, but that by the late nineteenth century the native peoples of this region had thoroughly adapted to Hispanic culture and that no member of the family would likely have been referred to as an "Indian woman"; e-mail and telephone conversations, 12 and 13 May 2002. The Avila family is also not remembered as having included any weavers. It is not impossible that a weaver from either New Mexico or Mexico made the two blankets while resident on the Avila ranch between 1880 and 1890.

4 For the history of blanket-weaving in New Mexico see Mera 1987; Lucero and Baizerman 1999; Jett 1976; and Weissman and Lavitt 1987, 212–231.

5 Lucero and Baizerman 1999, 14–16; Mera 1987, 22.

6 The Saltillo zig-zag motif was also adapted by the Mayo and Tarahumara tribes in northwestern Mexico (see Lucero and Baizerman 1999, 19 and plate 13).

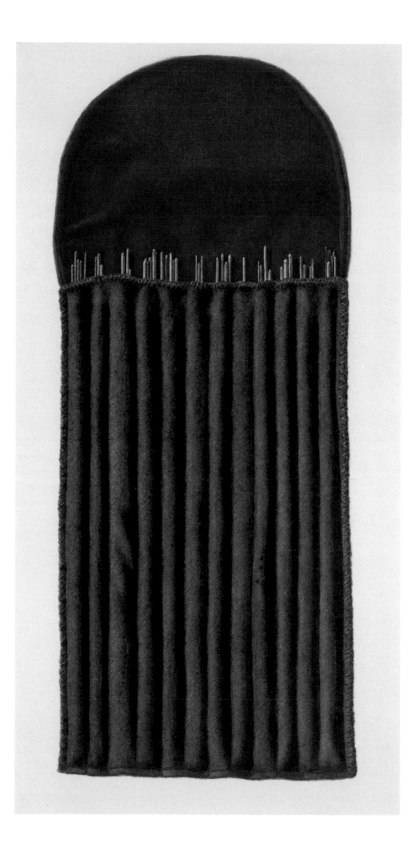

Elizabeth Moutal / active c. 1935

52 Shaker Knitting-Needle Case

1936 / watercolor over graphite / 37.7 x 26.1 cm (14 13/16 x 10 1/4 in.)

The Shaker religious philosophy is marked by an unwavering belief in the moral value of simplicity, and Shaker material culture functions as a "visual exhortation to conform to order and its attending moral virtues."[1] Believers crafted everything from architecture to the rungs on a ladder-back chair to express the value of uniformity and simplicity. Since material worldly objects were not to be idolized, practicality and usefulness were the key features of all items made and used in the Shaker community. Ornamental effects were strictly avoided; all objects were "relentlessly unadorned—causing Charles Dickens, a visitor to this community in 1842, to deride the buildings as no more sightly than English factories or barns."[2] The celibate sect focused on creating an environment of cleanliness, equality, and balance. Protecting their surroundings from disorder allowed the Shakers to follow the wisdom of their aphorism, "Put your hands to work, and your hearts to God, and a blessing will attend you."[3]

This Shaker needle case, rendered for the Massachusetts project by Elizabeth Moutal, is simple and unadorned in keeping with the ideals of the faith. Needle cases from "the world" beyond Shaker borders were often decorated with embroidery or colorful patterning. This case, made of broadcloth and lined with flannel, caused no distraction by idle pleasure for the knitter who stored her needles in it.

The needle case held in excess of sixty thin metal needles used for the intricate and exacting knitting for which the Shakers were known. Needles used by the sisters were purchased from the "world," because the Shaker elders realized the practical value of purchasing items that would be costly and inordinately difficult to make. Men and women were separate but equal, yet the task of knitting fell under the domestic duties of the female Shakers, while the men were responsible for farming and various other manual labors. At the time of its rendering this needle case was owned by Faith and Edward D. Andrews, early collectors of Shaker artifacts.[4] It is currently in the collection of Hancock Shaker Village in Pittsfield, Massachusetts.

LR

1 Sally M. Promey, *Spiritual Spectacles: Vision and Image in Mid-Nineteenth-Century Shakerism* (Indianapolis, Ind., 1993), 70.

2 Sprigg and Larkin 1987, 54.

3 Sprigg and Larkin 1987, 110.

4 See Stillinger, above, 47–48.

George V. Vezolles / 1894–1973

53 Shaker Rug with a Horse

1937 / watercolor over graphite / 53.4 x 60 cm (21 x 23⁵/₈ in.)

"Shaker sisters in all communities were heavily involved with textiles, from preparing thread and cloth, to cutting and sewing clothing, to making household textiles, including coverlets, sheets, towels, tapes for tying, and carpets."[1] A prime example of the sisters' mastery of textile work is this Shaker hooked-type shirred rug, which was made in the western Kentucky community of Pleasant Hill. Dated c. 1875, it fits into the stylistic traditions of the Shaker movement with only a few deviations. A scalloped border encircles the rectangular center, which features the image of a horse. "The definitive Shaker touch" is present in the thick, braided border.[2] A sense of order and balance pervades the composition, in keeping with the ideals of the religion. The portrayal of the horse is uncommon and somewhat unprecedented in Shaker design, as the Shakers discouraged representational art.[3]

The hooked-type rug was not a Shaker invention; derived from the American folk-art tradition of hooking, it was adapted by the Shakers in communities such as Pleasant Hill. Although not exactly a rag rug, "A hooked rug is made by drawing yarn or narrow cloth strips through a backing with a hook, creating a raised or pile surface on one side."[4] This rug combines the qualities of hooking and shirring. The shirring creates a higher pile on the surface than the technique of hooking. Dollar mats, small, round pieces of wool or cotton cut with a device resembling a hole puncher, are strung on a thread and tacked to the main surface to create a "caterpillar," a noticeably raised portion of the design. In this particular rug the horse is made of dollars folded in fourths. The pragmatic Shaker sisters were innovative and used old mattress ticking as the backing for this and many other rugs, an early example of the rural necessity of re-use. Utilitarian yet beautiful, this rug shows the fine attention to detail of an experienced rug-maker. The uniting of various elements of style and design in this particular rug expresses the intricacies of the Shaker religion, which was built on simplicity, yet dominated by a complexity of belief and skill.

LR

1 Sprigg and Larkin 1987, 188.

2 Gordon 1980, 123.

3 Gordon 1980, 121.

4 Gordon 1980, 112.

American 19th Century, *Shaker Rug with a Horse*, c. 1875, cotton and wool, 104.1 x 92.1 cm (41 x 36 ¼ in.), The Shaker Village of Pleasant Hill, Harrodsburg, Kentucky

Max Fernekes / 1905–1984

54 Child's Dress

1937 / watercolor over graphite / 67.9 x 49.1 cm (26³/₄ x 19⁵/₁₆ in.)

The owner of this dress, granddaughter of the child for whom it was made and great-granddaughter of the woman who made it, dated it 1862, presumably based on family history.[1] Fernekes rose to the challenge of reproducing the garment, crisply contrasting the rich black velvet of the buttons and striped decoration and the delicate lace trim, with the muted but varied colors of the patterned wool challis. To increase the saturation of the darkest elements in this image, he added additional medium to the pigments that is detectable in the glossy appearance of these areas.

DC

1 The owner was Mrs. A. H. Weber of Whitefish Bay in Milwaukee, Wisconsin, who also collected dolls. The present-day location of the dress and the dolls is not known. Shelly Foote, costume curator, NMAH, SI, agreed that the dress could be from the 1860s, adding that this "would also correspond to the yoke trim," but felt a date closer to 1867 than to 1862 might be more accurate; e-mail to the author, 28 February 2002.

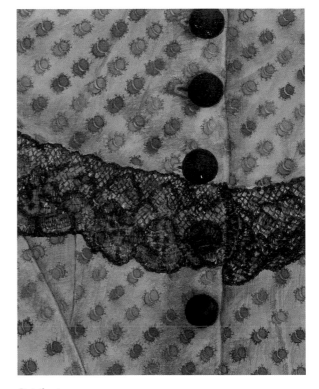

Detail cat. 54

Molly Bodenstein / 1902–1971

55 Doll

1938 / watercolor and gouache over graphite / 54.2 x 35.1 cm (21 $^5/_{16}$ x 13 $^{13}/_{16}$ in.)

The original documentation of this doll demonstrates the difficulties inherent in the limited knowledge available to researchers some sixty years ago. Often the Index data sheets provide indispensable information regarding the origins or use of an object, but sometimes the assumed or handed-down family history is inaccurate or incomplete.

While the data sheet for this doll lists a date of 1755–1765, the doll was probably made in the first quarter of the nineteenth century.[1] The lathe-turned wooden head indicates the late form of a type used in England from the late seventeenth century. On this example, the triangular wooden nose and the glass eyes were inserted into the wooden head, which was covered with a layer of gesso and then painted. A wooden doll of this type would generally have a tapering torso, here probably padded for a more childlike form.[2] Later versions, such as the one shown here, had arms and legs made of cloth or leather (in this case, kid) that were nailed on.

Although the Index information sheet indicates that the doll was clothed in its "original cotton printed dress," several authorities agree that the costume appears much more recent than the doll itself and may even be a twentieth-century collector's creation using late nineteenth-century fabric.[3]

Thus far, nothing is known about Annie Ruth Cole of Petersburg, Virginia, or what became of her collection of "authentic Amer. Dolls" described in Index records.

DC

1 The dating and other information concerning the doll was kindly provided by Elizabeth Ann Coleman, David and Roberta Logie Curator of Textiles and Fashion Arts, Museum of Fine Arts, Boston; correspondence with Virginia Clayton, 22 January 2002.

2 Coleman correspondence, 22 January 2002.

3 Shelly Foote, costume division, NMAH, SI, agrees that the clothing is later than the doll: "Claudia [Claudia Kidwell, costume curator, NMAH, SI] suggests that it was done in the twentieth century (hence lack of knowledge) using nineteenth-century fabric"; e-mail, 28 February 2002. Coleman writes that "the fabric looks later—1840–1880 period. Collectors historically have used old materials, but not always old material appropriate to the age of a doll." She describes in detail the areas in which the maker has missed the appropriate costume construction; correspondence, 22 January 2002.

Yolande Delasser / active c. 1935

56 Revolutionary Soldier

1939 / watercolor over graphite / 52 x 35.9 cm (20½ x 14⅛ in.)

Index artists of the New York project depicted a number of objects from the American Folk Art Gallery, the now legendary antique shop of Edith Halpert and Holger Cahill.[1] Works such as the revolutionary soldier, which Halpert found in New York in 1931, were included in exhibitions throughout the decade of the 1930s, an era of rediscovery and popularization of American folk art.[2] Electra Havemeyer Webb, founder of the Shelburne Museum and one of Halpert's most dedicated clients, purchased the piece in 1941.

This carving, likely from the early nineteenth century, may have been a child's toy and is probably part of a set. It is made from pine; the body and base are from a single piece of wood, with a movable head set into the neck socket and the arms loosely screwed on. The soldier was covered with gesso before painting.

DC

1   Tepfer 1989, 163–186.

2   According to Henry Joyce and Sloan Stephens in *American Folk Art at the Shelburne Museum* (Shelburne, Vt., 2001), 26, the work was found in 1931. Shelburne Museum records state "found in New York."

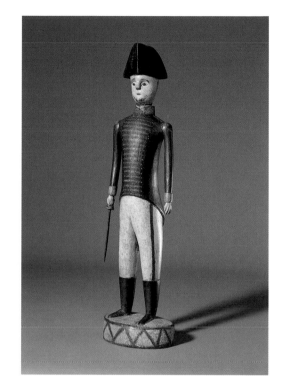

American 19th Century, *Revolutionary Soldier*, early nineteenth century, painted pine, 66 x 17.2 cm (26 x 6 ¾ in.), Shelburne Museum, Shelburne, Vermont

Mina Lowry / 1894–1942

57 Toy Horse

1939 / watercolor over graphite / 30.6 x 40.8 cm (12 1/16 x 16 1/16 in.)

This engaging toy horse was depicted three times by Index artists. The version by Lowry imparts more of the life and power of its small subject than the other renderings.[1] At the time it was documented by the Index, the carved creature was at Halpert and Cahill's American Folk Art Gallery. Many of the most important collectors of nonacademic art, including Abby Aldrich Rockerfeller, Electra Havemeyer Webb, and Edgar William and Bernice Chrysler Garbisch, turned to Halpert when forming their collections. Her wooden horse would appear frequently as an iconic folk art object in exhibitions beginning in the 1930s. It is now in the American Folk Art Museum, New York, the promised gift of Ralph Esmerian.

The spotted horse was found in Carlisle, Pennsylvania, one of several similar pieces created by an unidentified carver in the Cumberland County area.[2] From joined pieces of poplar, the maker created a marvelous, compact form of simplicity and swelling curves.

DC

American 19th Century, *Toy Horse*, c. 1860–1890, painted poplar, 29.9 x 31.4 cm (11 3/4 x 12 3/8 in.), American Folk Art Museum, New York, Promised Gift of Ralph Esmerian

1   All three Index renderings, one anonymous, one by Arsen Maralian, and another version by Lowry, bear the same data sheet number. The purpose of the multiple renderings is not known.

2   Exh. cat. New York 2001, 456. A nearly identical horse is in the collection of the Winterthur Museum.

Elizabeth Fairchild / active c. 1935

58 Rocking Horse

1938 / watercolor with white heightening over graphite / 31.5 x 50 cm (12 $\frac{3}{8}$ x 19 $^{11}/_{16}$ in.)

According to the Index data sheet, this horse was found near Lancaster, Pennsylvania, and was believed to be Pennsylvania German in origin. Although hobby horses from both Germany and England were imported to America, particularly in the second half of the nineteenth century, there are no characteristics that mark this toy as German in origin.

The graceful, elongated rockers emulate those seen on European models and follow "the design of bow rocker adopted in America…invariably English in origin with a central platform adjoining slim bows tapered at the ends and rounded off." This example, "like English models…was attached at the hooves to the outside of the rockers."[1] The sprightly, well-balanced steed already had a replaced tail, mane, and ears when it was recorded in watercolor. The maker cleverly carved a saddle onto the horse's back, giving it a sleek and practical design. In 1938 the rocking horse was in the Early American Shop in New York City; its present location is unknown.

DC

1 Patricia Mullins, *The Rocking Horse: A History of Moving Toy Horses* (London, 1992), 220.

Mina Lowry / 1894–1942

59 Rocking Horse

1941 / watercolor over graphite / 39 x 58.2 cm (15 3/8 x 22 15/16 in.)

This rocking horse is an early, somewhat crude example by a maker who would eventually become very well known in his field.[1] The single block of pine from which the body is carved is evident in the horse's simplified torso. The head and neck, carved from another block of wood, were attached with glue and the connection reinforced with iron plates. The animal's legs are straight and sturdy, rather than graceful and naturalistic. Burned with hot dies into the underside of the horse's body is the inscription: B.P. CRANDALL / 47 COURTLANDT ST. N.Y.

By consulting city directories from the period, we are able to place Benjamin Potter Crandall's workshop at the above address between 1853 and 1856. With his sons, Charles Thompson Crandall and William Edwin Crandall, joining him, the Crandall firm invented and manufactured rocking horses well into the twentieth century.[2]

DC

1   The rocking horse came from the antique shop of Helena Penrose and J. H. Edgette, yet the object's current location is unknown.

2   Patricia Mullins, *The Rocking Horse: A History of Moving Toy Horses* (London, 1992), 257–258.

Drawing on America's Past

Charles Henning / active c. 1935

60 Toy Locomotive: The "Grand Duke"

1940 / watercolor over graphite / 37.5 x 48.5 cm (14³/₄ x 19¹/₁₆ in.)

This toy locomotive was made by the Ives, Blakeslee and Williams Company of Bridgeport, Connecticut, one of the world's largest manufacturers of mechanical clockwork toys in the late nineteenth century, as well as one of the most inventive.[1] The "Grand Duke," the company's finest toy locomotive, was named to commemorate a visit by Grand Duke Alexis of Russia to Bridgeport in 1870.[2] Although the factory stenciled the name on the side of each "Grand Duke" it produced, this particular locomotive's aristocratic moniker, along with much of its paint, had chipped or peeled away before Charles Henning recorded the image for the Index of American Design.

Ives, Blakeslee and Williams sold its wares exclusively to toy dealers through wholesale catalogues. First made around 1880, the "Grand Duke" still appeared in the 1893 catalogue, described as "the largest mechanical toy locomotive made...21 inches long.... A fine show piece. Sure to sell."[3] Its wholesale cost, which included a bell on top, was $48 per dozen; without the bell, it was $45 per dozen. The retail price would have been about $5 for each—an expensive toy in the 1890s. The locomotive was primarily made of tin, with wheels of cast iron, the eagle in front of gilded lead, and the clockwork spring attached to the rear axle made of brass. When this spring was wound tight with a key, the rear wheels turned, driving the locomotive forward. The "Grand Duke," like other early toy trains, ran along the floor rather than on tracks. The model depicted for the Index by Charles Henning in 1940 was still in working condition. It was then in the antique shop of Helena Penrose and J. H. Edgette, but its present location is unknown.

Prior to the industrial revolution, children's toys were often handcrafted by their parents, but in the second half of the nineteenth century these made-at-home amusements had to compete for children's affections with mass-produced, mechanical playthings. Almost as soon as the railroads began to spread throughout the countryside in the 1840s, toy trains became a favorite novelty in great demand among children.[4] George W. Brown, a clock-maker in Forestville, Connecticut, made the first wind-up toy in 1856, and Ives, Blakeslee and Williams was soon designing and manufacturing both the greatest variety and the most innovative of these devices.[5] The factory was located beside the railroad tracks in Bridgeport, where the Housatonic and New Haven trains rolled by at frequent intervals. The real steam locomotives of the day, like the toys, were brightly painted and their names were prominently inscribed on them.[6]

VTC

1 Hertz 1950, 32–33. I am grateful to Jan Athey, librarian at the National Toy Train Museum in Strasbourg, Pennsylvania, for generously providing information, photocopies, and bibliography on the history of this toy locomotive.

2 Hertz 1956, 39. Henning's rendering of the *Toy Locomotive* appeared on the cover of this book.

3 *Ives, Blakeslee & Williams Co., Manufacturers: Iron Toys, Wood Toys, Tin Toys, Games and Novelties* (New York, 1893), 21.

4 *Toys and Games: Imaginative Playthings from America's Past* (Alexandria, Va., 1991), 139, 152–153.

5 Hertz 1950, 17.

6 Hertz 1956, 38–39.

Philip Johnson / active c. 1935

61 Toy Wagon

1939 / watercolor with gouache and white heightening over graphite / 32.8 x 48.8 cm (12^{15}/$_{16}$ x 19^{3}/$_{16}$ in.)

Emblazoned with its place and date of origin, this tin toy wagon not only served a child's fancy but also provided an advertisement for the Philadelphia merchant who sold it. The wagon appears to have been made by the firm of Francis, Field & Francis, a Philadelphia toy manufacturer working in the early 1860s; the style and construction of the wagon are strikingly similar to other tin wagons made by the firm at that time.[1] Francis, Field & Francis, later absorbed into the more famous James Fallows and Company, sold wagons of this kind at wholesale prices to merchants who would then label them with their name, specialty, and location.

This tin wagon is pulled by two horses that are mounted on small iron wheels set in front of the four main wheels. Other wagons, carriages, and carts produced by Francis, Field & Francis during this time included a small tin figure of a driver seated beneath the awning of the carriage. As these figures were often removable, this wagon had unfortunately lost its driver by 1939, the year of its inclusion in the Index. This object was in the Helena Penrose and J. H. Edgette antique shop in New York City at the time of its rendering (fig. 1); its present location is unknown.

LR

1 For photographs of similar Francis, Field & Francis and James Fallows tin wagons and a brief description, see Barenholtz and McClintock 1980, 80–95.

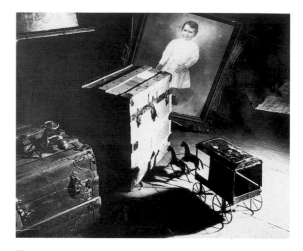

Fig 1

Toy wagon in Penrose and Edgette Shop, National Gallery of Art, Washington, Gallery archives

Edward L. Loper / born 1916

62 Toy Bank: Speaking Dog

1939 / watercolor with white heightening over graphite / 26.7 x 35.6 cm (10½ x 14 in.)

Mechanical toy banks, first manufactured in the late nineteenth and early twentieth centuries, combined the excitement of a toy with a lesson on the virtue of thrift. Children would stash away then valuable pennies in a cast-iron device that could chirp, sing, and swing at the insertion of a coin.[1] Complete with fairytale stories and patriotic images, mechanical banks reflected the values of the times in which they were made. An icon of the mechanical bank set, the *Speaking Dog* was patented in 1885 by the Shepard Brothers of Buffalo, New York.[2] This cleverly designed cast-iron bank became extremely popular soon after its introduction. Lighthearted in design and motif, it avoids much of the negative racial stereotyping and social parody prevalent in mechanical banks made in the last quarter of the nineteenth century. Depressing the lever next to the dog causes the girl's arm to swing back, dropping the coin that rests on the tray into the slot beside her. As the coin falls, the dog's mouth opens as if issuing a bark and his tail wags in excitement.[3] Although many examples of this toy bank have survived, this particular bank, privately owned in 1939, has not been identified.

LR

1 For a brief discussion of mechanical bank history and collecting, see "A Penny Saved: Collection of American Cast-iron Mechanical Banks Made before 1900," *Art and Antiques* 8 (January 1991), 19.

2 Patent records, 1885, NMAH, SI.

3 For photographs of various banks and information on the importance of cast iron in the design of mechanical banks, see *Toys and Games: Imaginative Playthings from America's Past* (Alexandria, Va., 1991).

Albert Rudin / active c. 1935

63 Roller Skates

1941 / watercolor with white heightening over graphite / 27.5 x 42.7 cm (10¹³⁄₁₆ x 16¹³⁄₁₆ in.)

The sport of roller skating was invented in Europe during the 1760s but was not introduced in America until the late 1830s. Created to provide the activity and exercise of the winter sport of ice skating, the early roller skate was of an in-line construction designed to imitate the formation of the ice-skate blade.[1] Pre-1863 American roller skates like the ones represented in this rendering were copied directly from ice-skate models of the time and featured either rubber or wooden wheels. According to the data sheet for the rendering, this specific pair of skates had an iron frame, hard rubber and wooden wheels, and leather straps. On the front wheel of the foreground skate, the words "Goodyear Pat." are visible, but the patent number is hidden by the part of the skate that holds the wheel. The back wheel is inscribed "1844–1858."

The in-line formation of early skates was abandoned in 1863 when James Plimpton invented the "guidable parlor skate," which was composed of a rocking-action steering mechanism; this new skate subsequently revolutionized the skating industry.[2] Skates such as the one represented in the rendering were replaced with four-wheel axle models capable of more precise breaking and steering. The skates in the rendering were owned by the Chicago Historical Society at the time of their inclusion in the Index project and are still in that collection today.

LR

1 Micheal Brooslin, *The First Fifty Years: American Roller Skates 1860–1910* (Lincoln, Nebr., 1983), 1.

2 Andrea Chesman, ed., *The Inventive Yankee: From Rockets to Roller Skates, 200 Years of Yankee Inventors & Inventions* (Dublin, N.H., 1989), 66.

Detail cat. 63

Albert Rudin.

Selma Sandler / active c. 1935

64 Partial Set of Nine Pins

1935/1942 / watercolor over graphite / 32.2 x 42.5 cm (12^{11}/$_{16}$ x 16^{3}/$_{4}$ in.)

The medieval indoor bowling game of nine pins, trace-able to AD 1200, was a popular pastime in nineteenth-century American life.[1] Introduced into the colonies by Dutch and English settlers, the game was outlawed by the austere Puritans around the middle of the seventeenth century, only to be revived later. The pins used for the game were rarely as detailed and anthropomorphic as this partial set. Remarkable in its attention to physiognomy, the set is believed to have been created by a Pennsylvania German artisan during the nineteenth century. Carved in the round of pine wood, covered with gesso, and then painted, each boot-shaped pin shows a distinct personality. The detailed coifs, skin color, and gender point to the attentive quality of a skilled craftsman. Once belonging to the collection of Juliana Force, founding director of the Whitney Museum of American Art, New York, this partial set was included in the first American folk sculpture exhibition held at the Newark Museum in 1931 [2]

LR

1 Henry Joyce and Sloane Stephens, *American Folk Art at the Shelburne Museum* (Shelburne, Vt., 2001), 6. I am grateful to Julie Edwards, formerly of the Shelburne Museum, for information on the history of nine pins.

2 For an extended discussion on folk sculpture as regarded in 1931, see exh. cat. Newark 1931.

American 19th Century, *Partial Set of Nine Pins*, nineteenth century, painted pine, 31.1 cm (12 ¼ in.), Shelburne Museum, Shelburne, Vermont

John Matulis / 1910–2000

65 Sign of the Bull's Head

1940 / watercolor and gouache over graphite / 55.1 x 40.6 cm (21 ^{11}/$_{16}$ x 16 in.)

The Connecticut Historical Society has sixty-six tavern signs in its collection, the largest group of such objects known.[1] Fourteen of these were reproduced in watercolor renderings made by Index artists more than sixty years ago, the signs' importance as historical artifacts clearly understood even then. At that time, the works were part of the collection of Morgan Brainard (1878–1957), having been gathered by him beginning in the 1910s; they were often purchased by Brainard from descendants of the original owners.[2] Brainard's collection was added to some dozen signs previously in the Historical Society's collection, and more recent examples were acquired by the society in the last decades of the twentieth century.

In her recent publication, Susan Schoelwer points out that there were ten thousand licensed establishments in the state of Connecticut offering food and lodging to the public between 1750 and 1850.[3] Each was required by law to be identified by a sign. These large numbers also applied to other states, but only a minute fraction of signs have survived to this day. The sign of the bull's head had been used to identify more than one establishment. Originally it advertised an inn belonging to Capt. Aaron Bissell (1722–1787), one of two brothers who were tavern owners in the vicinity of East Windsor (today part of South Windsor), Connecticut. Bissell's choice of the bull's head probably reflects his pride in the successful agricultural endeavors of the family through the years. The date of 1760, visible below the year 1797 on the sign's pediment, recalls the initial date of Captain Bissell's innkeeping business, but the sign's form suggests that it was constructed a decade or two later. The second owner of the sign, John Alderman (1768–1856), probably acquired it from Aaron Bissell Jr. (1761–1834) around 1804. The date of 1797 marks the opening of Alderman's tavern operation in East Windsor.[4]

DC

1 This collection is documented in detail and tavern signs are thoroughly discussed in exh. cat. Hartford 2000.

2 See biography by Ellsworth Grant in exh. cat. Hartford 2000, 179–180.

3 Schoelwer in exh. cat. Hartford 2000, 2.

4 Exh. cat. Hartford 2000, cat. 7.

John Matulis / 1910–2000

Sign for R. Angell's Inn

1939 / watercolor and gouche over graphite / 65.5 x 49.6 cm (25 $^{13}/_{16}$ x 19 $^{1}/_{2}$ in.)

Susan P. Schoelwer has characterized tavern and inn signs as "the public art of everyday life" in early America, the art that was most widely visible and shared by all members of society.[1] The popular imagery broadcast by signs is often symptomatic of wider cultural phenomena, allowing us to glean valuable historical information from signs if we perceive them—like other visual arts—as "the tip of a cultural iceberg."[2] The eagle on R. Angell's 1808 sign, for example, may offer pictorial evidence of Americans' eagerness to establish a distinct national identity for the United States during the early years of our republic. Prior to the late eighteenth and early nineteenth centuries, the figures on American tavern and inn signs were usually derived from European precedents. Perhaps manifesting America's growing nationalism in the early nineteenth century, the sign for R. Angell's inn brandished a version of the Great Seal of the United States, a patriotic emblem adopted by the nation in 1782. Featuring a spread-winged eagle holding an olive branch and a clutch of arrows, with a shield bearing one stripe for each state in the Union, variations of the Great Seal motif appeared frequently on tavern and inn signs at this time.[3] In one departure from the iconography of the Great Seal, the eagle on R. Angell's sign grasps an anchor rather than arrows. Since an anchor is an important part of the state seal of Rhode Island, this may indicate that the sign was made for an inn located in that state.[4] Early nineteenth-century tavern and inn signs, along with other types of American art, often aligned state and local insignia with national heraldic imagery as part of the ongoing effort to construct a unified national entity from a diverse collection of regional cultures.[5]

The vertical format of R. Angell's sign and the prominence of its pictorial rather than textual element are typical of signs made in America before the mid-nineteenth century, before the quickening pace of life and vehicular traffic made horizontal signs with large, easy-to-read lettering more practical.[6] As is frequently the case with early signs, this sign has also been repainted once or twice. The ghosts of earlier letters are emerging from beneath the weathered surface of the most recent paint film. The peculiar shape of the eagle

American 19th Century, *Sign for R. Angell's Inn*, 1808, painted wood, iron hardware, 72.4 x 45.1 cm (28 ½ x 17 ¾ in.), The Connecticut Historical Society, Hartford, Connecticut

and the idiosyncratic interpretation of a classical pediment at the top of the board have made R. Angell's sign a folk-art favorite, a validation of many Americans' notion of what such art should look like. This sign was part of the Morgan B. Brainard collection in Hartford, Connecticut, when it was rendered in 1939.

VTC

1 Schoelwer in exh. cat. Hartford 2000, 11.

2 Wolf in exh. cat. Hartford 2000, 14.

3 Wolf in exh. cat. Hartford 2000, 16–18; Vincent in exh. cat. Hartford 2000, 42–43; and Finlay in exh. cat. Hartford 2000, 59–61.

4 Although T. C. Stapleton found the sign in a garret in Brooklyn, Connecticut, around 1926, it may have been used for Richard Angell's Inn in Providence, Rhode Island (see exh. cat. Hartford 2000, 203–204).

5 Wolf in exh. cat. Hartford 2000, 18.

6 This evolution in design is discussed by Wolf in exh. cat. Hartford 2000, 21; Zimmerman in exh. cat. Hartford 2000, 24–25; and Vincent in exh. cat. Hartford 2000, 49–52.

John H. Tercuzzi / active c. 1935

67 Shop-Sign Spectacles

1941 / watercolor over graphite / 32.5 x 58.6 cm ($12^{13}/_{16}$ x $23^{1}/_{16}$ in.)

According to the Index data sheet, these spectacles once hung outside a jewelry store in Poughkeepsie, New York. Signs of this type would also have identified an optician's or optometrist's office. Instantly recognizable from a distance, commercial symbols such as this one were used from the earliest years of this country well into the twentieth century, until they were supplanted by the flashier properties of electric lighting.

Many early hanging signs were carved from wood. These eyeglasses, however, are fashioned from zinc tubing and may have been mass-produced. Oval inserts of sheet zinc are set halfway into the frames and display painted eyes both front and back. Similar in form and size is a sign in the collection of the Abby Aldrich Rockefeller Folk Art Collection. A trade catalogue, *E. G. Washburne & Co., Manufacturers of Optical and Jewelers Signs*, also illustrates a comparable "spectacle sign." Produced in nine sizes, the twenty-four inch variety (the approximate size of the sign depicted by Tercuzzi) was available for $6.25.[1] Such signs, with their staring, inescapable eyes, sometimes project an eeriness that belies their simple function as advertisements. F. Scott Fitzgerald used an oculist's sign, the "eyes of Doctor T. J. Eckleburg," as a recurring symbol in *The Great Gatsby*.

DC

1   New York, undated, page 8, Halpert Cushing Papers, NMAH, SI. Known in the Index files only through a photocopy, the exact source of this citation remains unclear.

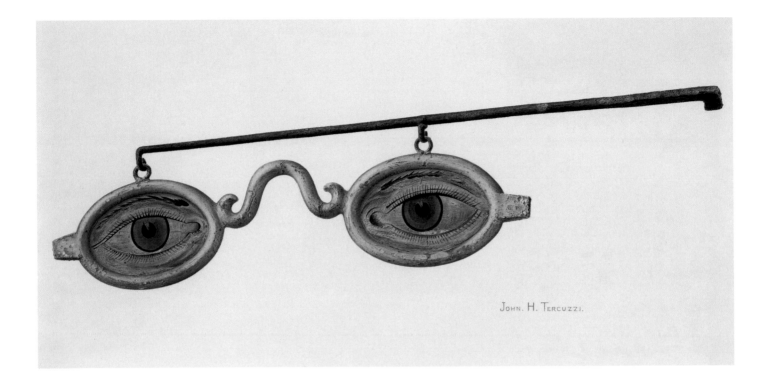

John. H. Tercuzzi.

Trade Signs and Figures

Ingrid Selmer-Larsen / active c. 1935

68 William Bliss Sled

1937 / watercolor over graphite / 37.2 x 27.1 cm (14⅝ x 10¹¹/₁₆ in.)

This sled was in the Wells Historical Museum in 1937 and today is part of the collection of Old Sturbridge Village in Massachusetts. It is notable for its odd blend of styles, its small dimensions, and its mysterious function. Lacking metal blades or runners, the sled was not made for speed or serious sport but was likely either a toy or a shop sign.[1] Crafted of wood and painted red with the inscription, "Wm Bliss 1840," this sled is modeled after a high-speed sled known as a Clipper.[2] If used as a sign, as the four mounting holes in the deck seem to indicate, the merchant or maker may have been advertising the Clipper as the type of sled he crafted or sold.[3] The style of the stenciled inscription is of the shop-sign variety, complete with the block letters and shadowing used to draw the eye in from afar. It is likely that the inscription, William Bliss, refers to the craftsman or merchant, and the date could indicate the year the business was established. The lack of paint chipping on the wooden blades of the sled seems to preclude the possibility of its use as a toy; a child would have pulled it along on the ground just like a full-size sled. If it was used as a sign, it was evidently not mounted outdoors for any extended period of time as the paint surface on the deck is not severely weathered. The business directories for cities in Massachusetts in the year 1840 list no maker or merchant by the name of William Bliss, leaving the true origin of this small sled a mystery.

LR

American 19th Century, *William Bliss Sled*, 1840, painted wood, 50.8 x 25.4 cm (20 x 10 in.), Old Sturbridge Village, Sturbridge, Massachusetts

1 David Shayt, museum specialist, cultural history, NMAH, SI, first suggested this was a doll-size sled; conversation, 12 December 2001.

2 For photographs, illustrations, and diagrams of various Clipper sleds, see Joan Palicia, *Flexible Flyer and Other Great Sleds for Collectors* (Atglen, Pa., 1997).

3 Frank G. White, curator of mechanical arts, Old Sturbridge Village, pointed out that the holes in the deck of the sled indicate a past wall mounting. He discussed the lack of serious weathering and wear and asserted the extreme likelihood of its use as a shop sign, but also recognized the conflicting elements of the sled's size, use, and history; e-mail, 25 February 2002.

Helen E. Gilman / born 1913

69 Shop Figure: Dapper Dan

1937 / watercolor over graphite / 49.1 x 33.7 cm (19 5/16 x 13 1/4 in.)

Unlike most nineteenth-century trade figures, produced in multiple versions in busy workshops, this sculpture appears to be unique, perhaps commissioned from a talented, self-taught carver. The gentleman's red-and-white striped cane suggests that he was used as a barbershop figure, probably in Washington, DC, where he was originally found, or possibly in Philadelphia. His imposing height of nearly six feet must have attracted considerable notice from passersby.

When this piece was depicted by Helen E. Gilman of the Massachusetts Index project, it was slightly different in appearance from its present state. The figure had a cigar in his mouth and wore rounded spectacles and a bow tie. Over time, these accoutrements, which may not have been original to the sculpture when it was created around 1880, were left behind, and a different necktie was added.

Dapper Dan has had an illustrious history as an example of the cleverness and creativity of American folk sculpture. At the time of the Index project, the figure was at the Wells Historical Museum, the private collection that later became the basis for Old Sturbridge Village. It was eventually deaccessioned because it was not appropriate to the earlier nineteenth-century focus of that collection. *Dapper Dan* became well known after being reproduced in Robert Bishop's *American Folk Sculpture* (1974, cat. 213) and was subsequently owned by a succession of folk-art collectors. The figure, a promised gift of Ralph Esmerian, is now an important presence in the American Folk Art Museum, New York.[1]

DC

1   Exh. cat. New York 2001, cat. 327, 549.

American 19th Century, *Shop Figure: Dapper Dan*, c. 1880, painted wood with metal, 173.4 x 56.2 cm (68 1/4 x 22 1/8 in.), American Folk Art Museum, New York, Promised Gift of Ralph Esmerian

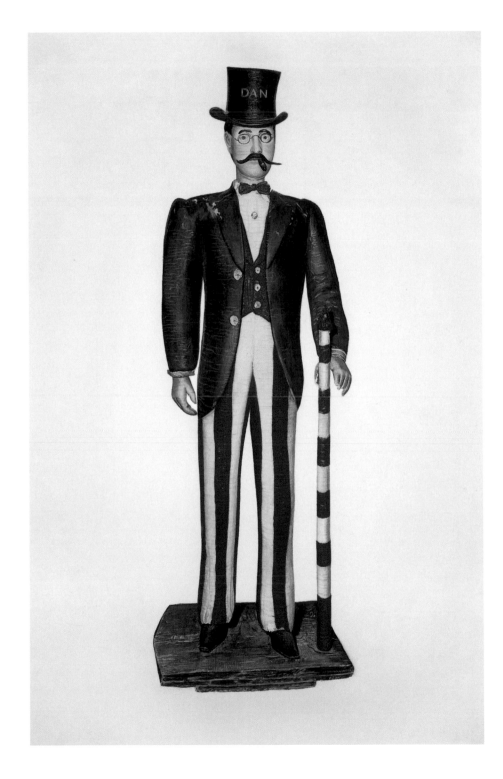

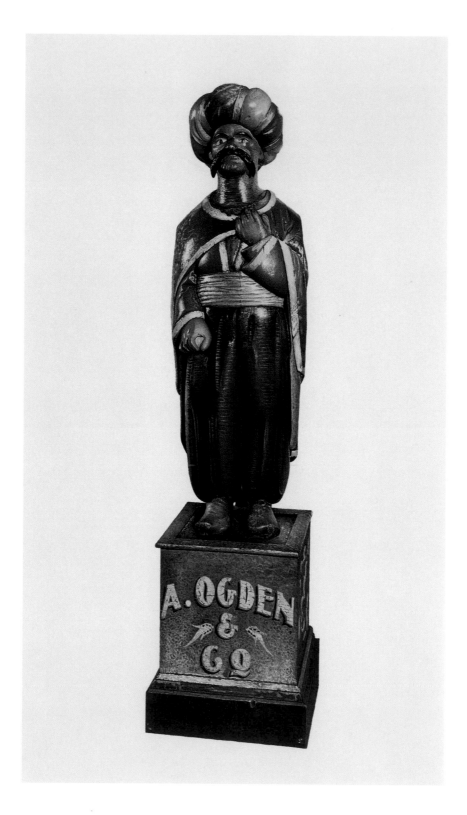

Robert Pohle / active c. 1935

70 Cigar-Store Turk

1935/1942 / watercolor over graphite / 44.6 x 35.5 cm (17 9/16 x 14 in.)

Although "Indians" were the most common type of cigar-store figure, other eye-catching subjects were featured as well. Exotic, turbaned "Turks" made their appearance as Turkish tobacco gained in popularity. Tobacco is advertised on the side of the base that supports this carving, a figure that may once have held a pipe in his right hand. Also inscribed on the base are the words "A. Ogden & Co.," possibly referring to Ogden & Co., Chicago, a manufacturer of stereoscopes, stereo photographs, and gaming devices.[1] This figure likely dates from the last quarter of the nineteenth century and may have been made by Thomas V. Brooks (1828–1895) of New York and Chicago. Brooks was for many years a ship carver but later turned his attention to trade figures. With a staff that could help him produce about two hundred figures per year, he eventually had the largest inventory of any carver in New York.[2] One of his apprentices, Samuel A. Robb, went on to become the most famous carver of cigar-store figures in America.

By the late 1930s *Cigar-Store Turk* was in a private collection in Rhode Island, presumably that of Carl W. Haffenreffer, who had purchased it from Dudley E. Waters of Grand Rapids, Michigan, another early collector of tobacconist figures. Waters owned a large number of trade figures, primarily "Indians," but also the handsome *Captain Jinks* (cat. 72).[3]

DC

1   Survey of the Van Alstyne Collection, NMAH, SI, files.

2   Fried 1970, 183.

3   The *Turk* and *Captain Jinks* are pictured together in an article on Waters' collection; see Lawrence F. Jessup, "The Tobacconists' Tribe of Treen," *Antiques* 18 (September 1930), 234, fig. 3.

Albert Ryder / active c. 1935

71 Cigar-Store Baseball Player

1939 / watercolor over graphite / 48.5 x 29.2 cm (19 ⅛ x 11 ½ in.)

The viewpoint of Albert Ryder's rendering clearly shows the beautifully lettered word "Lunch" on the figure's base. Less visible, but more important, is the inscription, "Robb MANUF'R. 114 Centre St. New York," which refers to the premier carver of show figures and trade signs at the time, Samuel A. Robb (1851–1928).

The son of Scottish immigrants, Robb was apprenticed as a young man to the carver Thomas V. Brooks. After five years, he went to work for the firm of William Demuth, all the while enhancing his considerable skills by studying drawing from life and from casts at the National Academy of Design and perspective drawing at Cooper Union. By 1875 he had set up his own shop, producing tobacconist's figures, shop signs, and other carvings for the next few decades. Around the turn of the century, demand for such objects was beginning to wane.

Samuel A. Robb
(American, 1851–1928),
Shop Figure: Baseball Player,
1888–1903, painted wood,
193 x 55.3 cm (76 x 21 ¾ in.),
American Folk Art Museum,
New York, Promised Gift of
Millie and Bill Gladstone

Baseball, invented in 1839 by Abner Doubleday in Cooperstown, New York, was so popular by the 1880s that Walt Whitman, caught up in his compatriots' enthusiasm for this sport, declared, "baseball is our game: the American game: I connect it with our national character."[1] During this decade baseball players became a favorite subject for cigar-store carvings; Robb's workshop produced several.[2] An 1890 inventory of his shop, published by the *New York Times*, identified one of these figures as "the counterfeit presentment" of baseball legend John L. Sullivan.[3] It is possible that the mustachioed batter in Ryder's rendering, probably carved between 1888 and 1903, is Mike "King" Kelly, to whom he bears a strong resemblance.[4] Kelly, a catcher who played for Cincinnati, Chicago, Boston, and New York between 1878 and 1893, and who was inducted into the Baseball Hall of Fame in 1945, has been called the "first superstar" of baseball.[5] He was so popular that a song, "Slide, Kelly, Slide," was written about him in 1889 and recorded for phonograph by Thomas Edison in 1892.[6]

This carving of a baseball player once belonged to Carl W. Haffenreffer, a major collector of cigar-store figures in Bristol, Rhode Island, who presented the figure as a gift to the Whitney Museum of American Art in New York. The player was later sold by the museum to a private collector, who has promised it as a gift to the American Folk Art Museum.[7]

DC and VTC

1 Quoted in National Geographic Society, ed., *Baseball as America: Seeing Ourselves through Our National Game* (New York, 2002), 37.

2 Fried 1970, 78. For examples of these players, see Fried 1970, 213. On Robb, see also Ralph Sessions, "The Image Business: Shop and Cigar Store Figures in America," *Folk Art* 21 (Winter 1996/1997), 57–58.

3 Fried 1970, 210.

4 For a photograph of Kelly that shows his remarkable likeness to the cigar-store carving, see Lawrence Lorimer, *Baseball Desk Reference* (New York, 2002), 18. The possibility that the sculpture might represent Kelly was first suggested in Stacy C. Hollander and Brooke Davis Anderson, *American Anthem: Masterpieces from the American Folk Art Museum* (New York, 2001), 354 n. 3. Baseball historian Neal McCabe, coauthor with Constance McCabe of *Baseball's Golden Age* (New York, 1993), kindly confirmed that the figure probably portrays Kelly.

5 Marty Appel, *Slide, Kelly, Slide: The Wild Life and Times of Mike "King" Kelly, Baseball's First Superstar* (New York, 1996).

6 The song is transcribed in Lorimer 2002, 518.

7 Stacy C. Hollander, "Grand Slam Addition to the Collection," *Folk Art* 24 (Fall 1999), 25.

Trade Signs and Figures

Albert Ryder / active c. 1935

72 Shop Figure: Captain Jinks

1935/1942 / watercolor over graphite / 52.3 x 31.8 cm (20⁹/₁₆ x 12½ in.)

Legend has it that the original *Captain Jinks* was created by Thomas J. White, an associate of and carver in the shop of Samuel A. Robb (see cat. 70), and that White based the sculpture on Robb dressed in his New York State National Guard uniform. The face, though caricatured, does bear a resemblance to the way Robb looked in photographs of about 1880, particularly to his dramatically extended mustache. The name of the figure type appears to be based on a Civil War–era song, "Captain Jinks of the Horse Marines," which described a dandified soldier.[1] The exaggerated curves and indentions of the figure's back and belly, the severe attenuation of his legs, and the beaklike nose lend a comic aspect to the character.

Several examples of the figure of *Captain Jinks* are known, including versions at the Shelburne Museum; the Newark Museum; and the National Museum of American History, Smithsonian Institution. The carving depicted by Ryder is alternately known as the "Bandmaster." It was in the Haffenreffer Collection at the time it was documented but had previously belonged to Dudley Waters.[2] It reportedly was once stationed in front of a cigar store in Coldwater, Michigan.[3]

DC

1 Fried 1970, 198–200.

2 Ralph Sessions kindly informed Virginia Clayton that this figure had once belonged to Waters.

3 Hornung 1972 (1997), 65.

John Matulis / 1910–2000

73 Circus-Wagon Figure: Muse with a Scroll

1939 / watercolor, gouache, and colored pencil over graphite / 55.7 x 25.9 cm (21¹⁵/₁₆ x 10³/₁₆ in.)

In 1938 William Lamson Warren, then director for the Connecticut project of the Index of American Design and later a well-known authority on early American art and antiques, purchased twenty-four wooden circus figures. These carvings, which he had discovered through a newspaper advertisement, had been left behind when the Barnum & Bailey Circus moved its headquarters from Bridgeport, Connecticut, to Sarasota, Florida.[1] Stripped of their original gold leaf and left in an open field, the beautifully sculpted figures were weathered but nevertheless appealing. Matulis made renderings of ten of the carvings, skillfully capturing the weather-beaten surface of each piece.

The sculptures appear to have been made in the workshop of Samuel A. Robb around 1880. Robb, America's premier producer of show figures, turned his talents as well to the creation of elaborate designs for circus parade wagons and figures.[2]

DC

1 Florence Thompson Howe, "Carved Wood Circus-Wagon Figures," *Antiques* (August 1947), 120–121. The *Muse with a Scroll* has not been located.

2 Fried 1970, 204–209.

Detail cat. 73

MUSE WITH A SCROLL

Marian Page / active c. 1935

74 Gilded Rooster Weather Vane

1939 / watercolor over graphite / 35.1 x 34.9 cm ($13^{13}/_{16}$ x $13^{3}/_{4}$ in.)

The best-known of all American weather-vane makers is Shem Drowne (1683–1774), the metalsmith who created the famous grasshopper that has decorated Boston's Faneuil Hall since 1742. In 1721 Drowne produced the impressive weathercock pictured in Page's rendering for the New Brick Church on Hanover Street, Boston, when its congregation separated from the New North Meeting House. With this striking creature flying overhead, the New Brick was alternately known as the Cockerel Church. Like Drowne's grasshopper, the rooster has glass eyes (these were replaced in 1822). It is made from gilded, hammered copper, is supposedly fashioned from two kettles, weighs 172 pounds, and is more than five feet long. Through the years it has been repaired and regilded several times. In 1869 the church spire on which it perched was blown down in a gale and the weathercock was badly damaged. It was repaired and kept inside the church until 1871, when the building was razed to widen the street. The Shephard Congregational Society (the First Church in Cambridge, Congregational) purchased the cock for $75 and in 1873 posted him atop their new stone church. He was removed when the tall spire of the church had to be dismantled in 1938 because of structural weakness, and was later returned to the new, shorter steeple, where he remains to this day.[1]

DC

1 Kaye 1975, 16–19.

Lucille Chabot / born 1908

75 # Rooster Weather Vane from the Fitch Tavern Barn

1938 / watercolor over graphite / 32.8 x 43.1 cm (12 $^{15}/_{16}$ x 16 $^{15}/_{16}$ in.)

Gilded weathercocks often perched above meeting houses and churches, while carved wooden fowl commonly roosted on barns. This cock, dated late eighteenth century, once sat atop the barn at the Old Fitch Tavern in Bedford, Massachusetts, where on 19 April 1775 Bedford's Minutemen gathered for a hasty breakfast before setting out to engage the British at North Bridge in Concord. Made of painted pine, with metal repairs in the serpentine neck and a crude bracket on the tail, the bird appears to balance unsteadily on its wrought-iron legs. In 1930 the barn was razed and the rooster was transferred to the roof of the tavern's woodshed. It was here that it was discovered by the Index of American Design.[1]

DC

1 Kaye 1975, 88–89.

American 18th Century, *Rooster Weather Vane from the Fitch Tavern Barn*, late eighteenth century, painted wood, wrought iron, and lead sheeting, 86.4 x 114.3 cm (34 x 45 in.), Shelburne Museum, Shelburne, Vermont

Weather Vanes, Whirligigs, and One Drum

Dorothy Hay Jensen / 1910–1999

76 Sea Serpent Weather Vane

1935/1942 / watercolor over graphite / 34.4 x 47.1 cm (13 9/16 x 18 9/16 in.)

Observing that the Index of American Design was covering the areas of textiles and furniture in other New England states, the artists of the Maine project chose as their focus wooden sculpture: shop figures, ship-carvings, and others. As the head of the Federal Art Project in Maine, Dorothy Hay Jensen traveled the state in many capacities, among them as locator of objects worthy of Index attention. She recalled:

> One day driving a country road near Warren I nearly went into a ditch when I saw on a barn roof a sea serpent weathervane. The owners of the house told me it had been there 40 years before when they bought the property, and the previous owner said the same things, so they could give me no history. They let me go up in their attic and take pictures out a window. It was 6' long [actually 6'7"] carved out of a pine board in an undulating shape, with a very Chinese dragon type head, and I can't help but feel that it was inspired by a dragon on a tray or box or kimono that came home to Maine in the China trade.[1]

The Newark Museum, in whose collection the fanciful sculpture now resides, provides some additional history. According to family tradition, the weather vane was carved by William Crane, China, Maine, for his brother Seth Crane of Warren around 1800. It remained on the Crane farm, which passed to nonfamily owners after 1932, until 1978–1979, when it was sold to an antique dealer and thereafter to several private owners.

Although Jensen based her rendering on a photograph and her color notes, she accurately captured the weathered appearance of the wood, with its faint traces of red and ocher, and the swoops and curves of the figure's extraordinary shape. Mythological weather vane subjects were not entirely unknown in the nineteenth century, but the fierce, imposing creature from Warren, Maine, is thought to be unique.[2]

DC

1 NGA/GA, Jensen Talk 1985, 14.

2 The Fiske Company offered a three-foot copper dragon in their 1893 catalogue; see Klamkin 1973, 166.

Attributed to William Crane (American, active c. 1800), *Sea Serpent Weather Vane*, c. 1800, painted wood and iron, 76.2 x 200.7 cm (30 x 79 in.), The Newark Museum, Purchase 1982, Membership Endowment Fund

Laura Bilodeau / 1896–1982

77 Butcher's Weather Vane

1939 / watercolor over graphite / 38.1 x 54.4 cm (15 x 21 ½ in.)

The grim humor of this vignette of a hog trotting atop the instrument of its own death might not be effective advertising in our time, but it was an image used more than once in the nineteenth century. Some versions, like this one, were made from wood. Others were cast from metal as weather vanes or as butcher-shop signs.[1]

This weather vane, of about 1835, originally belonged to Captain David West, owner of a slaughter-house in Fairhaven, Massachusetts. It is now in the collection of the New Bedford Whaling Museum in Massachusetts. In the summer and fall, drovers marched hogs, along with cattle and sheep, into New Bedford to be sold on the hoof, many of them to butchers like West.[2]

DC

1   Robert Bishop and Patricia Coblentz, *A Gallery of American Weathervanes and Whirligigs* (New York, 1981), 63.

2   Kaye 1975, 122–123.

American 19th Century,
Butcher's Weather Vane, c. 1835.
painted wood, 58.4 x 80.7 cm
(23 x 31 ¾ in.), New Bedford
Whaling Museum

Weather Vanes, Whirligigs, and One Drum

Lucille Chabot / born 1908

78 Angel Gabriel Weather Vane

1939 / watercolor over graphite / 36.2 x 52.4 cm (14¼ x 20⅝ in.)

The angel as a weather-vane subject is much less common than, for example, horses or roosters, and the image of Gabriel is rarer still. Although there are several known examples of the archangel blowing his horn, this version appears to be unique.

A slip of paper found in the weather vane's horn during repair by a WPA metalworker reads: "Boston June 26th, 1840 / Made by Gould and Hazlett / Charlestown Street / Haymarket Square / Boston."

No further information about the makers has been uncovered, but their creativity is apparent in the extraordinary weather vane depicted here. The work is graceful in the flowing contours of the angel's wings and robe, yet also crude, in the obvious, heavy bracing that supports the figure. Chabot was careful to show the vagaries of the object's life that could be read on its surface in 1939: worn gold leaf, rusted and pitted areas, and gray lead solder used to make repairs. The artist had to experiment to arrive at a technique that would "get the thing to glow…not to get it grainy." She achieved the desired effect by a "series of glazes, one color over another."[1]

Originally the angel graced the Universalist Church in Newburyport, Massachusetts, but it was sent to storage when the building was abandoned. The vane was subsequently purchased by a member of that town's People's Methodist Church and proudly installed on the church's steeple. In 1959 Gabriel's trumpet was blown off in a hurricane and for more than a decade the fallen instrument was stored in the minister's house.

In 1965 Chabot's Index rendering of the weather vane was reproduced on a United States postage stamp. The angel's feminine anatomy drew much comment at the time, but theologians were able to reassure those concerned that angels are genderless and, as such, could be depicted as masculine or feminine at the artist's discretion. When publicity from the stamp drew new attention to the weather vane, it was finally repaired and the detached trumpet returned to the angel. In the 1970s, following the theft of another important weather vane in a nearby town, the original Gabriel was removed once again from the church and this time replaced with a replica. The original was held for safekeeping in a Newburyport bank until its recent purchase by a private collector.[2]

DC

1 NGA/GA Chabot Interview 1986, 8.

2 Kaye 1975, 69–71.

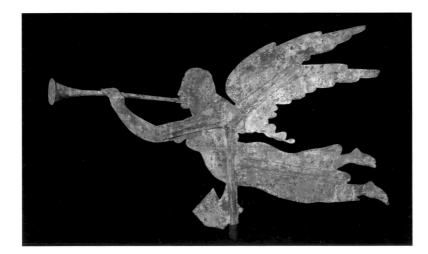

Gould and Hazlett (American, nineteenth century), *Angel Gabriel Weather Vane*, 1840, iron and copper with gold leaf, 91.4 x 166.4 cm (36 x 65½ in.), Kendra and Allan Daniel

Lucille Chabot / born 1908

79 Angel Gabriel Weather Vane: Demonstration Drawing

1939 / watercolor and graphite / 28 x 40.7 cm (11 x 16 in.)

Several particularly skillful Index artists used their talents to teach the methods of making renderings to other artists. Lucille Chabot, Suzanne Chapman, and Elizabeth Moutal, all of the Massachusetts project, instructed artists there and in other New England states.

Chabot's demonstration piece illustrates how each rendering might begin with a carefully drawn outline in pencil. Color was applied in thin washes, building layers to achieve the desired appearance. Chabot recalled that high-quality Windsor and Newton colors and brushes were used and that the renderings were generally executed on Whatman (English-made) board of the "best, beautiful texture."[1] The artist chose for the drawing "a good size to show the various transitions of color...[and] all the little flecks of color and clumsy kind of work that these two people [the weather vane's makers] did."[2]

DC

1 NGA/GA Chabot Interview 1986, 3.

2 NGA/GA Chabot Interview 1986, 6.

Weather Vanes, Whirligigs, and One Drum

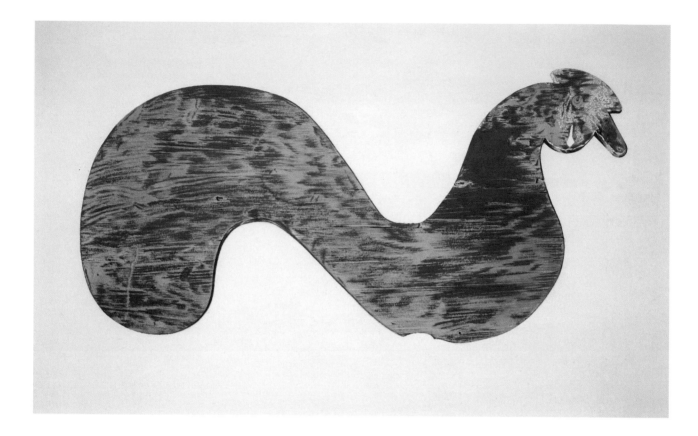

Zabelle Missirian / active c. 1935

80 Wooden Rooster Weather Vane

1939 / watercolor and gouache over graphite / 28.1 x 38.1 cm (11 1/16 x 15 in.)

Some connoisseurs of antiques might scorn this unprepossessing weathercock in preference for his fancier kin with gilding and full-bodied carving, but others have long admired him for the simplicity of his abstracted form, perceived by many as epitomizing the protomodernism inherent in American folk art. Cut from a pine plank, this weather vane was acquired in the early twentieth century by Russell Hawes Kettell, who illustrated it in his 1929 book, *The Pine Furniture of New England*, as part of a domestic setting for a seventeenth-century chest.[1] Kettell's book was highly influential on Americans' taste in antiques and home decorating, helping to inspire an appreciation for simple, homey artifacts. In the introduction to his book, Kettell wrote:

> probably it is the spirit of frank simplicity that gives this [pine] work its fundamental appeal. It is on friendly terms with open fires, with wrought-iron hinges, with hewn beams and corner posts, with rough-plastered walls or robin's-egg blue paneling and wide board flooring painted pumpkin yellow. All these things speak the same language. But 'ware lest you introduce a piece of mahogany to such company! The mahogany raises its eyebrows at favourite scratches and rounded edges of the pine, while the pine peeks out of the corners of its eyes at the painstaking satinwood inlay and wonders what it is all about.[2]

The red paint on this weathercock probably indicates that his creator meant to specifically represent a Rhode Island Red, a new and highly celebrated breed in nineteenth-century America, remarkable for its eggs as well as for its succulent flesh.[3] The rooster still resides in the Concord Museum in Concord, Massachusetts, as he did in 1939. A very similar weathercock is housed today in a private collection, and his printed image is widely circulated each month as the logo for the *Maine Antique Digest*. Another, with more elaborate tail feathers, is in the Shelburne Museum in Vermont. It is dated c. 1890.[4]

VTC

1 Russell Hawes Kettell, *The Pine Furniture of Early New England* (New York, 1929), no. 29. I am grateful to David F. Wood, curator at the Concord Museum, for sharing information about this piece, including references to the Kettell book and the significance of the fact that Kettell once owned the bird. Wood also mentioned its inclusion in Kaye 1975.

2 Kettell 1929, n.p.

3 Kaye 1975, 89.

4 *An American Sampler: Folk Art from the Shelburne Museum* [exh. cat., National Gallery of Art] (Washington, 1987), no. 74.

Mina Lowry / 1894–1942

81 Whirligig

1941 / watercolor with pen and ink over graphite / 71.9 x 35.6 cm (28 5/16 x 14 in.)

Like weather vanes, whirligigs indicate wind direction. With their movable paddles or other parts, they also show the velocity of passing breezes. Judging from the fanciful forms of surviving nineteenth- and early twentieth-century whirligigs, amusement was probably the primary purpose for such objects.

This large, painted wooden sculpture was for many years in the collection of the celebrated folk-art authorities Jean and Howard Lipman; it is now in the Fenimore Art Museum, Cooperstown, New York. Found in Quakerstown, Pennsylvania, it appears to depict a member of the Society of Friends, wearing the plain, dark, long coat and brimmed hat typical of that sect's early dress.[1] The piece is roughly carved and crudely constructed, with wooden dowels and glue joining the two halves lengthwise, a horizontal metal plate providing an area to hold the pole on which the object rotated, and ordinary iron pipe (probably of the late nineteenth century) providing the sockets for the movable arms. The Index data sheet suggested that the flat, tapering arm paddles were fashioned from pine shingles.

DC

1 Notes in the file suggest that the buttonless coat might indicate the subject was a member of the Dunkards; however, the rows of filled holes on the coat's front seem to show that buttons were once present there.

American 19th Century, *Whirligig*, c. 1890, painted wood and metal, 110.5 x 25.7 cm (43 1/2 x 10 1/8 in.), Fenimore Art Museum, Cooperstown, New York

Weather Vanes, Whirligigs, and One Drum

Wayne White / 1890–1978

82 Civil War Drum

1940 / watercolor over graphite / 53.9 x 39 cm (21 ¼ x 15 ⅝ in.)

This vibrantly decorated drum of wood, calfskin, and rope reflects the colorful history of the 9th Vermont Volunteers. The regiment was mustered into service on 9 July 1862, a mere six weeks after President Lincoln's summons for troops to protect the national capital. Since the regiment was the first to respond, it gained much attention as it made its way from Brattleboro through New York and Philadelphia to Washington. On 13 September 1862, at Harper's Ferry, the regiment surrendered to the Confederates and was sent to Chicago as paroled prisoners; it was exchanged on 10 January 1863. In subsequent weeks, fatigue, disease, and restlessness prompted several officers to resign and some enlisted men to join other units and head for the front. The remainder guarded captured Confederates in Chicago until about 1 April,

at which time the prisoners began to be escorted to Virginia. Presumably the drum found its way to a Chicago collector (and later to the Historical Society) through the regiment's sojourn there. Its drum major was Robert G. Hardie from Brattleboro, Vermont, who enlisted 25 June 1862, was mustered 9 July 1862, and was discharged 21 March 1863 by order of the War Department.[1]

The 9th Vermont went on to participate in the Battle of Gettysburg and several engagements in Virginia, including the Fall of Richmond.

DC

1 The Index data sheet reflects research compiled from an article by Hon. Joel C. Baker, 1st Lieut., 9th Regiment, Watchman Pub. Co., Montpelier, Vt., 1892 (Chicago Public Library). Baker's history of the regiment is also available on a Web site, *www.vermontcivilwar. org/9inf/history.shtml.*

American 19th Century, *Civil War Drum*, c. 1862, wood and calfskin, 42.2 cm (16 ⅞ in.), diam. 42.2 cm (16 ⅞ in.), Chicago Historical Society. This rope tension drum is now tied differently from the way it was when White portrayed it for the Index in 1940. According to Michael Collins, chief curator of the Civil War Antiques Preservation Society, it is now tied as it would have been during the Civil War. An undated black-and-white photograph in the files of the Chicago Historical Society shows the drum tied as in White's rendering. Sometime after the war and before 1940, this drum must have been disassembled and then retied incorrectly. After 1940, it was apparently disassembled again and the ropes returned to their original, correct position. At this time the top and bottom hoops were also shifted slightly to the right. Collins reports that the drum's ropes appear to be original and that the fife that belonged to the 9th Vermont Volunteers is now in the collection of the Civil War Antiques Preservation Society.

Select Bibliography

Books and Articles

Alexander 1980
Alexander, Charles. *Here the Country Lies: Nationalism and the Arts in Twentieth-Century America*. Bloomington, Ind., 1980.

Allyn 1982
Allyn, Nancy Elizabeth. "Defining American Design: A History of the Index of American Design, 1935–1942." Master's thesis, University of Maryland, 1982.

Anderson 1936
Anderson, Harry V. "Ruth Reeves." *Design* 37 (March 1936), 24–26, 39.

Bach in Leonard and Glassgold 1930; 1992
Bach, Richard F. "Industrial Design: The Resurgence of Quality." In Leonard and Glassgold 1930; reprint 1992, 79–81.

Barber 1903
Barber, Edward Atlee. *Tulip Ware of the Pennsylvania German Potters*. Philadelphia, 1903.

Barenholtz and McClintock 1980
Barenholtz, Bernard, and Inez McClintock. *American Antique Toys*. New York, 1980.

Benson 1934
Benson, E. M. "Wanted: An American Bauhaus." *The American Magazine of Art* 27 (June 1934), 307–311.

Berman 1988
Berman, Marshall. *All That Is Solid Melts into Air: The Experiences of Modernity*. New York, 1988.

Bibby 1996
Bibby, Brian. *The Fine Art of California Indian Basketry*. Berkeley, Calif., 1996.

Bishop and Coblentz 1981
Bishop, Robert, and Patricia Coblentz. *A Gallery of American Weathervanes and Whirligigs*. New York, 1981.

Boyd 1946
Boyd, E. *Saints and Saint Makers of New Mexico*. Santa Fe, 1946.

Brackman 1989
Brackman, Barbara. *Clues in the Calico: A Guide to Identifying and Dating Antique Quilts*. McLean, Va., 1989.

Brewington 1962
Brewington, M. V. *Shipcarvers of North America*. Barre, Mass., 1962.

Brooks 1908
Brooks, Van Wyck. *The Wine of the Puritans: A Study of Present-Day America*. New York, 1908.

Brooks 1918
Brooks, Van Wyck. "On Creating a Usable Past." *The Dial* 64, no. 764 (11 April 1918), 337–341.

Brooks in Rourke 1942
Brooks, Van Wyck. Preface in Rourke 1942.

Bustard 1997
Bustard, Bruce I. *A New Deal for the Arts*. Seattle, 1997.

Byars in Leonard and Glassgold 1930; 1992
Byars, Mel. Introduction to Leonard and Glassgold 1930; reprint 1992, v–xxvi.

Cahill 1932
Cahill, Holger. "Folk Art: Its Place in the American Tradition." *Parnassus* 4 (March 1932), 1–4.

Cahill in Christensen 1950
Cahill, Holger. Introduction to Christensen 1950, ix–xvii.

Cahill 1954
Cahill, Holger. Letter to Edgar Richardson, 30 June 1954. Published as "Document." *Archives of American Art Journal* 24, no. 3 (1984), 22–23.

Cahill 1957
Cahill, Holger. "The Reminiscences of Holger Cahill." Typescript of interviews conducted by Joan Pring for the oral history research office of Columbia University in 1957. Microfiche of typescript New York Times Oral History Program: Columbia University Collection; part 2, no. 24.

Cahill in O'Connor 1975
Cahill, Holger. "American Resources in the Arts." In O'Connor 1975, 33–44.

Cahill and Barr 1934
Cahill, Holger, and Alfred H. Barr Jr., eds. *Art in America in Modern Times*. New York, 1934.

Cahill and Wellman 1938
Cahill, Holger, and Rita Wellman. "American Design: From the Heritage of Our Styles Designers Are Drawing Inspiration to Mould a National Taste." *House and Garden* 74 (July 1938), 15–16.

Carlano and Shilliam 1993
Carlano, Marianne, and Nicola J. Shilliam. *Early Modern Textiles: From Arts and Crafts to Art Deco*. Boston, 1993.

Christensen 1950
Christensen, Erwin O. *The Index of American Design*. New York, 1950.

Corn 1999
Corn, Wanda M. *The Great American Thing: Modern Art and National Identity, 1915–1935*. Berkeley, Calif., 1999.

Cornelius in O'Connor 1975
Cornelius, Charles. "The New York Index." In O'Connor 1975, 170–172.

Dana 1926
Dana, John Cotton. "A Museum of, for, and by Newark." *The Survey* 55 (1 March 1926), 11.

Dana 1929
Dana, John Cotton. "Beauty Has No Relation to Price." *The Museum* 2 (February 1929), 40.

Dinger 1983
Dinger, Charlotte. *The Art of the Carousel*. Green Village, N.J., 1983.

Doss 1991
Doss, Erika. *Benton, Pollock, and the Politics of Modernism: From Regionalism to Abstract Expressionism*. Chicago, 1991.

Evans 1996
Evans, Nancy Goyne. *American Windsor Chairs*. New York, 1996.

Fabian 1978
Fabian, Monroe H. *The Pennsylvania-German Decorated Chest*. New York, 1978.

"Field Notes" 1936
"Field Notes: Design Laboratory, New York." *The American Magazine of Art* 29 (February 1936), 117.

Frankl in Leonard and Glassgold 1930; 1992
Frankl, Paul T. "The Home of Yesterday, To-day, and To-morrow." In Leonard and Glassgold 1930; reprint 1992, 25–27.

Fried 1970
Fried, Frederick. *Artists in Wood*. New York, 1970.

Glassgold 1928
Glassgold, [C.] Adolph. "The Modern Note in Decorative Arts II." *The Arts* 13 (April 1928), 221–235.

Glassgold in Leonard and Glassgold 1930; 1992
Glassgold, Adolph Cook. "Design in America." In Leonard and Glassgold 1930; reprint 1992, 174–175.

Glassgold 1931
Glassgold, Aldoph. "AUDAC Exhibit of Modern Industrial and Deorative Art at the Brooklyn Museum." *Creative Art: A Magazine of Fine and Applied Art* 8 (June 1931), 437–440.

Glassgold in O'Connor 1975
Glassgold, Adolph. "Recording American Design." In O'Connor 1975, 167–169.

Goldwater 1986
Goldwater, Robert John. *Primitivism in Modern Art*. 2d ed. Cambridge, Mass., 1986.

Gordon 1980
Gordon, Beverly. *Shaker Textile Arts*. Hanover, N.H., 1980.

Graham 1967
Graham, Otis L. Jr. *An Encore for Reform: The Old Progressives and the New Deal*. New York, 1967.

Greenberg in Rosenberg and White 1957
Greenberg, Clement. "Avant-Garde and Kitsch." In Rosenberg and White 1957, 98–107.

Greer 1981
Greer, Georgeanna H. *American Stonewares: The Art and Craft of the Utilitarian Potters*. Exton, Pa., 1981.

Harris 1995
Harris, Jonathan. *Federal Art and National Culture: The Politics of National Identity in New Deal America*. New York, 1995.

Hertz 1950
Hertz, Louis H. Messrs. *Ives of Bridgeport: The Saga of America's Greatest Toymakers*. Wethersfield, Conn., 1950.

Hertz 1956
Hertz, Louis H. *Collecting Model Trains*. New York, 1956.

Holstein 1991
Holstein, Jonathan. *Abstract Design in American Quilts. A Biography of an Exhibition*. Louisville, Ky., 1991.

Hornung 1972; 1997
Hornung, Clarence P. *Treasury of American Design: A Survey of Popular Folk Arts Based Upon Watercolor Renderings in the Index of American Design, at the National Gallery of Art*. New York, 1972, reprint 1997.

Jeffers 1991
Jeffers, Wendy. "Holger Cahill and American Art." Archives of American Art Journal 31 (1991), 2–11.

Jeffers 1995
Jeffers, Wendy. "Holger Cahill and American Folk Art." Antiques 148 (September 1995), 324–335.

Jensen 1987
Jensen, Dorothy Hay. "Art and the WPA." *Down East* 33 (June 1987), 78–81.

Jobe and Kaye 1984
Jobe, Brock, and Myrna Kaye. *New England Furniture: The Colonial Era, Selections from the Society for the Preservation of New England Antiquities*. Boston, 1984.

Jones 1971
Jones, Alfred Haworth. "The Search for a Usable Past in the New Deal Era." *American Quarterly* 23 (December 1971), 710–724.

Kainen in O'Connor 1972
Kainen, Jacob. "The Graphic Arts Division of the Federal Art Project." In O'Connor 1972, 155–175.

Kammen 1991
Kammen, Michael. *Mystic Chords of Memory: The Transformation of Tradition in American Culture*. New York, 1991.

Kane 1974a
Kane, Patricia. *300 Years of American Seating Furniture: Chairs and Beds from the Mabel Brady Garvan and Other Collections at Yale University*. Boston, 1974.

Kane 1974b
Kane, Patricia. "The Seventeenth-Century Furniture of the Connecticut Valley: The Hadley Chest Reappraised." In *Arts of the Anglo-American Community in the Seventeenth Century*. Ed. Ian M.G. Quimby, Winterthur Conference Report, 1974.

Kaye 1975
Kaye, Myrna. *Yankee Weathervanes*. New York, 1975.

Ketchum 1987
Ketchum, William C. Jr. *Potters and Potteries of New York State, 1650–1900*. Syracuse, 1987.

Ketchum 1991
Ketchum, William C. Jr. *American Redware*. New York, 1991.

Kiracofe 1993
Kiracofe, Roderick. *The American Quilt*. New York, 1993.

Kirstein 1938; 1975
Kirstein, Lincoln. *Walker Evans: American Photographs*. New York, 1938, reprint 1975.

Klamkin 1973
Klamkin, Charles. *Weather Vanes: The History, Design and Manufacture of an American Folk Art*. New York, 1973.

Lasansky 1988
Lasansky, Jeanette, ed. *Pieced by Mother: Symposium Papers*. Lewisburg, Pa., 1988.

Lea 1960
Lea, Zilla Rider. *The Ornamented Chair: Its Development in America (1700–1890)*. Rutland, Vt., 1960.

Leonard and Glassgold 1930; 1992
Leonard, R. L., and C. A. [A. C.] Glassgold, eds. *Modern American Design by the American Union of Decorative Artists and Craftsmen*. New York, 1930; reprint with introduction by Mel Byars, 1992.

Levine 1988
Levine, Lawrence. "The Historian and the Icon." In *Documenting America, 1935–1943*, 15–42. Edited by Carl Fleishhauer and Beverly W. Brannan. Berkeley, Calif., 1988.

Lucero and Baizerman 1999
Lucero, Helen R., and Suzanne Baizerman. *Chimayo Weaving: The Transformation of a Tradition*. Albuquerque, 1999.

Luther 1935
Luther, Rev. Clair Franklin. *The Hadley Chest*. Hartford, Conn., 1935.

MacDonald in Rosenberg and White 1957
MacDonald, Dwight. "A Theory of Mass Culture." In Rosenberg and White 1957, 59–73.

MacLeish 1937a
MacLeish, Archibald. "Unemployed Arts." *Fortune* 15 (May 1937), 109–117, 168, 171–172.

MacLeish 1937b
MacLeish, Archibald. "The Index of American Design: A Portfolio." *Fortune* 15 (June 1937), 103–110.

Mackey 1965
Mackey, William J. Jr. *American Bird Decoys*. Exton, Pa., 1965.

Mandeles 1995
Mandeles, Chad. "Meaning of the Art of William Harnett." Ph.D. diss., City University of New York, 1995.

Mangione 1983
Mangione, Jerre. *The Dream and the Deal: The Federal Writers' Project, 1935–1943*. Philadelphia, 1983.

Martin and Tucker 1997
Martin, Gina, and Lois Tucker. *American Painted Tinware: A Guide to Its Identification*. New York, 1997.

Mather 1978
Mather, Christine. "The Arts of the Spanish in New Mexico." *Antiques* 113 (February 1978), 422–429.

McDonald 1969
McDonald, William F. *Federal Relief Administration and the Arts*. Columbus, Ohio, 1969.

McKinzie 1973
McKinzie, Richard D. *The New Deal for Artists*. Princeton, N.J., 1973.

Meikle 2001
Meikle, Jeffrey L. *Twentieth Century Limited: Industrial Design in America, 1925–1939*. 2d ed. Philadelphia, 2001.

Mera 1987
Mera, H. P. *Spanish-American Blanketry: Its Relationship to Aboriginal Weaving in the Southwest*. Santa Fe, 1987.

Mercer 1961
Mercer, Henry C. *The Bible in Iron: Pictured Stoveplates of the Pennsylvania Germans*. 3d ed. Doylestowne, Pa., 1961.

Mumford 1926
Mumford, Lewis. *The Golden Day: A Study in American Experience and Culture*. New York, 1926.

Mumford in Leonard and Glassgold 1930; 1992
Mumford, Lewis. "Culture and Machine Art." In Leonard and Glassgold 1930; reprint 1992, 9–10.

Nuttal 1924
Nuttal, Zelia. "Two Remarkable California Baskets." *California Historical Society Quarterly* 2 (1924), 341–344.

O'Connor 1972
O'Connor, Francis V. *The New Deal Art Projects: An Anthology of Memoirs*. Washington, 1972.

O'Connor 1975
O'Connor, Francis V. *Art for the Millions: Essays from the 1930s by Artists and Administrators of the WPA Federal Art Project*. Boston, 1975.

Park and Markowitz 1977
Park, Marlene, and Gerald E. Markowitz. *New Deal for Art: The Government Art Projects of the 1930s with Examples from New York City and State*. Hamilton, N.Y., 1977.

Peniston 1999
Peniston, William A. *The New Museum: Selected Writings by John Cotton Dana*. Newark, N.J., 1999.

Pierce 1991
Pierce, John T. Sr. *Historical Tracts of the Town of Portsmouth, Rhode Island*. Portsmouth, R.I., 1991.

Pulos 1983
Pulos, Arthur J. *American Design Ethic: A History of Industrial Design to 1940*. Cambridge, Mass., 1983.

Quimby and Swank 1980
Quimby, Ian M. G., and Scott T. Swank, eds. *Perspectives on American Folk Art*. New York, 1980.

Ring 1993
Ring, Betty. *Girlhood Embroidery: American Samplers & Pictorial Needlework, 1650–1850*. 2 vols. New York, 1993.

Rohde 1936
Rohde, Gilbert. "The Design Laboratory." *The American Magazine of Art* 29 (October 1936), 638–643, 686.

Rosenberg in Rosenberg and White 1957
Rosenberg, Bernard. "Mass Culture in America." In Rosenberg and White 1957, 3–12.

Rosenberg and White 1957
Rosenberg, Bernard, and David Manning White, eds. *Mass Culture: The Popular Arts in America.* Chicago, 1957.

Rosenberg 1959
Rosenberg, Harold. *Tradition of the New.* New York, 1959.

Rothschild in O'Connor 1972
Rothschild, Lincoln. "The Index of American Design of the WPA Federal Art Project." In O'Connor 1972, 177–196.

Rourke 1935
Rourke, Constance. "American Art: A Possible Future." *The American Magazine of Art* 27 (June 1935), 390–405.

Rourke 1937
Rourke, Constance. "The Index of American Design." *The Magazine of Art* 30 (April 1937), 207–211, 260.

Rourke 1938
Rourke, Constance. *Charles Sheeler: Artist in the American Tradition.* New York, 1938.

Rourke 1942
Rourke, Constance. *The Roots of American Culture and Other Essays.* Edited and with a preface by Van Wyck Brooks. New York, 1942.

Rourke in O'Connor 1975
Rourke, Constance. "What Is American Design?" In O'Connor 1975, 165–166.

Rowe 1973
Rowe, Ann Pollard. "Crewel Embroidered Bed Hangings in Old and New England." *Bulletin: Museum of Fine Arts, Boston,* 71 (1973), 101–163.

Rubin 1980
Rubin, Joan Shelley. *Constance Rourke and American Culture.* Chapel Hill, N.C., 1980.

Rubin 1990
Rubin, Joan Shelley. "A Convergence of Vision: Constance Rourke, Charles Sheeler, and American Art." *American Quarterly* 42 (June 1990), 191–221.

Rumford in Quimby and Swank 1980
Rumford, Beatrix T. "Uncommon Art of the Common People: A Review of Trends in the Collecting and Exhibiting of American Folk Art." In Quimby and Swank 1980, 13–33.

Sasser 1989
Sasser, Elizabeth Skidmore, "Under the Protection of the Saints: New Mexican Retablos and Bultos." *Southwest Art* 19 (July 1989), 86–90, 92.

Seldes in Rosenberg and White 1957
Seldes, Gilbert. "The People and the Arts." In Rosenberg and White 1957, 74–97.

Smith 1982
Smith, Lillian. "Three Inscribed Chumash Baskets with Design from Spanish Colonial Coins." *American Indian Art Magazine* 7 (Summer 1982), 62–68.

Smith 1987
Smith, Lillian. "A Fourth Chumash Inscribed Basket with a Design from a Spanish Colonial Coin." *The Ventura County History Society Quarterly* 32 (Summer 1987), 12–21.

Sprigg and Larkin 1987
Sprigg, June, and David Larkin. *Shaker Life, Work, and Art.* Boston, 1987.

Stott 1973
Stott, William. *Documentary Expression and Thirties America.* New York, 1973.

Swan 1995
Swan, Susan Burrows. *Plain and Fancy: American Women and Their Needlework, 1650–1850.* Rev. ed. Austin, Tex., 1995.

Taylor and Warren 1975
Taylor, Lonn, and David B. Warren. *Texas Furniture: The Cabinetmakers and Their Work, 1840–1880.* Austin, Tex., 1975.

Tepfer 1989
Tepfer, Diane. "Edith Gregor Halpert and the Downtown Gallery Downtown, 1926–1940: A Study in American Art Patronage." Ph.D. diss., University of Michigan, 1989.

Troncale 1995
Troncale, Anthony T. "Worth beyond Words: Romana Javitz and the New York Public Library's Picture Collection." *Bulletin of the New York Public Library* 4 (Fall 1995), 115–138.

Veblen 1899
Veblen, Thorstein. *The Theory of the Leisure Class.* New York, 1899. Reprinted 1912, 1927, and 1934.

Vlach 1980
Vlach, John Michael. "American Folk Art: Questions and Quandaries." *Winterthur Portfolio* 15 (1980), 345–355.

Vlach 1985
Vlach, John Michael. "Holger Cahill as Folklorist." *Journal of American Folklore* 98 (1985), 148–162.

Vlach and Bronner 1992
Vlach, John Michael and Simon J. Bronner, eds. *Folk Art and Folk Worlds.* Expanded ed. Logan, Utah, 1992.

Votolato 1998
Votolato, Gregory. *American Design in the Twentieth Century: Personality and Performance.* New York, 1998.

Webster and Kehoe 1971
Webster, David S., and William Kehoe. *Decoys at Shelburne Museum.* Shelburne, Vt., 1971.

Weissman and Lavitt 1987
Weissman, Judith Reiter, and Wendy Lavitt. *Labors of Love: America's Textiles and Needlework, 1650–1930.* New York, 1987.

Wroth 1982
Wroth, William. *Christian Images in Hispanic New Mexico.* Colorado Springs, Colo., 1982.

Exhibitions

Exh. cat. Berkeley 1968
Elsasser, Albert B. *Treasures of the Lowie Museum.* Robert H. Lowie Museum of Anthropology, University of California at Berkeley. Berkeley, Calif., 1968.

Exh. cat. Boston 1987a
Kaplan, Wendy, et al. *"The Art That Is Life": The Arts and Crafts Movement in America, 1875–1920.* Museum of Fine Arts, Boston. Boston, 1987.

Exh. cat. Boston 1987b
Troyen, Carol, and Erica H. Hirshler, *Charles Sheeler: Paintings and Drawings.* See Troyon, Carol. "From the Eyes Inward," 21–26. Museum of Fine Arts, Boston. Boston, 1987.

Exh. cat. Columbia 2001
Koverman, Jill Beute. *Making Faces: Southern Face Vessels from 1840–1990.* McKissick Museum, College of Liberal Arts, University of South Carolina. Columbia, S.C., 2001.

Exh. cat. Deerfield 1992
Zea, Philip, and Suzanne L. Flynt. *Hadley Chests.* Pocumtuck Valley Memorial Association. Deerfield, Mass., 1992.

Exh. cat. Hartford 2000
Schoelwer, Susan P., ed. *Lions & Eagles & Bulls: Early American Tavern & Inn Signs from the Connecticut Historical Society.* See Finlay, Nancy. "Lions and Eagles and Other Images on Early Inn Signs," 56–65; Schoelwer, Susan P. "Introduction," 2–13; Vincent, Margaret C. "Some Suitable Signe...For the Direction of Strangers," 36–55; Wolf, Bryan J. "Signs of the Times: A Brief Cultural History of Sign Painting," 14–21; Zimmerman, Philip D. "Reading the Signs: An Object History of Tavern Sign from Connecticut, 1750–1850," 22–35. Connecticut Historical Society. Hartford, Conn., 2000.

Exh. cat. Lexington 1988
Becker, Jane S., and Barbara Franco. *Folk Roots, New Roots: Folklore in American Life.* Museum of Our National Heritage. See Metcalf, Eugene W. Jr., and Claudine Weatherford. "Modernism, Edith Halpert, Holger Cahill, and the Fine Art Meaning of American Folk Art." 141–166. The Museum of Our National Heritage. Lexington, Mass., 1988.

Exh. cat. London 1995
Kaplan, Wendy, ed. *Designing Modernity: The Arts of Reform and Persuasion, 1885–1945.* See Kaplan, Wendy. "Traditions Transformed," 19–47; Stein, Laurie A. "German Design and National Identity, 1890–1914," 70–73. Wolfsonian, Miami Beach. London, 1995.

Exh. cat. Newark 1930
Cahill, Holger. *American Primitives: An Exhibit of the Paintings of Nineteenth Century Folk Artists.* Newark Museum. Newark, N.J., 1930.

Exh. cat. Newark 1931
Cahill, Holger. *American Folk Sculpture: The Work of Eighteenth and Nineteenth Century Craftsmen.* Newark Museum. Newark, N.J., 1930.

Exh. cat. Newark 1936
Cahill, Holger. *Old and New Paths in American Design.* Newark Museum. Newark, N.J., 1936.

Exh. cat. Newark 1944
Cahill, Holger. *A Museum in Action, Presenting the Museum's Activities: Catalogue of an Exhibition of American Paintings and Sculpture from the Museum's Collections.* Newark Museum. Newark, N.J., 1944.

Exh. cat. New Haven 1983
Karen Davies. *At Home in Manhattan: Modern Decorative Arts, 1925 to the Depression.* Yale University Art Gallery. New Haven, Conn., 1983.

Exh. cat. New Haven 1987
Fillin-Yeh, Susan. *Charles Sheeler: American Interiors.* Yale University Art Gallery. New Haven, Conn., 1987.

Exh. cat. New York 1932
Cahill, Holger. *American Folk Art: The Art of the Common Man.* The Museum of Modern Art. New York, 1932.

Exh. cat. New York 1934
Barr, Alfred H. Jr., and Philip Johnson. *Machine Art.* See Barr, Alfred H. Jr. "Foreword;" Johnson, Philip. "History of Machine Art." The Museum of Modern Art. New York, 1934.

Exh. cat. New York 1936
Cahill, Holger. *New Horizons in American Art.* The Museum of Modern Art. New York, 1936.

Exh. cat. New York 1984
Rubin, William. *"Primitivism" in Twentieth-Century Art: Affinity of the Tribal and the Modern.* 2 vols. The Museum of Modern Art. New York, 1984.

Exh. cat. New York 1991
Brix, Michael, and Birgit Mayer, eds. *Walker Evans: America.* See Brix, Michael. "Walker Evans' Photographs, 1928–1938: A Campaign against Right-Thinking Optimism," 9–31. Städtische Galerie im Lenbachhaus, Munich. New York, 1991.

Exh. cat. New York 1998
New York Public Library. *Subject Matters: Photography, Romana Javitz, and the New Public Library's Picture Collection.* New York Public Library. New York, 1998.

Exh. cat. New York 2000
Johnson, J. Stewart. *American Modern, 1925–1940: Design for a New Age.* The Metropolitan Museum of Art. New York, 2000.

Exh. cat. New York 2001
Hollander, Stacy C. *American Radiance: The Ralph Esmerian Gift to the American Folk Art Museum.* American Folk Art Museum. New York, 2001.

Exh. cat. Washington 1990
Hartigan, Lynda Roscoe. *Made with Passion: The Hemphill Folk Art Collection.* National Museum of American Art, Smithsonian Institution. Washington, DC, 1990.

Exh. cat. Wintherthur 1977
Ames, Kenneth L. *Beyond Necessity: Art in the Folk Tradition.* Winterthur Museum. Winterthur, Del., 1977.

Archival Documents

AAA

AAA (Archives of American Art) Holger Cahill Papers (unless otherwise noted) on microfilm.

Cahill FAP/WPA
Holger Cahill. "The Federal Art Project of the Works Progress Administration" (Reel 1105, frames 282–292).

Cahill 1941
Holger Cahill. "Speech to the Tenth Anniversary Conference of the American Institute of Decorators," 1941 (Reel NDA 15, frames 512–519).

Drozdoff
Leo Drozdoff. "Documentary Art," n.d. (Reel 1107, frame 1202).

Glassgold 1937
Adolph C. Glassgold. "Index of American Design," December 1937 (Reel 1107, frame 1309).

Glassgold 1939
Adolph C. Glassgold. "Recording American Design." This text is undated but probably was written in 1939 (Reel 1107, frames 1148–1150).

Javitz to Cahill 1949
Romana Javitz letter to Holger Cahill, 29 April 1949 (Reel 5286, frames 1044–1047).

Reeves to Cahill 1949
Ruth Reeves letter to Holger Cahill, 15 April 1949 (Reel 5286, frames 1029–1033).

Reeves to Collier 1950
Ruth Reeves letter to Nina Collier, 16 June 1950 (Nina Collier Papers, Reel NDA 6, frames 68–71).

NGA/GA
NGA/GA (National Gallery of Art, Gallery Archives) Record Group 17b, Index of American Design.

Angus to Fukui 1982
Letter from Charlotte Angus Stefanak to Lisa J. Fukui, 17 November 1982 (Artists' Files, Charlotte Angus folder).

Chabot Interview 1986
Interview with Lucille Chabot conducted by Laurie Weitzenkorn, 10 June 1986 (Artists' Files, Lucille Chabot folder).

Chapman Interview 1986
Interview with Suzanne Chapman conducted by Laurie Weitzenkorn and Charles Ritchie, 9 June 1986 (Artists' Files, Suzanne Chapman folder).

Crockett 1996
Crockett, K. Ginger. *Index of American Design: Research Guide,* 1996 (Finding Aid).

Davison 1982
Austin L. Davison. "Some Observations Regarding the Creation of an Index Plate for the Index of American Design," 17 December 1982 (Artists' Files, Austin Davison folder).

Davison to Steele 1983
Letter from Austin Davison to Lina Steele, 30 September 1983 (Artists' Files, Austin Davison folder).

Davison to Ritchie 1985
Letter from Austin Davison to Charles Ritchie, 15 June 1985 (Artists' Files, Austin Davison folder).

Ellinger Interview 1985
Interview with David Ellinger conducted by Laurie Weitzenkorn, 23 October 1985 (Artists' Files, David Ellinger folder).

Gautier Interview 1985
Interview with Lucille Lacoursiere Gauthier conducted by Laurie Weitzenkorn, 23 October 1985 (Artists' Files, Lucille Lacoursiere Gauthier folder).

Glassgold to Christensen 1946
Memorandum from Aldolph C. Glassgold to Erwin O. Christensen, 14 September 1946, "Analysis of Index of American Design Collection" (Correspondence-Alphabetical, Adolph C. Glassgold folder).

Glassgold to Christensen 1947
"Copy of information on the development of the Index of American Design contained in Adolph C. Glassgold's letter to Mr. Christensen of 24 January 1947" (Correspondence–Alphabetical, Adolph C. Glassgold folder).

Index Manual 1936
Supplement No. 1 to the Federal Art Project Manual: Instructions for Index of American Design, Works Progress Administration, Washington, DC, January 1936 (Research File, Manual).

Index Manual 1938
Index of American Design Manual. W.P.A. Technical Series, Art Circular No. 3, 3 November 1938, Works Progress Administration, Division of Women's and Professional Projects, Washington, DC (Research File, Manual).

Jensen Interview 1986
Interview with Dorothy Hay Jensen conducted by Laurie Weitzenkorn, 6 June 1986 (Artists' Files, Dorothy Hay Jensen folder).

Jensen to Weitzenkorn 1984
Dorothy Hay Jensen's summary of notes on recommended colors from lessons given by Suzanne Chapman of the Massachusetts project, October 1984 (Artists' Files, Dorothy Hay Jensen folder).

Jensen Talk 1985
The transcript of a talk presented by Dorothy Hay Jensen, "Art and the WPA," at Westbrook College, 16 April 1985 (Artists' Files, Dorothy Hay Jensen folder).

Kottcamp Interview 1985
Interview with Elmer R. Kottcamp conducted by Laurie Weitzenkorn, 24 January 1985 (Artists' Files, Elmer R. Kottcamp folder).

Loper Interview 1985
Interview with Edward Loper conducted by Laurie Weitzenkorn, 25 January 1985 (Artists' Files, Edward Loper folder).

Warren Interview 1965
Interview with William L. Warren conducted by Geoffrey R. Swift, 11 October 1965. Archives of American Art Oral History Program (Artists' Files, William L. Warren folder).

Appendix I
Artists' Biographies

Biographical information is sparse or unavailable for most of the artists who participated in the Index of American Design. Few artists achieved national acclaim after the Index was terminated, and many went on to other professions. Some artists moved to states different from those in which they had worked while on an Index project. Among the women, several assumed new names by marriage.

Using the Social Security Death Index (SSDI), best guesses have been provided here for the life dates of several artists, but it is not certain that the individuals have been correctly identified. For many others, life dates have not yet been discovered.

During the 1980s a few of the Index participants provided information to the National Gallery of Art archives, often through oral interviews. It is apparent in these documents that the artists took great pride in their technical proficiency and that they had a sense of contributing to a worthwhile, lasting effort. Some had felt ill at ease accepting benefits from the government, yet all were grateful for the opportunity to earn a living in economically desperate times. Several of the participants had received formal training in museum art schools; most appear to have been dedicated to the finest standards of craftsmanship. Finally, while these artists were entrusted with documenting objects of early American ingenuity and pride, many were themselves of recent immigrant stock and thoroughly representative of a growing segment of the population in the United States in the first decades of the twentieth century.

Jenny Almgren
(1881–1962 SSDI)
New York project: 4 renderings

Nicholas Amantea
(1900–1978 SSDI)
New York project: 104 renderings

Elmer G. Anderson
Pennsylvania project: 51 renderings

Charlotte Angus (Stefanak)
(1911–1989)
Pennsylvania project: 67 renderings

Born in Kansas City, Missouri, Charlotte Angus grew up in Philadelphia. She attended the School of Industrial Art there and took lessons at the Graphic Sketch Club. In 1936 she went to work for the Federal Art Project, at first doing scene painting for the Federal Theater Project and then working on the Index. Angus found the discipline she learned there to be very beneficial in her later career. In 1942, after a course in detailing and tracing, she found employment in the engineering department of the Naval Air Material Center, where she began as a draftsman and advanced to doing industrial illustration.

Angus was married in 1947, lived in Pennsylvania, and continued to exhibit her work in local art shows throughout her life.

Laura Bilodeau
(1896–1982 SSDI)
Massachusetts project: 16 renderings

Molly Bodenstein
(1902–1971 SSDI)
Virginia project: 10 renderings

Amos Brinton
(1888–1982)
Delaware project: 20 renderings

Giacinto Capelli
New York project: 97 renderings

Ferdinand Cartier
New York project: 48 renderings

Lucille Chabot
(born 1908)
Massachusetts project: 27 renderings

Like several of the women who worked on the Index, Lucille Chabot was a product of the traditional museum art school training. She graduated in 1931 from the Worcester Art Museum School in Worcester, Massachusetts, and for the next few years tried her hand at free-lance illustration and writing in New York City and Boston. Beginning about 1934 she became involved in various WPA art projects, joining the Index of American Design in 1937. From 1943 to 1973 Chabot worked at the Raytheon Company in Lexington, Massachusetts, "learning various aspects of the electronics industry," in her words, and eventually founding the company's technical publications department. In addition to her precise work as a technical illustrator, she pursued portraiture, where she employed the broader and more liberating medium of pastels.

In a 1986 oral interview regarding the Index and its artists, Chabot acknowledged, "I think it deepened our appreciation for this country. It also gave us an insight on how the early settlers, under great difficulty, produced some beautiful work, and it deepened our love for this kind of thing..." (interview, 10 June 1986, Index of American Design, NGA archives).

Suzanne Chapman
(1904–1990)
Massachusetts project: 5 renderings

Suzanne Chapman graduated from the Museum of Fine Arts School, Boston, in 1929 and began to work on the Index in 1935. She instructed fellow Index artists in the Massachusetts and Maine projects on how to produce detailed watercolor renderings, particularly teaching the complex methods for reproducing the appearance of textiles. In 1937 she went

Nicholas Amantea,
April 1939, National
Gallery of Art,
Washington, Gallery
archives, photo-
graph Herman

the Great Depression. In 1934, while working at a Florida hotel, an accident cost him his left hand. Drawing skills developed in his childhood made it possible for him to be placed with the Index. His daughter reported, "he used to bring home his work and paint on it at nights and weekends…[using] a magnifying glass and drafting instruments to ensure accuracy of reproduction. People used to try to pick up pieces he painted, thinking they were the real thing" (correspondence of 10 May 1982 from Patricia F. Waller, Fossum's daughter, NGA archives).

An insurance settlement received in 1937 allowed Fossum to acquire ten acres of land, whereupon he left the art project, became a farmer, and rarely produced a picture again.

to work at the Museum of Fine Arts, Boston, in the Egyptian and classical departments, and became well known for her remarkable depictions of Greek vases and gold artifacts. Her illustrations enhanced numerous scholarly publications. She also served on the faculty of the Museum of Fine Arts School as a teacher of drawing in jewelry design. Although she officially retired as special assistant in the museum's Egyptian department in 1970, she continued to contribute her expertise there throughout the following decade.

Mae A. Clarke
New York project: 20 renderings

Yolande Delasser
New York project: 161 renderings

Edward DiGennaro
Connecticut project

Donald Donovan
Rhode Island project: 10 renderings

Donald Donovan was the Index supervisor of the Rhode Island Index project and a graduate of the Rhode Island School of Design.

Ethel Dougan
(1898–1976 SSDI)
California project: 33 renderings

Hester Duany
(1891–1964)
New York project: 86 renderings

Harry Eisman
New York project: 38 renderings

Martha Elliot
Connecticut project: 4 renderings

Elizabeth Fairchild
New York project: 13 renderings

Max Fernekes
(1905–1984 SSDI)
Wisconsin project: 23 renderings

Magnus S. Fossum
(1888–1980)
Florida project: 29 renderings

The son of a Lutheran minister and his wife, both Norwegian immigrants, Magnus S. Fossum was born in what is now Madison, South Dakota. For twenty-five years he managed a wheat farm in Manitoba but was forced to relocate to the South with his wife and children during

Frank Fumagalli
New York project: 96 renderings

Helen E. Gilman
(born 1913)
Massachusetts project: 24 renderings

Like Suzanne Chapman, Gilman attended the Museum of Fine Arts School in Boston. Her work has been exhibited at the 1937 International Exposition in Paris, at the Fogg Art Museum in Cambridge, Massachusetts, and at the Worcester Museum in Worcester, Massachusetts.

Isadore Goldberg II
New York project: 41 renderings

Flora G. Guerra
(1900–1989)
Texas project: 3 renderings

Charles Henning
New York project: 38 renderings

Hazel Hyde
Massachusetts project: 10 renderings

Gordena Jackson
(1900–1993 SSDI)
California project: 35 renderings

Dorothy Hay Jensen
(1910–1999)
Maine project: 4 renderings in Index

As director of the Federal Arts Project for the state of Maine, Dorothy Hay Jensen oversaw the work of about forty artists and traveled throughout the state, matching the talents of various artists to the placement of works of art in schools, libraries, and local government offices. She found her work for the Index of American Design, however, to be the most valuable and engaging of her FAP efforts. The Maine Index project concentrated on wooden sculpture such as shop figures, ship carvings, and weather vanes (see page 11, fig. 9). Jensen writes, "we photographed them from various angles in black and white, of course. Color photography was still in the laboratories. We took measurements, we got from the owner all possible historical data, and then we sat down and made a quick color sketch…we tried to get all the accurate color detail possible, including worn or rusty spots, the color of the wood, if the paint was chipped, stains, everything. Then we took all the notes home and spent perhaps a month making as precise and careful a watercolor drawing as possible" (from talk delivered by Dorothy Hay Jensen at Westbrook College, 16 April 1985).

Dorothy Hay Jensen received her education and training at Smith College, where she majored in art, and at the Portland, Maine, School of Art. After her work with the FAP, she continued to create and exhibit prints and watercolors. She later became interested in pottery and devoted thirty years to this discipline.

Philip Johnson
New York project: 48 renderings

Albert Jean Levone
Pennsylvania project: 60 renderings

Edward L. Loper
(born 1916)
Delaware project: 113 renderings

Between 1936 and 1941 Edward L. Loper worked on both the Index of American Design and the WPA's easel project. He eventually became a well-known artist and teacher. Born in Wilmington, he was exposed to works by the great American illustrator N. C. Wyeth at the public library and to the Howard Pyle collection at the Philadelphia Museum of Art. At the Index he was trained in meticulous observation by David Reyam, himself a student of William-Adolphe Bouguereau (1825–1905). In 1937 Loper began to fully explore his own style when he turned to local subjects, and his painting of a rain-soaked Wilmington street received an honorable mention at the Annual Delaware Art Show. He subsequently taught art and exhibited his own works in many locations, and through his Philadelphia dealer, Robert Carlen, befriended the much-admired African American artist Horace Pippin. Loper's works can be found in such collections as Howard University, The Pennsylvania Academy of Fine Arts, and the Delaware Art Museum. He has had several solo exhibitions and received numerous prizes and honors, as well as recognition of his special achievements as an African American artist.

Elodora P. Lorenzini
(1910–1993)
Colorado project: 20 renderings

Elodora P. Lorenzini was born in Colorado and studied art in Denver and Colorado Springs. In addition to her participation in the Index of American Design, she assisted Frank Mechau with a WPA mural in the Colorado Springs post office and was commissioned to create a mural for the Hebron, Nebraska, post office, for which she chose the subject of bison stampeding a train. She is also said to have worked as an illustrator, printmaker, and decorator. (Tey Marianna

Nunn, Museum of International Folk Art, Santa Fe, kindly indicated the following source: *http://communitydisc.wst.esu3.k12.ne.us/html/colette/muralsSIG/Hebron Page.html*.)

Mina Lowry
(1894–1942)
New York project: 204 renderings

John Matulis
(1910–2000)
Connecticut project: 43 renderings

John Matulis began working with the Index of American Design not long after his graduation from the Hartford Art School in 1933. He found it easy to adapt the prescribed exact style of the Index renderings to his own meticulously observed work. The Connecticut project paid special attention to the Connecticut Historical Society's collection of tavern signs and to other antiques discovered by William Lamson Warren, the project's knowledgeable director. Matulis also worked briefly on the WPA easel project and on a mural for a Hartford bank. During World War II he drew topographical maps from aerial photographs.

From 1945 to 1975 he was a technical illustrator for the publications of an aircraft corporation. He also continued to

Max Fernekes (left) and Eugene Barth, National Gallery of Art, Gallery archives

Magnus S. Fossum copying the 1770 coverlet Boston Town Pattern, Coral Gables, Florida, February 1940, National Archives, Washington, DC, Records of the Works Progress Administration (the Index data sheet lists a date of 14 February 1941)

create and exhibit his own paintings throughout New England and to teach art privately in his hometown of New Britain, Connecticut. After his retirement he found a second career as a teacher of art to seniors and won awards for poster design.

Zabelle Missirian
Massachusetts project: 5 renderings

Esther Molina
(1895–1988 SSDI)
Texas project: 3 renderings

Elizabeth Moutal (Beckwith)
Massachusetts project: 41 renderings
Her colleague, Lucille Chabot, remembers Elizabeth Moutal (see page 14, fig. 11) as brilliant, beautiful, and charming, and as a respected and skillful instructor to other Index artists.

Marian Page
Massachusetts project: 9 renderings

Arlene Perkins
New York project: 8 renderings

Robert Pohle
Rhode Island project: 38 entries

Rosa Rivero
(1905–1998)
Texas project: 7 renderings

M. Rosenshield-von-Paulin
New York project: 53 renderings

Albert Rudin
Illinois project: 19 renderings

Albert Ryder
Rhode Island project: 29 renderings

Selma Sandler
New York project: 25 renderings

Ingrid Selmer-Larsen
Massachusetts project: 26 renderings

Ingrid Selmer-Larsen was born in Boston as the daughter of a sculptor and instructor of architecture. She studied at the School of the Museum of Fine Arts, Boston, finishing with a scholarship to the Ecole des Beaux-Arts at Fontainebleau. In addition to producing images for the Massachusetts project of the Index, she served as instructor to Index artists in New Hampshire and New York City. After World War II she began to decorate furni-

ture and to restore antiques, opening her own shop in Marblehead, Massachusetts. She also pursued an interest in landscape painting (correspondence from Selmer-Larsen, 1 June 1982, NGA archives).

Alfred Smith
Massachusetts project: 47 renderings

John Tarantino
New York project: 153 renderings

John H. Tercuzzi
New York project: 54 renderings

George Vezolles
(1894–1973 SSDI)
Kentucky project: 40 renderings

Howard Weld
Connecticut project: 18 renderings

Wayne White
(1890–1978)
Illinois project: 13 renderings

Wayne White studied at the School of the Art Institute of Chicago and was a commercial artist throughout his life (interview by Charles Ritchie, assistant curator of modern prints and drawings, National Gallery of Art, with Richard Rogers, White's grandson, 15 December 1997).

Appendix II
Annotated List of State Projects

The thirty-seven state projects of the Index of American Design varied greatly, probably influenced by such factors as each state's WPA administration; its Index supervisor and artists; the types of artifacts, museums, and collectors in the state; and its history, its geography, and the size and distribution of its population. The following notes are based on a brief survey of data sheets compiled for each state—however, they barely begin to describe the character of the projects. In-depth studies of the individual state projects have yet to be undertaken and would be of tremendous value to an overall understanding of the Index. Many questions remain to be investigated, for example, why a few projects relied heavily on black-and-white photography. Further study would require thorough examination of the extensive documents on each state project that are available in the National Archives in Washington, DC, as well as in the archives of each state.

Alabama
This very small project produced about thirty black-and-white photographs of artifacts in the Montgomery Museum of Fine Arts, all made in fall 1941.

Arizona
The Arizona project was also small. Artists produced about forty renderings, all dated 1942; most were of branding irons from a private collection.

California
(Southern California had a separate project; see below). In northern California the Index represented a variety of objects, many of them pioneer artifacts from the De Young Museum in San Francisco and the Oakland Public Museum. Private collections in San Francisco also offered material to be rendered, much of it imported by early settlers from the eastern and mid-western United States (cats. 24, 51).

Colorado
The focus of this state was on the abundant collections of Spanish colonial art in the Denver Art Museum and the Taylor Museum in Colorado Springs (cat. 7).

Connecticut
In addition to early American works in all media from the Wadsworth Atheneum, the New Haven Historical Society, the Garvan Collection at Yale University, and the Connecticut Historical Society (where artists made many renderings of inn and tavern signs), the Index drew from private collections in Branford, Greenwich, Hartford, Middlebury, and Mystic. Artist Charles Sheeler's collection of Shaker furniture was rendered. Early wall paintings from homes in Old Lyme, Windsor, and Washington were of special interest in this state (cats. 6, 9, 43, 65, 66, 73).

Delaware
This project's focus was on furniture, and about one quarter of the pieces were photographed rather than rendered. All photographs date to 1936; later work was in watercolor. Great private collections of early American furniture existed in Delaware, many of them in Wilmington homes. Delaware Index artists also rendered some furniture from private collections in nearby Chester County, Pennsylvania (cats. 17, 32, 36, 62).

District of Columbia
Nearly all the renderings made by artists in this small project were from the collections of the Smithsonian Institution, the Daughters of the American Revolution, the National Society of Colonial Dames, and the Lee Mansion in Fort Myer, Virginia; very little was recorded from private collections. About half the renderings were of furniture. Although the resources were ample in this city, the project lacked a sufficient number of skilled artists.

Florida
Florida Index artists drew from the collections of the State Museum in Gainesville and the winter quarters of the Ringling Brothers Circus in Sarasota, as well as from private collections throughout the state, but mainly in Miami, Coral Gables, and Coconut Grove. Most of the material in private collections was originally from states other than Florida. Some of the Florida artists produced renderings of works that they themselves owned (cat. 49).

Illinois
The Illinois Index project was very productive, especially in depicting metal objects such as small household appliances, toys, and tools. Many of the pieces had been made in states farther east and later brought to Illinois. The greatest source for this material was the Chicago Historical Society. The Swedish community at Bishop's Hill was also an excellent resource (cats. 25, 28, 63. 82).

Iowa
Artists in this project recorded many artifacts created by the numerous Americans of Norwegian descent in this state, as well as works by members of the Community of True Inspiration in Amana. The Amana pieces include primarily furniture and bakery equipment.

Kansas
This fairly small project benefited from the collection of the Kansas State Historical Society in Topeka. Some unusual pieces, such as corn husk dolls, were rendered at a Shawnee mission.

Kentucky
The greatest emphasis of this state project was on Shaker artifacts made at Pleasant Hill. Artists rendered tools, textiles, furniture, and other objects from this community. The objects then belonged to private collectors in Harrodsburg and Louisville (cat. 53).

Louisiana

A large number of the artifacts portrayed by the artists in this project were made in Louisiana. More than one hundred costume renderings depict items drawn from private collections as well as from the Louisiana State Museum in New Orleans.

Maine

Artists rendered Shaker furniture and domestic goods from the Sabbathday community and carved works from the folk-art collection of modernist sculptor Robert Laurent. Many images depict ships' carvings (including a large private collection of figureheads from Isleboro, Maine), weather vanes, and cigar-store figures. Antique shops in coastal towns were an important source for objects rendered in Maine (cat. 76).

Maryland

Private collections in Baltimore, along with the Maryland Historic Society and the Baltimore Museum of Art, provided Index artists with a large assortment of Maryland costumes to render. Early American furniture, mainly made in Baltimore and Philadelphia, was the favored subject of this state project. Most was located in the mansions of Baltimore, Annapolis, and Hagerstown, as well as in Maryland country estates. This extensive inventory of furniture from the great homes of Maryland primarily consists of black-and-white photography rather than renderings.

Massachusetts

Massachusetts had a very large and successful Index project. Artists completed hundreds of renderings of ships' carvings from private collections, museums, historical societies, and antique shops located along the coast. Hundreds of lighting fixtures were recorded, mainly from the Society for the Preservation of New England Antiquities and the Essex Institute, as were weather vanes from private collections and antique shops.

Artists rendered the textile collection of the Museum of Fine Arts, Boston. The western region of the state provided many Shaker artifacts originally from Hancock Shaker Village and New Lebanon (just across the border in New York), objects that were then part of the collection of Faith and Edward D. Andrews (cats. 2, 5, 12–15, 27, 39–41, 52, 68, 69, 74, 75, 77–80).

Michigan

The Dudley Waters collection of cigar-store figures in Grand Rapids was an important focus of this project. Artists also rendered carvings and toys from the Edison Institute of Technology in Dearborn (today Greenfield Village and the Henry Ford Museum). In September 1936 photographers made about eighty photographs of Michigan ceramics. The Detroit Institute of Art and private collectors in Detroit and Flint offered many glass objects, as well as marionettes and hand puppets. A large private collection of toy banks in Farmington, and one of dolls in Kalamazoo, were also portrayed by Michigan artists.

Minnesota

Minnesota artists produced renderings of many types of carvings—such as pipe bowls, wooden spoons, decoys, and cigar-store figures—from private collections and historical societies.

Missouri

This was a small project in which nearly all the renderings were completed in 1938. They include furniture, tools, household items, and quilts from private homes in Saint Louis.

New Hampshire

A series of black-and-white photographs show architecture and furniture from the Shaker communities in Enfield and Canterbury. Renderings portray cigar-store figures and ships' carvings from private collections in Meredith, Keene, and Manchester.

New Jersey

Artists in this project mainly recorded items from public and private collections in the metropolitan New York area. Included were many ceramic and glass pieces made in Passaic, Jersey City, Trenton, and Newark. Artists depicted nineteenth-century costumes from private collections, as well as furniture from Washington's Headquarters, located in Rocky Hill, and from other sites. A private collector of pewter in Princeton contributed material, as did a New Brunswick family with extensive holdings in textiles.

New Mexico

Artists in New Mexico produced renderings and photographs of blankets and other textiles from Spanish and Indian trading posts and curio shops in Santa Fe and from the well-known Candelario Museum. There are also renderings of santos, carved crosses, beadwork, and jewelry from Taos, Albuquerque, and Santa Fe, as well as photographs of branding irons.

New York City

The largest project was the one in New York City, whose artists were responsible for between one quarter and one third of the renderings produced by the entire Index of American Design. Many talented commercial artists were unemployed in New York City during the depression, and the quality of the work they were able to contribute to this project was very high. Great attention was also given to research. The many museums in the city made their enormous holdings available, as did numerous private collectors and well-stocked antique shops. New York City artists rendered every type of artifact, from all regions of the United States, present in the city's eclectic collections (cats. 1, 3, 4, 10, 18–20, 22, 23, 26, 29–31, 33–35, 44, 45, 47, 56–61, 64, 67, 81).

New York State

Artists in this fairly small project specialized in depicting furniture from private homes in Utica, Buffalo, Syracuse, Tarrytown, and Amsterdam. A fine representation of New York coverlets included those of Harry Tyler from a private collection in Butterville.

North Carolina
Only a few renderings were produced in North Carolina, and these were primarily of furniture from private homes in Raleigh.

Ohio
Ceramic objects made in Ohio were one focus of this project; Ohio-made quilts and coverlets were another. Two large private collections, in Ashland and Cleveland, contributed numerous artifacts to the effort: furniture, kitchen tools, painted tin, wallpaper, hatboxes, fraktur, and textiles. Items from the religious community of Zoar Separatists—many of them privately owned by a collector in Cleveland—were also well represented.

Pennsylvania
Pennsylvania had a very large project, but artists recorded many items in black-and-white photographs rather than in renderings. This was especially true in the western part of Pennsylvania, where more than one thousand glass and metal artifacts were photographed from collections in and around Pittsburgh. In the east, in Philadelphia and its suburbs, more objects were depicted in watercolor renderings, especially after 1936. Artists in the eastern project primarily recorded Pennsylvania German artifacts, although early fire-company equipment was another keen interest of the Index in Philadelphia. Objects came from the Philadelphia Museum of Art and the Historical Society of Pennsylvania, as well as from the Barnes Foundation and from extensive private collections in the area (cats. 16, 21, 42, 46).

Rhode Island
Eighteenth- and nineteenth-century furniture in private homes, the Haffenreffer collection of cigar-store figures, along with ships' carvings and carousel animals from public and private collections were the main concerns of the Rhode Island project. (cats. 8, 70–72).

South Carolina
Artists in this small project made black-and-white photographs of mid-nineteenth-century anchors, bells, pumps, and other naval artifacts in the Charleston ship yard, and of spoons in the Charleston Museum. One rendering featured a jar in the Charleston Museum made by an African American slave.

Southern California
The artists employed by this project primarily recorded Spanish colonial works, especially those associated with the California missions. They rendered carved wooden decoration from the missions, *retablos* and *bultos*, church furniture, religious wall paintings, ecclesiastical vestments, candlesticks, fonts, and wrought-iron window grilles. Items from private collections in Los Angeles were also rendered, including saddles, spurs, and belt buckles. A large number of quilts, coverlets, and rugs were depicted that had been made in eastern states and imported to California by early settlers, and photographs were made of branding irons.

Tennessee
Tennessee-made furniture from private homes in Nashville, along with Tennessee quilts and coverlets, were rendered by the artists of this small project.

Texas
Gifted artists in Texas made outstanding renderings of early Texas furniture and textiles. Private collections and museums in San Antonio and Fredericksburg provided many fine examples of German colonial furniture. Spanish colonial artifacts, primarily furniture, were also of great interest to this project. The Sam Houston House in Huntsville, the University of Texas in Austin, Baylor University in Waco, the collections of Mrs. Hobart Key in Marshall and of Mrs. Jean Pinckney in Austin, along with many other collections, both private and public, large and small, offered great resources (cats. 37, 38, 48, 50).

Utah
The most brilliant renderings produced by Index artists in this state depicted the early homespun textiles of Utah. Many such pieces were located at the University of Utah in Salt Lake, as well as in private homes. The artists typically focused on small sections of the fabrics and were able to give them almost a trompe l'oeil presence.

Vermont
This very small project resulted in just a few renderings of ceramics.

Virginia
Virginia artists rendered figureheads at the Mariners' Museum in Newport News. Other than forays into Newport News, the project did not venture from Richmond, despite the obvious potential in other locations such as Charlottesville. Nearly all the renderings were made in the Valentine Museum, the Virginia Historical Society, the Confederate Museum, and the John Marshall Museum in Richmond. Only a few private collections were included (cat. 55).

Washington
Probably the most significant single achievement of this small project, which was largely confined to Seattle, Spokane, and Tacoma, was to render a very large private collection of toy banks in Seattle.

Wisconsin
A number of accomplished artists were at work in this project. They devoted their efforts primarily to rendering locally made objects, most of them metallic. Public and private collections in Milwaukee, Kenosha, Manitowoc, Racine, and Baraboo offered chopping knives, ice skates, lanterns, kettles, shop tools, agricultural equipment, and ship furnishings to be rendered. A fine collection of dolls that belonged to Mrs. A. H. Weber of Whitefish Bay was also pictured by this project (cats. 11, 54).

Index of Renderings in the Exhibition

Photographic Credits